The Emergence and Revival of Charismatic Movements

Political movements founded by charismatic leaders are often considered ephemeral. Existing literature argues that because they rest on unmediated, emotional attachments between leaders and followers, these movements either fade quickly after their leaders disappear or transform into routinized parties. Yet, charismatic movements around the world have proven surprisingly resilient and have retained their personalistic core. Focusing on Argentine Peronism and Venezuelan Chavismo, this book investigates the nature and trajectory of charismatic movements from the perspectives of both leaders and followers. Using interviews, focus groups, and survey experiments, Caitlin Andrews-Lee reveals that charismatic movements can emerge, survive, and become politically revived by sustaining – not discarding – their personalistic character. Followers' charismatic attachments to the movement founder can develop into an enduring, deeply affective political identity that successors can reactivate under certain conditions by portraying themselves as symbolic reincarnations of the founder. Consequently, charismatic movements can have lasting, deleterious effects on democracy.

CAITLIN ANDREWS-LEE is Assistant Professor of Politics and Public Administration at Ryerson University. Previously, she was a postdoctoral fellow at the Center for Inter-American Policy and Research (CIPR) at Tulane University. She has published articles on charismatic politics, political behavior, and democracy in journals such as *Comparative Political Studies*, *Comparative Politics*, *Political Research Quarterly*, and *Journal of Politics in Latin America*.

T0384604

The Emergence and Revival of Charismatic Movements

Argentine Peronism and Venezuelan Chavismo

CAITLIN ANDREWS-LEE

Ryerson University

CAMBRIDGE
UNIVERSITY PRESS

Shaftesbury Road, Cambridge CB2 8EA, United Kingdom

One Liberty Plaza, 20th Floor, New York, NY 10006, USA

477 Williamstown Road, Port Melbourne, VIC 3207, Australia

314–321, 3rd Floor, Plot 3, Splendor Forum, Jasola District Centre, New Delhi – 110025, India

103 Penang Road, #05–06/07, Visioncrest Commercial, Singapore 238467

Cambridge University Press is part of Cambridge University Press & Assessment, a department of the University of Cambridge.

We share the University's mission to contribute to society through the pursuit of education, learning and research at the highest international levels of excellence.

www.cambridge.org
Information on this title: www.cambridge.org/9781009462709

DOI: 10.1017/9781108917353

First published 2021
First paperback edition 2024

A catalogue record for this publication is available from the British Library

ISBN   978-1-108-83147-5   Hardback
ISBN   978-1-009-46270-9   Paperback

Cambridge University Press & Assessment has no responsibility for the persistence or accuracy of URLs for external or third-party internet websites referred to in this publication and does not guarantee that any content on such websites is, or will remain, accurate or appropriate.

For Mark and Jamie.

Contents

Figures

Tables

Acknowledgments

I first encountered Peronism as an undergraduate study abroad student in 2007, during the election that would bring Cristina Fernández de Kirchner to power as Argentina's first democratically elected woman president. As I observed the presidential campaign, I marveled at the flexibility and resilience of Peronism. The political movement had endured for more than sixty years, despite the exile and subsequent death of its charismatic founder – not to mention several coups, a ruthless military dictatorship, tumultuous economic crises, and dramatic ideological swings. Through it all, Peronism had maintained its place as Argentina's predominant political force, a fact evidenced in part by Cristina's decisive electoral victory that year. What, I wondered, was the basis of so many citizens' ongoing attraction to this remarkably persistent yet notoriously chameleonic movement?

Four years later in 2013, I was attending Raúl Madrid's graduate seminar on democratic consolidation at the University of Texas at Austin when a fellow student exclaimed in class that Hugo Chávez's death had just been announced. In the years that followed, Venezuelans suffered a humanitarian crisis of epic proportions – a crisis that worsens today as a political stalemate, international sanctions, rock-bottom oil prices, and, most recently, the novel Coronavirus plague the country. That the devastating consequences of this complex humanitarian emergency have fallen on the shoulders of millions of innocent Venezuelans is an unspeakable tragedy.

While Chavismo emerged in a different temporal, geographical, and cultural context than Peronism, in graduate school I noted the striking resemblances between the two movements. Both were founded by a charismatic leader who vowed to rescue the country from a terrible crisis. Both movements underwent ideological transformations that made them difficult to define along programmatic lines. And perhaps most importantly, both movements attracted the fervent adoration of millions of citizens and dominated politics, not only during the lifetimes of their founders but also in the years after the founders' deaths. This book seeks to explain the remarkable power and persistence of charismatic movements like Peronism and Chavismo and teases out the consequences of their resilience for democracy.

The multi-year process of planning, researching, writing, and completing this book would not have been possible without the support of many individuals and institutions. I am especially indebted to my dissertation supervisor at the University of Texas at Austin, Kurt Weyland. Kurt's mentorship, tireless enthusiasm, and extremely generous contributions of time and feedback were instrumental in shaping both this book project and my career as a scholar. From our initial correspondence when I was a prospective graduate student in 2011 to the completion of this book project nine years later, I have benefited enormously from Kurt's teaching, wisdom, and guidance. I strive to be as dedicated a mentor to my future students.

I am also deeply grateful to the other members of my dissertation committee at UT Austin for their advice, feedback, and encouragement. Bethany Albertson introduced me to political psychology and the experimental method. She encouraged me to think creatively and enrich my project by incorporating original survey experiments. During my first year of graduate school, Raúl Madrid's course on Democratic Consolidation pushed me to rigorously assess the effects of charismatic leadership on democracy. Over the years, Raúl posed challenging questions and offered thoughtful suggestions that helped me improve my theory and evidence. Daron Shaw shared great wisdom and literature on campaigns and elections, consistently urging me to think about the "big picture" beyond Latin America. Discussions with Javier Auyero, along with his written work, greatly deepened my understanding of Peronism. Javier also introduced me to contacts in Argentina who became some of my most invaluable and rewarding partners in research. Last but not least, my undergraduate advisor, Juan Lindau, helped sow the seeds for this project fourteen years ago, nurtured my intellectual curiosity, and profoundly influenced my decision to pursue an academic career.

During my fifteen combined months of fieldwork in Argentina and Venezuela, many others made generous contributions of knowledge, time, and encouragement without which this book would not have reached its completion. In Argentina, I am especially grateful to Shila Vilker, Carlos Gervasoni, Natalia Arnuado, and Nicolás Papalía for their advice, support, and friendship. I also thank María Matilde Ollier, Sebastián Mazzuca, and Lucas González at Universidad Nacional de San Martín, whose help with my pilot survey experiment in 2013 was instrumental to the success of my full survey experiment three years later. I am grateful to Noam Lupu and Luis Schiumerini for including my survey questions about charisma in the 2015 Argentine Panel Election Study. Universidad Torcuato Di Tella provided an institutional home away from home as well as the opportunity to present my research and receive feedback from some of Argentina's foremost experts on

Peronism. In Venezuela, I thank Thais Maingon, Gerardo González, Alexandra Panzarelli, Fernando Pires, Félix Seijas Rodríguez, José Vicente Carrasquero, Deborah Vega, Ricardo Méndez, Douglas and Sonia Méndez, Elsa Fernández, Jael Palacios, and Ricardo Romero for entertaining my questions, deepening my understanding of Chavismo during hours-long conversations, and helping me navigate the challenges of daily life in Caracas, which were substantial. I thank Benigno Alarcón and the Universidad Católica Andrés Bello for generously offering an institutional affiliation during my fieldwork. In Peru, Carlos Meléndez and Eduardo Dargent provided valuable insights and guidance. I am indebted to hundreds of other scholars, politicians, country experts, and voters in Argentina and Venezuela who generously shared their time and experiences with me in the context of informal conversations, interviews, focus groups, and survey experiments.

I am also grateful for the incisive feedback offered by numerous scholars in the contexts of workshops and conferences. In addition to the scholars mentioned above, my friends and colleagues at UT Austin including Kate Bersch, Jake Dizard, Riitta-Illona Koivumaeki, Calla Hummel, Ken Miller, Katie Putnam, Kim Guiler, Iasmin Goes, Daniel Weitzel, Nathalia Sandoval-Rojas, Tommy Burt, Brendan Apfeld, Matt Rhodes-Purdy, Chieh Kao, Wendy Hunter, Amy Liu, Mike Findley, Xiaobo Lu, Ken Green, Jason Brownlee, Chris Wlezien, Tse-Min Lin, Henry Dietz, and Stephen Jessee provided encouraging and thoughtful comments that helped me improve the central arguments and empirical analyses advanced in this book. Beyond Texas, I am grateful for the feedback and support of Laura Gamboa, Jordan Kyle, Brett Meyer, Dave Ohls, Cathy Schneider, Adam Auerbach, and Gina Lambright, who patiently listened as I presented the book's central arguments to them. I also benefited tremendously from the excellent comments of several discussants on different sections of this book, including Ken Roberts, Mollie Cohen, and Matthew Layton. Two anonymous reviewers at Cambridge University Press read the entire book manuscript and provided several pages of invaluable comments and suggestions that greatly improved the book. Finally, my colleagues at the Center for Inter-American Policy and Research (CIPR) at Tulane University, including Ludovico Feoli, Moisés Arce, David Smilde, Ann Mische, Francisco Rodríguez, Rachel Schwartz, Stefanie Israel de Souza, David de Micheli, Alexander Slaski, and Sefira Fialkoff, as well as members of the Department of Political Science at Tulane, including Mirya Holman and Ruth Carlitz, offered generous feedback and a stimulating intellectual environment in which to complete my book manuscript as a postdoctoral fellow.

Several institutions provided financial support for my project. The Lozano Long Institute for Latin American Studies at the University of Texas at Austin funded summer fieldwork trips to Argentina and Venezuela through the Argentine Studies Program Grant and the Tinker Summer Field Research Grant, respectively. Fulbright and the Institute for International Education provided the nine-month US Student Scholarship with which I conducted the rest of my fieldwork in Argentina. The National Science Foundation generously funded my survey experiment through a Doctoral Dissertation Research Improvement Grant. UT Austin's Graduate School Continuing Fellowship supported an additional four semesters of my graduate education, including one semester of fieldwork in Venezuela and three semesters of dissertation writing. P.E.O. International funded my final year of graduate school as I completed my dissertation. Finally, the Faculty of Arts at Ryerson University provided a Special Projects Grant to fund the indexing of this book.

I would also like to acknowledge the outstanding assistance of Ashely Beene, whose careful comments on the manuscript greatly sharpened my prose. Additionally, I thank Sarah Doskow and Cameron Daddis for expertly guiding me through the publication process of my first book at Cambridge University Press. I also appreciate the permission granted by SAGE Publications to reproduce parts of my articles, "The Revival of Charisma: Experimental Evidence from Argentina and Venezuela," published in *Comparative Political Studies* 52:5 (2019): 687–719, and "The Power of Charisma: Investigating the Neglected Citizen-Politician Linkages in Hugo Chávez's Venezuela," published in the *Journal of Politics in Latin America* 11:3 (2019): 298–322. I thank the *Journal of Comparative Politics* at the City University of New York for permission to reproduce part of my article, "The Politics of Succession in Charismatic Movements: Routinization versus Revival in Argentina, Venezuela, and Peru" 52:2 (2020): 289–316.

Finally, I am grateful to my family for their unconditional love and support throughout the process of developing this book. My parents have always welcomed my pursuit of a liberal arts education, applauded my successes, and taught me to learn and grow from my mistakes. They have also followed me around the world, bringing a piece of home to me regardless of how far I have strayed from Colorado. My in-laws have graciously supported my ambitious career, even though it has meant moving their son and family thousands of miles away from their home in Denver. Both sets of parents have doted on our son, Jamie, and have provided invaluable support when his parents have had to work during nights, weekends, and a global pandemic. Last but not least, I owe an enormous debt of gratitude to my husband, Mark, who has lifted me up, made me laugh during even the most challenging times, and joined me on the wild and exhilarating adventure of parenthood. It is to him and our beautiful son that I dedicate this book.

PART I

THEORETICAL DISCUSSION

I

Introduction

Political movements founded by charismatic leaders are widely considered to be ephemeral. Indeed, scholars argue that the unmediated, deeply emotional bonds linking charismatic leaders to their followers fade quickly after the leaders disappear. For charismatic movements to survive, then, the existing literature claims that followers' emotional attachments must be transformed into indirect ties sustained by evaluations of policies and programs or membership in affiliated social groups (Jowitt 1992, 107; Madsen and Snow 1991, 24; Weber 1922/1978, 246). This process of depersonalization, or "routinization," replaces the leader's personal authority with a party organization capable of coordinating voters' and politicians' complex preferences over the long term (Kitschelt 2000, 847; Weber 1922/1978, 246).

Curiously, however, charismatic movements have proven surprisingly resilient and have retained their personalistic core in countries across the world, including Argentina, Venezuela, Peru, Italy, and Thailand. In Latin America, charismatic movements have become particularly prevalent and enduring. For instance, Argentina's Peronist movement, founded over seventy years ago by Juan Perón, has continued to attract charismatic leaders who reinforce, rather than overcome, the movement's weak institutional structure (Gervasoni 2018, 2; Levitsky 2003, 17). Though younger than Peronism, Hugo Chávez's movement in Venezuela has sustained a surprisingly large base of loyal supporters for over twenty years. Even in the face of deteriorating economic and social conditions since Chávez's death in March 2013, about one-third of Venezuelans continue to express deep, personalistic attachments to Chavismo (Briceño 2015a; GBAO Strategies 2019). In Peru, Alberto Fujimori's paradigm-shifting movement from the 1990s has sustained a larger support base than any other party (Tanaka 2011, 80). In fact, Fujimori's daughter, Keiko, has tied herself to her father's movement in recent years to gain political support. Consequently, she received 40 percent of the vote in the first round of the 2016 presidential elections – over eighteen points more than the second-place candidate (Dargent and Muñoz 2016, 145). While these movements have developed some party structures, each remains characterized primarily by entrenched personalism and institutional weakness (Dargent and Muñoz 2016; Gervasoni 2018; Levitsky and Zavaleta 2016; Mainwaring 2016, 2018).

This book offers a novel explanation for the emergence and surprising resilience of charismatic political movements and sheds light on the resulting challenges for democracy. Rather than necessarily routinizing, I argue that these movements can endure after the death or disappearance of their founders by sustaining their original personalistic nature. As Chapters 3 and 4 demonstrate, survival is possible because citizens' deep, emotional attachments to charismatic leaders can form a resilient political identity that shapes the citizens' worldview and expectations of future politicians.[1] Thus, new leaders who portray themselves as symbolic reincarnations of the founder can reactivate these attachments, garner support, and restore the movement to power in their own name. Chapter 5 illustrates the mechanisms underlying this process of charismatic reactivation, while Chapter 6 identifies the conditions under which new leaders are most likely to succeed in reviving the movement. Finally, Chapter 7 demonstrates the self-reinforcing nature of this process. The results indicate that charismatic movements can perpetually evade routinization and dominate politics after the founder's departure, repeatedly undermining the development of strong party institutions and compromising citizens' democratic representation.

1.2 THE MAIN ARGUMENT

Scholars of routinization cannot account for the strikingly personalistic trajectory that charismatic movements have taken since the disappearance of their founders. Indeed, the routinization thesis views these movements as resting on two pillars: (1) citizens' fleeting emotional attachments to the founder and (2) the founder's exercise of uninstitutionalized, personalistic authority. According to this view, charismatic movement survival requires both the depersonalization of followers' attachments and the institutionalization of the

[1] In keeping with the literature on political identity and partisanship, I understand citizens' political attachments – their perceived psychological connections to a leader or group – as foundational to their identification with that person or group (Campbell et al. 1960; Conover 1984; Green, Palmquist, and Schickler 2002; Huddy 2013; Lupu 2013). Throughout the book, when discussing the reactivation of charismatic movements from the followers' perspective, I therefore refer to the terms "attachment" and "identity" interchangeably. I also treat the terms "linkage," "attachment," and "bond" synonymously.

movement. Yet Peronism and Chavismo, the most prominent charismatic movements in Latin America, have persisted while remaining intensely personalistic and plagued by institutional weakness. In both cases, my research shows that followers have continued to express profoundly affective attachments to the founder and to subsequent leaders of the movement. Meanwhile, the programmatic principles guiding each movement remain ambiguous at best and contradictory at worst, participation in movement-affiliated organizations remains low, and leaders routinely tie themselves to the movement's charismatic founder and exercise personalistic authority rather than working through institutional channels. These factors suggest that both Peronism and Chavismo have failed to routinize.

In contrast to existing literature, I therefore contend that charismatic movements can survive by sustaining, rather than discarding, their personalistic core. The reason is that followers' original attachments to the founder are not fleeting, as scholars of routinization would suggest. Rather, these attachments foster the development of a resilient political identity that remains rooted in charismatic bonds and divides society along a cleavage defined by support for (or opposition to) the founder and movement. Consequently, citizens' attachments need not transform into depersonalized partisan linkages when the founder disappears. Instead, the ties can endure in their original personalistic state. In the years after the founder has gone, citizens' charismatic identity can make them long for a leader who is capable of picking up the founder's baton and single-handedly delivering them peace and prosperity. This identity also deepens citizens' suspicions of politicians who do not align themselves with the founder and movement. As I will demonstrate, new leaders who effectively implement two strategies – (1) tying themselves symbolically to the charismatic founder and (2) achieving bold performance to demonstrate their capacity to "rescue" society – can politically reactivate citizens' unmediated and profoundly emotional connections to the movement and thereby garner support as its new standard-bearers.

However, while many successors attempt to replace the founder, few are able to enact the abovementioned strategies and consolidate power. Thus, the new leaders' success is heavily shaped by three conditions. The first condition concerns the way in which successors emerge. Those who are handpicked by the founder for immediate replacement encounter formidable obstacles that severely encumber their attempts to become effective leaders of the movement. Conversely, self-starters who rise on their own – often years after the founder's disappearance – have greater latitude to convince followers that they are worthy of the founder's mantle. Yet while many self-starters attempt to rise to power, most of them also fail. Self-starters are far more likely to be considered true heirs when they fulfill two additional conditions. First, those who seek power during a crisis increase their chances of success because followers' demand for a savior intensifies under difficult, crisis-induced circumstances. In addition to this exogenous condition, self-starters who exercise individual agency – namely, the willingness and ability to adopt the founder's charismatic leadership style – appeal directly to the followers and therefore claim the followers' deeply emotional bonds with the movement for themselves, as righteous heirs of the charismatic founder.

In short, citizens' profoundly affective attachments to the founder and movement function as a remarkably stable political identity that cleaves society into two groups – followers and opponents – and structures political competition along the lines of charismatic leadership rather than policy "packages" (Lipset and Rokkan 1967, 3). Yet, the successful revival of the movement by new leaders depends on conditions that occur sporadically. Consequently, charismatic movements do not unfold in the linear fashion of conventional parties, gathering programmatic strength and stability over time (Converse 1969). Instead, these movements tend to develop spasmodic trajectories that involve periods with powerful charismatic leadership as well as periods with no leader at all. This is because, similar to the founder, successful self-starters prioritize bold, shortsighted policies and foster symbolic ties to win the followers' loyalty. While these initiatives earn self-starters popularity at the outset, the inevitable collapse of their audacious programs eventually discredits them. Furthermore, because these personalistic leaders typically loathe sharing power, they hesitate to groom talented successors. Thus, in the wake of self-starters' rule, charismatic movements experience a leadership vacuum. Sooner or later, however, the ensuing crisis encourages the suffering followers to seek out a more convincing successor to take up their beloved founder's mantle, causing the cycle of charismatic leadership to repeat.

1.3 THE RELEVANCE AND CONTRIBUTIONS OF THIS STUDY

1.3.1 Theoretical Contributions

My investigation of emergence and revival of charismatic movements holds several important theoretical implications. To my knowledge, this analysis is the first to challenge the routinization thesis and offer an alternative explanation for persistent personalism and institutional weakness in countries where charismatic movements have developed. In doing so, the study contributes to the growing literature in political science that reintroduces charisma as a concept worthy of systematic, empirically driven analysis (e.g., Madsen and Snow 1991; Merolla and Zechmeister 2009b, 2011; Pappas 2019). In particular, the investigation empirically captures the relational nature of charisma by combining quantitative, qualitative, and experimental methods to examine both the demand for and supply of charismatic leadership – highlighting the perspectives of followers and leaders, respectively. This pluralistic methodological approach addresses challenges of conceptualization and measurement with which many studies of charisma have struggled.

Second, this study contributes to the literature on political identity and partisanship by shedding new light on a unique yet resilient form of identity that is rooted in charismatic attachments. Because existing research perceives such personalistic bonds to be short-lived, it overlooks their potential to develop into a stable and enduring form of political identification. In contrast, my analysis indicates how charismatic attachments compete with and undermine the development of programmatic and organizational linkages thought to be foundational to conventional forms of partisanship. By overpowering alternative linkage types and sowing deep roots in the leader's narrative of salvation, I show that charismatic attachments can develop into a stable yet deeply personalistic political identity. Although the substantive content of this identity differs from that of programmatic and organizational forms of partisanship, I demonstrate that it shares important characteristics, including the capacity to endure over time and split society based on a cleavage that crystallizes "in" and "out" groups defined by allegiance or aversion to the founder and his mission to transform society (Cyr and Meléndez 2015; Huddy 2013; Lipset and Rokkan 1967; Meléndez and Rovira Kaltwasser 2019; Roberts 2014; Tajfel 1974). By recognizing charismatic attachments as foundational to a specific and enduring type of political identity, this study clarifies the precise ways in which charisma can exert a more lasting influence on political systems than previously thought.

Through its historical analysis, this study also addresses important debates regarding the roles of structure and agency in charismatic politics. In particular, I underscore the crucial importance of structural conditions, such as the presence of an acute crisis, for both the emergence and revival of charismatic movements. While scholars acknowledge crisis as an important factor for the consolidation of charismatic attachments (Madsen and Snow 1991; Merolla and Zechmeister 2009b; Pappas 2019; Weber 1922/1978), I document precisely when and why crisis matters – not only for the solidification of an individual leaders' charismatic authority, but also for the perpetuation of these leaders' movements.

I also acknowledge the important role of leader agency in reviving charismatic movements. Self-starters simply cannot portray themselves as heirs of the founder without generating their own personal appeal – that is, signaling their own charisma. Yet self-starters' agency only goes so far: the leaders are inherently constrained by the preexisting, personalistic structure of the movement. Thus, as I will demonstrate in the case of the unsuccessful presidential candidate Antonio Cafiero in Argentina, even talented self-starters cannot rely on their skill and appeal to fundamentally restructure the movement into a depersonalized, programmatic party. Indeed, a programmatic strategy, even if well executed, will fail to resonate with the followers, who are in search of a savior – not an ordinary representative. Thus, while recognizing the role of agency as important, this study paradoxically stresses structural factors as central to the vitality of charismatic movements.

Next, this book contributes to the growing literature on challenges to democracy by clarifying how charismatic movements encourage authoritarian tendencies in their leaders, undermine citizens' representation, and impede party system development – all of which make democratic regimes vulnerable to illiberal threats. Leaders who draw their legitimacy from charismatic attachments develop authoritarian behaviors to sustain their image of invincibility. For example, they demand unquestioning loyalty from their followers and display intolerance toward critics. This intolerance can manifest itself in various ways, from public haranguing to discriminatory legalism to, occasionally, outright repression (Weyland 2013). Moreover, to prove their heroic capacities, charismatic leaders seek to concentrate their executive power, undermining the institutional checks and balances that are critical to representative democracy. Finally, to minimize challenges to their authority, these leaders surround themselves with personal cronies rather than professional advisers and experienced bureaucrats, which, in turn, fosters nepotism, corruption, and scant political accountability.

In addition to authoritarian leader tendencies, I demonstrate that charismatic movements dilute the quality of citizens' democratic representation. This is because, in their quest to appear heroic, the leaders of these movements introduce bold programs that demonstrate their miraculous image and openly defy "rational, and particularly bureaucratic, authority" (Weber 1922/1978, 244). While such daring reforms may provide benefits at the outset, the leaders' disregard for bureaucratic rules and sustainable practices eventually compromises the welfare and interests of the movement's supporters. Because the leaders' legitimacy rests not on the supporters' "reasoned deliberation," rather, it rests on deeply affective bonds, the leaders also enjoy far more leeway in their performance than do politicians in programmatic contexts (Urbinati 2019, 119). Further, over time, the volatility in the substance of charismatic leaders' policies generates a programmatically ambiguous party brand (see Lupu 2013). For all of these reasons, citizens cannot be certain what policies they are supporting when they vote for a charismatic leader. Peronist leaders, who are known for their dramatic policy reversals that span the left–right ideological spectrum, exemplify this programmatic volatility and uncertainty (Ostiguy 2009). In short, citizens' democratic representation suffers because they base their support on the personal appeal and immediate impact of each new leader rather than on the substantive consistency and coherence of the leader's policies.

Finally, the emergence and revival of charismatic movements inhibit the development of stable, institutionalized party systems. Each leader who comes to power must overcome institutional limitations and exercise direct authority in order to prove the capacity to fulfill a heroic and transformative mission. Moreover, these leaders' audacious policies, while successful in the short term, contain the kernel of their own collapse. When the collapse finally occurs, the country enters a period of crisis with no leader to guide the way. Rather than opening a path to routinization, these circumstances make followers crave a new savior to resolve the crisis, perpetuating the cycle of political and economic volatility. Thus, unlike routinization, which suggests that charismatic movements eventually transform into institutionalized parties, my theory of charismatic movement revival indicates that these movements can expose societies to frequent and severe crises, tenacious personalism, and persistent institutional weakness. Argentine history exemplifies these neurotic cycles.

1.3.2 Empirical Contributions

Substantively, Peronism and Chavismo have irrevocably transformed their respective countries. From the rise of Juan Perón in 1946 to the time of writing in 2020, Peronism has dominated the Argentine political system. Until Mauricio Macri's recent presidency (2015–19), only Peronist presidents had managed to complete full terms in office, earning the movement a reputation as the only force capable of governing the country (Mora y Araujo 2011; Ollier 2015). Existing literature suggests that Peronism owes its longevity and power to the fact that it has transformed into an organized and largely depersonalized political party (Levitsky 2003; Loxton and Levitsky 2018). Yet, the movement has remained characterized by intense personalism and profound institutional weakness (Gervasoni 2018; McGuire 2014). In fact, its most successful leaders – Juan Perón, Carlos Menem, and Néstor and Cristina Kirchner – have subordinated the party (and the political system writ-large) to their individual authority, governing based on their bold, nearsighted policies and captivating personal appeal.

In Venezuela, Chavismo has also upended politics and mobilized poor citizens in an unprecedented fashion. Chávez's anointed successor, Nicolás Maduro, has doubled down on his symbolic connection to his beloved predecessor since rising to power in 2013, widely disseminating images of Chávez in public spaces across Venezuela and even constructing a hologram of the founder to walk the streets of Caracas (@VTVcanal8 2016). Simultaneously, Maduro has overseen a devastating crisis and has resorted to brutal authoritarian tactics to remain in power. Maduro's failed leadership has been widely interpreted as evidence of Chavismo's inevitable death (Denis 2015; López Maya 2014). Nevertheless, my research shows that followers, many of whom disavow Maduro as the true son of Chávez, remain profoundly attached to Chavismo, proclaim devout loyalty to Chávez, and express hope that a more capable successor will emerge in the future (see also Briceño 2015a; Morales 2016). Thus, like Peronism, Chavismo challenges the predominant view in the literature that routinization is the only viable path for charismatic movement survival.

This book moves beyond routinization to explore a different explanation for the remarkable persistence of Peronism and Chavismo. Using an array of methodological tools that shed new light on the perspectives of followers and leaders, my research reveals a personalistic mechanism of survival that causes these movements to persist in society while taking power in fits and starts.

On the followers' side, I demonstrate that charismatic attachments endure in a fairly steady fashion. This is due to followers' deep, emotional identification with the movement, which they establish and preserve through personal narratives that glorify the founder as the ultimate savior, reinforce his mission to combat the people's enemies, and promise a more prosperous future. In contrast to the stability of followers' attachments, both the founder and subsequent leaders bring the movement to political predominance in a temporary and intermittent manner. My analysis indicates that these leaders can only consolidate power under favorable conditions, at which point they must exercise individual agency to portray themselves as heroes in their own right – and, in the case of successors, as symbolic reincarnations of the founder. Moreover, successors who effectively claim the founder's mantle can only do so temporarily, as their shortsighted policies eventually collapse and reveal their weaknesses to the followers. While these leaders never fully replace the adored founder, they play a crucial role in perpetuating the movement because they reinvigorate the political relevance of followers' charismatic bonds, incorporate new supporters from different groups, such as from younger generations, and temporarily restore the movement's supreme power.

The spasmodic trajectory highlighted in this study shows how political movements such as Peronism and Chavismo have risen and persisted by sustaining a fundamentally charismatic core, despite having experienced periods without strong leadership, such as under Isabel Perón in Argentina and Nicolás Maduro in Venezuela. Indeed, such leaderless periods are bound to occur when initially successful self-starters have fallen from grace and conditions have not yet aligned for a new leader to pick up the founder's baton. By illustrating how the tumultuous cycle of charismatic leadership unfolds in these movements, my theory better accounts for the ongoing personalism, institutional weakness, and frequent crises that characterize politics in both countries.

1.4 RESEARCH DESIGN

Scholars have hesitated to parse out and examine factors that have caused charismatic movements to persist. After all, defining, operationalizing, and measuring the psychological mechanisms underlying citizens' loyalty to such movements presents unique difficulties. To confront these challenges, I adopt a pluralistic methodological approach that examines the establishment and revival of charismatic movements in terms of demand and supply, focusing on the perspectives of both followers and leaders.

1.4.1 The Demand Side of Charisma: Follower Support for Charismatic Leaders and Movements

On the demand side, I first draw on public opinion data to quantitatively examine the extent to which citizens' charismatic perceptions of the founder influence their initial attachments to the movement relative to competing factors rooted in evaluations of movement-affiliated programs and participation in relevant social organizations. While existing literature notes the central role of charisma in generating citizens' original bonds to these movements (e.g., Hawkins 2010; Madsen and Snow 1991; Zúquete 2008), it rarely examines the influence of competing linkage mechanisms. I assess these different mechanisms and confirm that the followers' initial attachments to the movement are primarily charismatic rather than programmatic or organizational in nature. Moreover, I demonstrate that these charismatic attachments are more than short-lived ties to the original leader; rather, they develop into a resilient form of political identity with both the leader and his movement. Due to limited availability of relevant public opinion data from Argentina during Perón's first two presidencies (1946–55), this portion of the analysis focuses on the more recent Venezuelan case.

Next, I analyze the trajectory of citizens' charismatic attachments after the death of the founder. In particular, I examine citizens' bonds at distinct junctures across the two movements: about forty years after the founder's death in Argentina (2013–16), and fewer than five years after the founder's death in Venezuela (2014–17). I begin with semi-structured interviews and focus groups with self-identified followers of Peronism and Chavismo. This exploratory investigation provides crucial insights regarding followers' relationship to the movement from their own perspectives. The interviews reveal detailed information about individual followers' experiences, whereas the focus groups allow for thought-provoking discussion among followers regarding their shared understandings of their connections to the movement (Berg 2001; Cyr 2016; Sugiyama and Hunter 2013). I use these data to explain the mechanisms through which followers' charismatic attachments to the movement cultivate an important and enduring political identity that can be reactivated by subsequent leaders.

In the third and final stage of follower-focused research, I conduct a survey experiment with 999 followers of Peronism and Chavismo in three diverse regions of Argentina and Venezuela, respectively, to test my theory on the reactivation of charismatic attachments. Specifically, I test the extent to which two strategies of new leaders – (1) the fulfillment of bold, initially impressive performance and (2) symbolic ties to the charismatic founder – strengthen followers' emotional bonds with the movement and increase political support for the successor. In the experimental setup, participants are randomly assigned to one of four conditions in which a new leader uses both of these strategies, only one of the two strategies, or neither strategy. By controlling for observable *and* unobservable factors that might otherwise confound the analysis, this random assignment allows me to parse out and directly assess the causal impact of the two (often-overlapping) strategies on followers' emotional ties (Druckman et al. 2011). In sum, I use public opinion data, interviews, focus groups, and survey experiments with followers of Peronism and Chavismo to clarify the mechanisms through which their charismatic attachments form, endure, and become politically reactivated by new leaders.

1.4.2 The Supply Side of Charisma: Leader Strategies for Charismatic Movement Revival

On the supply side, I turn to elite interviews and archival research to trace the process through which new leaders succeeded or failed to reactivate citizens' charismatic attachments and restore the movement to power under their own authority. This method, which highlights the roles of timing and sequence (Bennett 2009; Collier 2011), permits a careful examination of important junctures in the development of Peronism and Chavismo and of the conditions that facilitated or impeded new leaders' attempts to employ strategies of reactivation and pick up the founder's charismatic mantle. Though it is difficult to obtain fresh insights from the perspective of movement leaders on these historical cases, my interviews with former leaders, campaign managers, and political strategists provide crucial information regarding the nature and effectiveness of the leaders' tactics for consolidating support, as well as whether and how the leaders associated themselves with the charismatic founders of the movement. Archival materials including newspaper articles, campaign posters, and public opinion polls from the relevant historical periods shed additional light on the context in which successors sought power, the leadership style they adopted, and the extent to which their campaigns resonated with the public.

Finally, I integrate the perspectives of followers and leaders to examine how charismatic movements unfold over time. Focusing on the case of Peronism, this historical analysis demonstrates how charismatic movements emerge with the meteoric rise of the founder and proceed in a wave-like pattern of booms and busts in which subsequent leaders come to power, temporarily reactivate the emotional vigor of citizens' identification with the movement, and inevitably sow the seeds of their own collapse. Specifically, I examine four waves of Peronism led by the founder Juan Perón (waves 1 and 2), Carlos Menem (wave 3), and Néstor and Cristina Kirchner (wave 4). I also briefly review the fifth and most recent wave of Peronism, which began with Alberto Fernández's rise to the presidency in 2019. The results illustrate the endogenous and fitful pattern that characterizes charismatic movements.

1.5 KEY CONCEPTS: CHARISMA, POPULISM, AND CHARISMATIC MOVEMENTS

This study lies at the intersection of two (in)famously contested concepts: charisma and populism. The former has long been invoked by scholars, pundits, and ordinary citizens to describe alluring leaders in diverse contexts, yet the precise meaning of the term remains ambiguous. This has led many social scientists to spurn charisma as a "non-falsifiable" concept (Mudde 2007, 262) that is no more useful than an "amorphous and soggy sponge" (Worsley 1957).

Recently, populism has also become a political buzzword for academics and nonacademics alike. As Grzymala-Busse notes, "the term is everywhere: usually applied to political parties, but also used to characterize politicians, movements, grievances, demonstrations, policies, and electorates" (in Bernhard et al. 2020, 20). In fact, while the concept first appeared in the nineteenth century, references to it have exploded in the twenty-first century (Rovira Kaltwasser et al. 2017, 1–2). Yet, like charisma, populism's slippery definition has stirred intense debate among scholars, earning it the label "weasel word," which Bernhard describes as "a term ... whose meaning is so imprecise or badly defined that it impedes the formulation of coherent thought on the subject to which it is applied, or leads to unsubstantiated conclusions" (Bernhard et al. 2020, 2).

Compounding the conceptual confusion around charisma and populism is the fact that the two terms are often used synonymously. Indeed, individual leaders whom people consider to be "populist" are often described as "charismatic"; similarly, the political movements and parties these leaders control are referred to with both terms. Nevertheless, many scholars claim that neither concept constitutes a definitional property of the other. For example, Weyland states that "a widespread belief in a leader's amazing, extra-ordinary, and 'supernatural' capacities is a prime way in which the connection between leaders and followers can acquire the special intensity that gives rise to and sustains populism," yet he also indicates that "charisma is not a definitional component of populism" (2017, 54). Similarly, Mudde and Rovira Kaltwasser acknowledge that "populism is generally associated with a strong (male) leader, whose charismatic personal appeal, rather than ideological program, is the basis of *his* support" (2017, 6). However, the authors conclude that "populism is neither defined by nor wedded to a specific type of leader," charismatic or otherwise (ibid., 77).

I argue that the relationship between charisma and populism remains contested and uncertain due to an imbalance in the scholarly literature. Specifically, while research on populism has proliferated (e.g., Hawkins 2010; Hawkins et al. 2019; Kenny 2017; Mudde and Rovira Kaltwasser 2017; Urbinati 2019; Weyland 2001, 2017), charisma has "rarely [been] analyzed and measured in political science" (Merolla and Zechmeister 2011, 29). To remedy this disparity and shed new light on the important connections between charisma and populism, this book places charisma front and center by tracing the development of charismatic attachments between leaders and followers in political settings that most would describe as populist.

To clarify my approach, I briefly review contrasting conceptualizations of charisma and populism that appear in the contemporary literature, identifying the definition of each that I find most valid and useful for the purposes of this study. I then introduce the concept of "charismatic movement," which stands at the heart of my analysis and best captures the intersection of charisma and populism. The subsequent section justifies the selection of Peronism and Chavismo, the two cases that constitute the main focus of this book.

1.5.1 Charisma

Weber, who developed the most important, seminal conceptualization of charisma, defines it as "a certain quality of individual personality by virtue of which he is considered extraordinary and treated as endowed with supernatural, superhuman, or at least specifically exceptional powers or qualities" (1922/1978, 241). Charisma has since been adopted in a widespread fashion to describe individuals – usually leaders – who possess intrinsic, magnetic appeal.

While intuitive, this interpretation of charisma has drawn criticism for two reasons. First, it suggests that charisma consists of a set of fixed, objective leader traits such as divine grace and extraordinariness, which are notoriously ambiguous and difficult to pin down (Antonakis et al. 2016, 301; Mudde and Rovira Kaltwasser 2017, 66). Second, this interpretation tends to treat charisma dichotomously: someone "is either charismatic or is not" (Eberhardt and Merolla 2017, 103). Approaching charisma as a set of universally understood, black-and-white, yet frustratingly elusive characteristics has resulted in much debate over who qualifies as "charismatic" and why, if at all, it matters.

In an effort to address these issues, others have emphasized a more subjective definition of charisma that highlights followers' perceptions of the leader rather than the leader's objective characteristics (e.g., Eberhardt and Merolla 2017; Haslam, Reicher, and Platow 2011; Madsen and Snow 1991; Merolla, Ramos, and Zechmeister 2007; Merolla and Zechmeister 2011; Urbinati 2019). These scholars look to Weber's insistence that it is followers' *recognition* of the leader's traits – rather than the independent existence of those traits – that form the foundation of charismatic authority. Thus, these authors conclude that charisma is a characteristic or attribute that is *conferred* on the leader by the followers (Eberhardt and Merolla 2017, 104; Haslam, Reicher, and Platow 2011, 245; Steffens et al. 2017, 530). This subjective understanding of charisma has important advantages. For one, it does not require universal consensus regarding what it is that makes the leader inherently "exceptional"; instead, it suggests that charisma exists to the extent that the followers *regard* their leader as exceptional, however defined. Second, it interprets charisma in relative rather than absolute terms: charismatic perceptions can range on a continuum from weak to strong and can shift in intensity across time, contexts, and individual followers (Bass and Avolio 1995; Eberhardt and Merolla 2017; Merolla, Ramos, and Zechmeister 2007).

Despite these improvements, the subjective conceptualization of charisma introduces another problem: It highlights the charismatic "effect," or the intended outcome of charismatic leadership, rather than charisma itself

(Antonakis et al. 2016, 302). In fact, charisma does not consist of connections between leaders and followers; rather, it creates those connections. Examining the establishment and impact of charismatic attachments is itself a worthy endeavor – indeed, it is the primary objective of this book – yet it would be misguided to conflate these bonds with the phenomenon that led to their formation in the first place.

In light of these issues and debates, I contend that charisma is a property of leadership that, when applied under certain conditions, encounters massive receptivity and therefore results in the establishment (or reactivation) of charismatic attachments between leaders and their followers. Specifically, in keeping with Antonakis and his colleagues in the field of business management, I define charisma as a type of leadership that signals through both words and actions a particular set of symbols and values that, in certain circumstances, resonates on a deeply personal and affective level with the intended audience (Antonakis et al. 2016, 304). As I will elaborate in Chapters 2 and 3, leaders signal and exert their charisma in three ways: They (1) directly recognize the genuine and undeserved suffering of their followers, (2) vow to personally resolve the people's misery through bold action, and (3) use emotional, quasi-religious symbols and rhetoric to cultivate a mission of profound societal transformation designed to defeat evil forces and provide the followers with a prosperous future. The extent to which followers recognize, fall for, and respond to a leader's charisma is influenced by both the leader's individual characteristics (e.g., their personality, communication skills, and experience) and contextual circumstances.

If executed when many people suffer from serious problems and therefore long for a savior, charisma allows the leader to establish (or reactivate) charismatic attachments: linkages with followers that are unmediated, asymmetrical, and deeply emotional in nature. The *unmediated* quality of these attachments implies that the leader communicates directly with the followers rather than using intermediary bureaucratic channels. The *asymmetry* of the bonds arises because the leader maintains an exalted position over the followers and therefore enjoys unmatched power and commands their unwavering loyalty. Indeed, the qualities that followers perceive in the leader "are not accessible to the ordinary person, but are regarded as of divine origin or as exemplary" (Weber 1922/1978, 231). Although the leader is unlikely to possess divine roots in reality, the followers' perception of divinity substantiates the leader's charisma and justifies his/her influence over them. Finally, the *emotional* character of charismatic attachments inspires the followers to feel "intense devotion to and extraordinary reverence for the leader" (Madsen and Snow 1991, 5). The combination of these features makes the followers feel that they have a unique and intimate relationship with the leader. It also convinces them to relinquish control over their lives to the leader, whom they perceive as their savior.

How, then, does charisma apply to the political arena? I argue that politicians can exercise charisma to cultivate unmediated, asymmetrical, and emotional attachments with their followers across a wide spectrum of organizational settings. Just as voters in the United States can worship Franklin Delano Roosevelt or Barack Obama as their redeemer, so can Chinese citizens praise Mao Zedong as their ultimate hero. While these leaders vastly differed in ruling strategy and organization, they all may be considered charismatic because they recognized the unjust suffering of their people, vowed to boldly resolve it, and, in doing so, crafted a mission of salvation. Despite their many differences, these signals enabled these leaders to develop unmediated, top-down, and deeply affective connections to their most devout supporters; thus, all three came to be viewed by these supporters as quasi-divine saviors.

Though charismatic attachments can develop in strikingly diverse contexts, the political relevance of these attachments varies based on the extent to which leaders rely on the personalistic authority they derive from these attachments to govern. Neither fully democratic nor clearly totalitarian leaders use charisma as their primary source of power. On the democratic end of the spectrum, leaders such as FDR, Obama, and Brazil's Luiz Inácio Lula da Silva cultivated charismatic attachments with a significant number of voters, yet they governed primarily based on "rational" laws and institutions. On the totalitarian end of the spectrum, Mao and Adolf Hitler also enjoyed the unwavering, emotionally driven loyalty of many citizens, but relied far more on ruthless, overt repression than charismatic bonds to rule. In contrast to these liberal–democratic and totalitarian extremes, as I will explain subsequently, leaders who rely predominantly on charismatic attachments to assert their authority thrive best in "populist" settings.

1.5.2 Populism

An "essentially contested concept," populism has undergone various definitional transformations since it emerged in the nineteenth century in the United States, Russia, and France (Rovira Kaltwasser et al. 2017, 2–4). While scholars have debated the term's true meaning for decades, the recent surge in political leaders and parties considered "populist" has injected these discussions with renewed urgency. Although several conceptualizations of populism exist, contemporary scholars tend to subscribe to one of two approaches: one ideational and the other political-strategic.[2]

Proponents of the ideational approach define populism as "a thin-centered ideology that considers society to be ultimately separated into two homogeneous and antagonistic camps, 'the pure people' versus 'the corrupt elite,' and which argues that politics should be an expression of the *volonté générale* (general will) of the people" (Mudde and Rovira Kaltwasser 2017, 5). This

---

[2] Other conceptualizations understand populism as an expression of popular agency (Goodwyn 1978), a political style (Moffitt and Tormey 2014), an economic program (Sachs 1989), a sociocultural identity (Ostiguy 2017), and a form of political emancipation (Laclau 2005).

definition emphasizes three components: the virtuous "people," who are the key protagonists of the populist cause; the malevolent "elites," who encompass all who oppose the populist cause; and the "general will," or the source that unites the people and justifies their mission to vanquish the selfish and morally bankrupt elites (ibid., 9–14).

At its core, the ideational approach understands populism to be independent of the context from which it emerges. It is a highly flexible discourse that virtually anybody can adopt and perform, for any period of time. As a "thin-centered" ideology, it can be combined with any left–right ideological position, political project, or regime type (ibid., 5). Theoretically, then, any leader, party, or ordinary citizen could become populist simply by taking up the rhetoric dividing "the people" and "the elites." Moreover, while charismatic leaders are by far the greatest producers of populist rhetoric, charisma has no place in the ideational definition (ibid., 77).

In contrast, the political–strategic approach promotes a more specific definition of populism that incorporates the political context and focuses on the connection between "the people" and the leader who claims to represent them. Weyland, an early adopter of this approach, states that "Populism is best defined as a political strategy through which a personalistic leader seeks or exercises government power based on direct, unmediated, unistitutionalized support from large numbers of mostly unorganized followers" (2001, 14). Rather than mere discourse that praises "the people" while attacking "the elites," this interpretation defines populism as a holistic strategy used by political leaders to mobilize support and *take power* (ibid., 12; Urbinati 2019, 34). In other words, populism constitutes a distinct political force characterized by intense personalism. Unlike leaders in programmatic parties who mobilize support through the party's firmly established apparatus, populist leaders bypass institutional channels to connect with and secure the devotion of their supporters in a quasi-direct and seemingly intimate fashion. Only through establishing unmediated linkages with voters can populists achieve their ultimate goal: leveraging the fervent support of the masses to exercise unchecked authority.

To be sure, the political-strategic definition of populism acknowledges the important role of Manichean rhetoric outlined by the ideational approach. However, it maintains that this discourse matters only insofar as it helps the leader convince the supporters that he/she personally embodies their will and therefore deserves their unfaltering loyalty (Weyland 2017, 58–59). As Urbinati states, "The populist leader is *emotionally* and *propagandistically* active in his daily effort to reconquer the authorization of the people" (2019, 117, emphasis added). In contrast to liberal democracy, which embraces a spirit of pluralism, promotes competition between multiple parties, and imposes a system of institutional checks and balances, populist movements stress that sacred leaders and their "people" constitute the *only* source of legitimate power and deem all opponents to be unworthy of representation (ibid., 114–15).

I contend that the political–strategic approach offers the most precise definition of populism because it makes clear the important role of charismatic
attachments. Specifically, this interpretation suggests that the populist leader's
objective of obtaining and exercising power rests fundamentally on his/her
capacity to cultivate charismatic – unmediated, asymmetrical, and emotional –
attachments with his/her followers. As mentioned previously, it is true that non-
populist leaders ranging from democratic presidents and prime ministers to
totalitarian dictators can use charisma to establish these attachments with their
supporters. Whereas these leaders complement their charismatic influence with
other strategies and mechanisms, charismatic connections form the basis by
which populist leaders win and exercise power.

1.5.3 Charismatic Movement

Throughout this book, I use the term "charismatic movement" to describe the
group of people bound together by unmediated, asymmetrical, and emotional
bonds to the charismatic leader and his/her mission of redemption. While each
follower perceives their connection to the leader as profoundly personal, the
shared identity that emerges from these attachments, and the influence these
bonds grant the charismatic leader, constitute a powerful and potentially
transformational force.

Because populist leaders rely so heavily on charismatic attachments to
establish and exercise power, I argue that populism constitutes the purest
and most powerful form of charismatic movement in the political sphere.
However, charismatic movements – like charisma itself – can complement
other forms of authority across a range of regime types and can even emerge
outside of politics.

As mentioned earlier, in Brazil's liberal-democratic setting, Lula governed as
the head of a programmatic, center-left political party (Hunter 2010). He also
consolidated the fervent support of an important base of followers from the
country's impoverished Northern and Northeastern regions using his charismatic appeal rather than his party affiliation. Consequently, the number of
citizens who identified personally with the leader and who viewed him as their
savior (*lulistas*) outnumbered those who identified with his party (*petistas*) (de
Souza 2011, 75, 88; Hunter and Power 2019, 69; Samuels and Zucco 2014,
130). Furthermore, though Lula's charismatic movement never subsumed the
programmatic Workers' Party he helped found, its resilient influence unques-
tionably impacted succession politics – a process I explain in Chapter 6. Indeed,
like other charismatic movement founders, Lula struggled to anoint a compelling presidential successor. His first handpicked heir, Dilma Rousseff, suffered a
terrible crisis of legitimacy and was ultimately impeached in 2016. In the 2018
elections, after Lula was barred from running at the eleventh hour, he personally selected yet another uninspiring presidential candidate, Fernando Haddad,
who covered his own face with a mask of Lula on the campaign trail in a

desperate attempt to borrow Lula's appeal, but lost the election to the right-wing fringe candidate, Jair Bolsonaro (Hunter and Power 2019).

Charismatic movements can also emerge within totalitarian regimes. For example, as discussed earlier, Mao relied primarily on his well-organized and ideologically cohesive Chinese Communist Party (CCP) to assert totalitarian control. Yet, he also used charisma to establish profound, unmediated bonds with millions of Chinese citizens – especially with those who became his Red Guard, the "true believers" who were "blindly devoted to Mao" (Andreas 2007, 438). Periodically, Mao leveraged his charismatic movement to shake up the CCP and reassert his personal grip on power, most notably by launching the Cultural Revolution in 1966.

Finally, charismatic movements can develop outside of politics, often in the form of (pseudo-)religious cults such as Sun Myung Moon's Unification Church (known as the "Moonies"), Marshall Applewhite's Heaven's Gate, Jim Jones' People's Temple, and Keith Raniere's NXIVM. Similar to their political counterparts, Singer states that these groups take the shape of "an inverted T," in which "the leader is alone at the top, and the followers are all at the bottom" (Singer 2003, 8). Cult leaders use charisma to entice their followers: They recognize their followers' suffering, claim to be endowed with unique – even miraculous – power to resolve this suffering, and declare a mission to forge a "simple path to happiness, to success, to salvation" (Zimbardo 1997). These leaders establish profound, emotional bonds with their followers and thus enjoy tremendous influence over them. Using these bonds, cult leaders build charismatic movements that often engage in a range of controlling and destructive behaviors, some of which even culminate in mass homicidal and suicidal acts (Bohm and Alison 2001; Hassan 1990).

As I explain in the subsequent section, this book focuses on charismatic movements in the political sphere. In fact, I focus on charismatic movements that constitute a leader's main basis for winning and exercising power and that therefore also qualify as populist. However, I use the former concept rather than the latter as the foundation of my analysis in order to shed light on charisma's essential role in the establishment and revival of these movements. Although many populism experts view charisma as a prominent feature of these movements, few consider it to be a definitional property. In contrast, I view charisma as the indispensable glue that holds these movements together – even after their original leaders disappear. Moreover, my analysis may be extended in the future to study charismatic movements in other contexts, including diverse political regimes and nonpolitical settings.

1.6 CASE SELECTION

This book focuses on two charismatic movements in Latin America that emerged, survived, and profoundly transformed the political trajectories of their respective countries: Peronism and Chavismo. I prioritize these cases for several reasons. First, they represent *typical* cases of charismatic movement survival (Seawright and Gerring 2008, 299). As will be detailed in subsequent chapters, both movements have survived beyond the deaths of their founders and have had a dramatic and enduring impact on political behavior and the organization of the party system. Yet the causal mechanisms underlying the resilience of the two movements remain poorly understood. Concentrating on these important instances of charismatic movement survival allows for a deep exploration of causal mechanisms involved.

Second, while examining only "positive" cases, my examination of followers and leaders within each movement provides variation on important dimensions of the dependent variable, charismatic movement survival. At the level of the followers, I analyze variation in the strength of charismatic attachments and political support for successors. At the level of the leaders, I assess variation in successors' attempts to revive the movement. In particular, I investigate the process through which some leaders succeeded while others failed to return the movement to power. The variation in these two dimensions – the intensity of followers' charismatic attachments and new leaders' ability to restore the movement to power – provides me with the analytic leverage to assess, on one hand, the competing explanations rooted in routinization and, on the other hand, personalistic revival.

Third, Peronism and Chavismo have unfolded in different geographical and historical contexts, allowing for a direct analysis of charismatic movement survival at distinct junctures. Peronism emerged in Latin America's Southern Cone with Juan Perón's rise to power in the mid-1940s, whereas Chavismo came to power in the Andean region with Hugo Chávez's presidential victory in 1998, over fifty years later. Peronism has survived for over seven decades and has experienced rule under several successors, including Isabel Perón, Carlos Menem, Eduardo Duhalde, Néstor Kirchner, Cristina Kirchner, and most recently, Alberto Fernández. Conversely, at the time of writing, Chavismo has survived just seven years since the death of its founder and has been governed by a single successor: Nicolás Maduro. I take advantage of these differences to examine first-hand two important stages in charismatic movement survival: long-lasting (in Argentina) and still developing (in Venezuela).

1.7 OVERVIEW

The remainder of the book is organized as follows. Part I (the present chapter and Chapter 2) lays out the theoretical discussion. Specifically, Chapter 2 details explanations for the survival of charismatic movements that are rooted in the logic of routinization and presents my alternative theory of charismatic movement revival.

Part II analyzes the establishment and revival of charismatic movements from the demand side by investigating the formation (Chapter 3), survival (Chapter 4), and political reactivation (Chapter 5) of followers' attachments.

Chapter 3 identifies how these attachments initially develop, overwhelm alternative linkage types, and contribute to the formation of powerful political movements. I focus this analysis on the case of Venezuela due to the relatively fresh status of citizens' attachments to Chavismo. Combining insights from classic studies of charisma with empirical analyses of voters devoted to Chávez and his movement, I develop a compact theory on the formation of charismatic attachments. Subsequently, I use data from a 2007 survey by the Latin American Public Opinion Project to test the influence of charismatic perceptions of Chávez on citizens' attachments to the movement relative to competing factors rooted in the movement's substantive programs and grassroots organizations. The results indicate the disproportionate influence of charismatic leadership on citizens' ties to the movement.

Chapter 4 examines the staying power of charismatic movements by exploring the mechanisms through which followers' attachments cultivate a resilient, charismatic political identity that survives after the disappearance of the founder. Focus group discussions with followers of Peronism and Chavismo reveal how the factors involved in the original formation of citizens' affective bonds – including the leader's direct recognition of the followers, impressive performance, and narrative of salvation – facilitate the perpetuation of those attachments and reinforce their profound identification with the movement. In particular, the focus groups illustrate how followers sustain their unmediated, deeply emotional bonds with the founder by holding onto stories and material possessions symbolizing their transformative experiences under the founder. The discussions also indicate how followers' resilient charismatic identity shapes their understanding of politics and provide a pathway for new politicians who portray themselves as heroic reincarnations of the founder to win the followers' loyalty.

To complete the analysis from the demand side, Chapter 5 investigates how followers' emotional attachments to the movement can be politically reactivated to facilitate new leaders' consolidation of power. Face-to-face survey experiments conducted with movement followers in Argentina and Venezuela indicate that leaders who implement two strategies – (1) bold, initially impressive policies and (2) symbolic associations with the charismatic founder – cause citizens to express stronger emotional attachment to the movement and increased support for the new leader. The results further challenge the notion that charismatic attachments are short-lived and underscore the potential of new leaders to resurrect the political salience of those attachments.

Part III turns to the supply side by examining the conditions under which new leaders can implement the abovementioned strategies to consolidate power as new standard-bearers of the movement. Chapter 6 identifies three conditions that successors must fulfill to accomplish this task: They must seek power on their own terms after the founder's disappearance, rise in the midst of a crisis to portray themselves as desperately needed saviors, and adopt the founder's personalistic style to revitalize and take ownership of the followers' preexisting emotional bonds to the movement. To demonstrate the relevance of these conditions, I examine the process through which several successors failed while others succeeded in reviving three charismatic movements in Latin America: Peronism, Chavismo, and Fujimorismo in Peru.

Given the conditions that facilitate new leaders' successful revival of charismatic movements, Chapter 7 investigates the trajectories of these movements starting from the moment when their founders disappear. Focusing on Peronism, which has survived over forty years since the death of its founder, I trace the history of the movement from Perón's rise in 1943 until 2019, when Peronist candidate Alberto Fernández rose to power after defeating the non-Peronist incumbent president, Mauricio Macri. The analysis illustrates how, by sustaining its personalistic nature, Peronism has unfolded in a spasmodic fashion that contrasts with the more stable, linear trajectories of conventional parties.

Chapter 8 summarizes key empirical findings of the study, draws theoretical conclusions about the potential for charismatic movements to bypass routinization and live on in personalistic form, and reflects on the challenges these movements pose for democracy. It also extends the analysis to cases beyond Argentina and Venezuela where charismatic movements persisted or reemerged after the disappearance of their founders, including Fujimorismo in Peru, Forza Italia in Italy, the Pheu Thai Party in Thailand, and Maoism in China. Finally, I explore the broader implications that my theory of personalistic revival holds for the potential staying power and consequences of charismatic populist leaders, who are on the rise in countries across the world.

2

A Theory of Charismatic Movement Revival

The survival of charismatic movements beyond the lifetimes of their founders is puzzling. Indeed, these movements are considered to be fundamentally unstable because they hinge on the captivating and "strictly personal" authority of their founders. Extant literature, therefore, concludes that charismatic movements tend to disintegrate when their founders disappear (Weber 1968, 21–22; Kostadinova and Levitt 2014, 500–1; Weber 1922/1978, 246).

What, then, explains the surprising resilience of Peronism and Chavismo? Two theories offer potential explanations: routinization and revival in personalistic form. Routinization constitutes the predominant view in the literature (Jowitt 1992; Loxton and Levitsky 2018; Madsen and Snow 1991; Shils 1965; Weber 1922/1978). Originally proposed by Weber, this theory states that the founder's charismatic authority must be reshaped into an institutionalized party for the movement to survive. In contrast, my theory of charismatic movement revival contends that the founder's deep, emotional bonds with the followers can be preserved and reactivated by future politicians to restore the movement to power. In other words, these movements can survive by perpetuating a cycle that reinforces citizens' affective attachments and subordinates political institutions to the authority of personalistic leaders.

This chapter begins with a discussion of the logic of routinization and indicates why this theory falls short of explaining the survival of Peronism and Chavismo. Specifically, I argue that routinization overstates the ephemerality of citizens' emotional ties to the charismatic founder while minimizing the immense difficulty of transforming the founder's authority into a depersonalized party organization.

Next, I propose my alternative theory of charismatic movement revival. Drawing on insights from political and social psychology, I contend that followers' charismatic bonds can turn into a resilient identity that remains personalistic in nature and shapes the followers' perceptions, attitudes, and behaviors after the founder's disappearance. Because these attachments survive in personalistic form, I explain that new leaders who portray themselves as the founder's heirs have the potential to reactivate followers' affective identity, restore its political significance, and garner support. Subsequently, I outline the conditions under which this process of charismatic reactivation is possible. Finally, I demonstrate that charismatic movements can survive in latent form during periods of poor leadership and reemerge when conditions are more favorable. Rather than establishing an institutionalized party, as routinization would predict, I argue that the revival of charismatic movements generates a cycle of political and economic volatility that perpetuates personalistic leadership and undermines party system institutionalization. In subsequent chapters, I substantiate my theory using a wide array of evidence that focuses primarily on the Peronist and Chavista movements.

2.1 CENTRAL TENETS OF THE ROUTINIZATION THESIS

Adherents of the routinization argument claim that the survival of charismatic movements in personalistic form is impossible. First, they stress that successors cannot take over the founder's direct, emotional bonds with the followers. Second, because they lack the founder's magnetic appeal, successors cannot exercise the concentrated authority of the charismatic predecessor. For these reasons, scholars conclude that the survival of charismatic movements depends on routinization. During this process, the followers' emotional bonds with the founder are said to transform into depersonalized partisan linkages. An organizational structure staffed with lower-level politicians and bureaucrats also develops to replace the concentrated authority of the charismatic founder. In short, routinization suggests that charismatic movements survive by shedding their true nature and becoming institutionalized parties. In the following two sections, I outline the process of routinization at the level of the followers and the leaders who emerge in the wake of the founder's death.

2.1.1 The Depersonalization of Followers' Charismatic Attachments

According to Weber, attachments between charismatic leaders and their followers are "strictly personal, based on the validity and practice of [the leader's] charismatic personal qualities," as those qualities are perceived by the followers (1922/1978, 246). Scholars identify two such qualities as especially important for shaping the "leader-to-mass flow of communications and benefits" (Madsen and Snow 1991, 25). First is the leader's seemingly miraculous performance, which provides the followers with tangible benefits and demonstrates his heroic capacity to resolve their suffering.[1] The second quality is the leader's frequent,

---

[1] Charismatic leaders can be female or male. For the sake of simplicity, and because the majority of charismatic founders under study are male, I use the pronoun "his" throughout this chapter.

direct communication with his followers, which gives the followers the illusion of an intimate relationship with their beloved savior.

Existing studies suggest that the survival of charismatic movements depends on routinization in part because new leaders cannot replicate the founder's charismatic qualities in the eyes of the followers. To begin, proving super-human abilities would require "the constant achievement of 'miracles'" (Eatwell 2006, 141). The founder's chosen successor, typically "a functionary who is not remotely comparable with the predecessor" (Kostadinova and Levitt 2014, 500–1), is unlikely to achieve this ambitious feat. Compounding this issue of lackluster performance, especially in comparison to the almighty founder, the chosen successor struggles to sustain unmediated ties with the followers (Madsen and Snow 1991, 25). Unable to tap into these intimate connections, the successor cannot control the masses through "symbolic manipulation" in a manner reminiscent of the founder (Jowitt 1992, 107).

Because successors cannot perform miracles or captivate the masses using magnetic appeal, they cannot uphold the founder's deep, emotional attachments with the followers. This leads scholars of routinization to conclude that the nature of followers' attachments must undergo a fundamental change if an initially charismatic movement is to survive. In particular, the literature suggests that, because the emotional intensity of citizens' attachments to the founder irreversibly dissipates upon his disappearance, the agents of routinization must replace those attachments with alternative linkage types (Jowitt 1992, 107; Madsen and Snow 1991, 29; Shils 1965, 202; Weber 1922/1978, 246).

Studies of partisanship suggest two alternative party–voter linkages that could replace citizens' charismatic attachments to the movement. First, programmatic attachments could emerge based on the ambitious policies enacted by the founder. These policies, validated by their initially impressive success and their association with the founder's valiant promises to rescue society, could develop into a programmatic trademark for the movement (Lupu 2013, 51–52). To sustain followers' loyalty based on this mechanism, the movement's new leadership would need to preserve the substantive content and positive performance of the founder's policies. If successful, first-generation followers who recognized and supported this set of policies would reinforce their attachment to the movement; those who disagreed or were simply unaware of the policies would become less attached after the founder's disappearance (Key 1966, 7–8). Subsequent generations of citizens whose issue preferences coincided with the content of the movement's programmatic trademark – due to a combination of parental socialization, preference formation occurring during young adulthood, and retrospective evaluation of the movement's past performance – would be more likely to develop strong attachments to the movement in the future (Achen 2002; Fiorina 1981; Niemi and Kent Jennings 1991). However, if their issue preferences deviated over time or the movement's programmatic trademark became diluted, the basis for citizens' programmatic attachments would break down, resulting in the erosion of the movement's core of supporters (Lupu 2013, 52; Roberts 2014, 26).

A second linkage that could routinize the followers' charismatic attachments rests on an organizational mechanism. Specifically, the followers could sustain their devotion to the movement based on their participation in the network of movement-affiliated organizations, social clubs, and neighborhood associations created under the charismatic founder (Campbell et al. 1960; Granovetter 1973; Green, Palmquist, and Schickler 2002; Huckfeldt and Sprague 1992). Crucially, the persistence of followers' organizational ties to the movement would depend on the followers' ongoing (informal or formal) membership in these social groups (Green, Palmquist, and Schickler 2002, 4, 91; Roberts 2014, 27). Moreover, the movement's new leaders would have to actively mobilize the movement's organizational network to remain politically relevant and win follower support (Huckfeldt and Sprague 1992, 70; Samuels and Zucco 2015, 758–59). Subsequent generations of followers would then be socialized into the network during childhood or through their social groups during young adulthood, perpetuating the strength of the movement over time (Lewis-Beck et al. 2008, 138–41; Niemi and Kent Jennings 1991, 979–81). In contrast, the disintegration of movement-affiliated groups would weaken followers' connections to the movement and would undermine their loyalty as a result.

In sum, the routinization thesis posits that successors to the charismatic founder cannot replicate the founder's seemingly miraculous performance; moreover, these successors struggle to maintain direct, intimate connections with the followers. Given these weaknesses, the survival of the movement requires that citizens' deep, emotional attachments to the founder transform into depersonalized linkages based on either a steady, substantively meaningful programmatic trademark or a strong network of movement-affiliated organizations that generate feelings of belonging among the followers.

2.1.2 The Replacement of the Leader's Charismatic Authority with a Party Organization

In addition to the transformation of the followers' profoundly affective attachments, routinization studies claim that the founder's concentrated, charismatic authority invariably dissipates. Thus, the founder's subordinates must work together to develop an organizational structure that can substitute for his authority (Madsen and Snow 1991, 29). Crucially, these intermediary agents do not *personally* inherit a dose of the founder's charismatic appeal. Rather, the founder's appeal becomes associated with the *offices* that the agents occupy and with the *rules* that govern the agents' behavior. Eventually, the institutional "roles and rules" acquire independent legitimacy rather than leaning on their (increasingly distant) association with the founder (Shils 1965, 205). In other words, a depersonalized type of authority that rests on institutions rather than on individuals stands in place of the founder's charismatic authority.

To successfully replace the founder's charismatic authority in this fashion, scholars stress that the movement must develop a party structure with at least a moderate degree of organizational capacity (Jowitt 1992, 107; Kostadinova and Levitt 2014, 500–1; Madsen and Snow 1991, 25–29; Shils 1965, 202–5). In fact, the more extensive the organizational structure, the better the chances of movement survival. As Shils explains, "the more widely dispersed, unintense operation of the charismatic element in corporate bodies governed by the rational-legal type of authority," the greater the possibility of establishing a powerful, lasting, and firmly institutionalized party (1965, 202).

2.2 THE INSUFFICIENCY OF THE ROUTINIZATION THESIS

While routinization studies attempt to theorize the evolution of charisma after the death of the founder, they underestimate the potential of the followers' charismatic attachments to endure. Moreover, they overlook the tremendous difficulties of constructing a party organization to replace the charismatic founder's deeply entrenched authority. Consequently, these studies fail to explain the trajectory of charismatic movements such as Peronism and Chavismo, which have persisted in a strikingly personalistic manner since the deaths of their founders.

2.2.1 Theoretical Limitations of the Routinization Thesis

To begin, scholars of routinization suggest that followers' charismatic attachments fade away upon the founder's disappearance. Yet it seems unlikely that citizens' fervent bonds would be so fragile. During the founder's rule, these bonds are so strong that they cause a "searing reorientation" in the lives and identities of the followers (Madsen and Snow 1991, 24). The founder's promise to provide the followers with salvation inspires a deep devotion that is missionary, even Christ-like (Zúquete 2008, 107). Indeed, charismatic attachments transcend the mundane world of self-interest, inspiring the followers to "rise above, and to go beyond, mercenary concerns of contractual obligation and exchange" (Haslam, Reicher, and Platow 2011, 31). Given the deeply emotional and quasi-religious nature of these ties, it seems unreasonable to conclude that the founder's death would cause them to disappear. To the contrary, social psychology research on the "death positivity bias" and "postmortem charisma" suggests that the founder's death – an emotional and tragic event for the followers – could actually *intensify* their love for the founder and strengthen their loyalty to his movement (Allison et al. 2009, 116; Steffens et al. 2017, 532).

A second issue overlooked by routinization studies is the difficulty of developing an institutional structure that can supplant the founder's charismatic authority. Scholars describe the transfer of authority from the founder to his intermediaries as an inevitable, if gradual, process. For example, Madsen and Snow explain, "The emergence of such intermediary roles...occurs gradually as the leader finds it more and more difficult to maintain frequent and direct ties with his or her following" (1991, 25). Similarly, Shils states that charisma "*flows* from the central authority ... [to] a multitude of others who live within a territory ruled by the central authority" (1965, 212, emphasis added).

Yet, charismatic founders prioritize concentrating authority above all else, casting doubt on the notion that their authority would transfer in such a smooth and inexorable fashion. In fact, these leaders take extraordinary measures to *undermine* the development of structure in their movements and ensure that their influence cannot be easily shared during or after their lifetimes. For example, they exercise authority on a whim, relying on spontaneity and capriciousness to prevent others from sharing or challenging their power (Carroll 2013, 135). Furthermore, rather than constructing a hierarchy of officials, charismatic leaders allow and even intentionally generate feelings of jealousy and competition among their inner circle of agents in order to keep the structure of their movements weak and reduce threats to their unmatched superiority (Burns 1978, 125; Roberts 2014, 37; Weber 1922/1978, 243). Finally, to keep their legacies from being overshadowed, charismatic leaders tend to anoint weak, inexperienced, and fervently loyal successors (Lasswell 1948, 101; Weber 1922/1978, 246).

Due to their extraordinary efforts to preserve their concentrated influence, the disappearance of charismatic founders results in a tumultuous and disorganized power vacuum in the movement's leadership. It seems unlikely that routinization would take place under these circumstances. The movement's intermediaries would struggle to develop party structures through which to disperse the founder's authority. Moreover, these mid-level agents would likely be suspicious of and hostile toward one another – a result of the founder's efforts to keep his underlings weak and divided. Thus, it would be unrealistic to expect these individuals to willingly and effectively share power among themselves. Indeed, the personalistic structure of the movement would incentivize new leaders to consolidate power for themselves in the style of their predecessors rather than behaving as disciplined bureaucrats committed to the task of institutionalization.

2.2.2 Empirical Limitations of the Routinization Thesis

The trajectories of Peronism and Chavismo reflect the shortcomings of the routinization thesis. In Argentina, the behaviors of both followers and leaders of Peronism call into question the viability of routinization. More than forty years after Perón's death, many Peronists have continued to express direct, deeply emotional attachments to the founder and his wife, Eva, as well as to subsequent leaders, including Carlos Menem, Néstor Kirchner, and Cristina Fernández de Kirchner. At the same time, followers have expressed little understanding of the movement's programmatic principles and few have consistently participated in Peronist-affiliated organizations, suggesting that followers' affective attachments have not been replaced by more conventional partisan ties (Levitsky 2003, 84–90; McGuire 1995, 201–2).

In addition to citizens' persistent emotional bonds with the movement, prominent successors of Perón have tied themselves to his charismatic legacy and have deliberately weakened institutions in order to exercise power in a direct and personalistic manner. For instance, Menem relied heavily on personal appeal to rise to the presidency in 1989 (McGuire 1997, 208; Ostiguy 2009, 13–14). During his presidential campaign, he attracted the support of millions of Peronists and thus won the presidency by emphasizing his allegiance to the charismatic foundations of Peronism, explicitly invoking the names of Juan and Eva Perón, and demonizing establishment politicians. As president, Menem enacted bold reforms via emergency decree to combat hyperinflation and portray himself as the people's savior (Weyland 2002, 134–47). Notably, the neoliberal substance of these reforms contradicted Perón's original platform of economic nationalism! Yet Menem declared that Perón would have behaved identically if he had governed during the same period (Comas 1993). As this behavior demonstrates, Menem sought to embody Perón's charismatic appeal and had little interest in developing a programmatic trademark to carry the movement forward.

While Menem's brazen economic policies ended in collapse and unleashed a severe crisis in 2001, Peronism survived and was returned to power in 2003 with the election of Néstor Kirchner. As president, Kirchner secured overwhelming popular support by implementing unilateral decrees to address the crisis and attacking rapacious foreign bondholders and human rights abusers from the 1976–83 military dictatorship (Gantman 2012, 345; Gervasoni 2015). Furthermore, Kirchner and his wife, Cristina – who succeeded him as president in 2007 – explicitly evoked the legacies of Juan and Eva, portraying themselves as symbolic reincarnations of the charismatic couple. Moreover, to ensure their power went unquestioned, both Kirchners regularly intervened in political institutions ranging from the Supreme Court to the National Institute of Statistics and Census (Gervasoni and Peruzzotti 2015). In short, similar to Menem, the Kirchners used personalistic tactics to further concentrate their authority, declaring that they would save the Argentine people from misery and deliver their followers a better future (Ollier 2015; Wortman 2015).

In Venezuela, Chavismo has likewise endured in personalistic form, casting further doubt on the logic of routinization. Chavistas have sustained profoundly affective attachments to Chávez since his death in March 2013. Indeed, they have openly mourned their beloved founder, worshipping him at shrines constructed in homes and public spaces. Followers have also commemorated Chávez by sporting images of his face in the form of T-shirts and tattoos, listening to recordings of his speeches and television shows, and singing songs about his heroic impact. However, while continuing to revere Chávez, these individuals have grown disillusioned with the movement's collapsing programs; furthermore, their participation in movement-affiliated organizations has remained low. These factors suggest that programmatic and social attachments to Chavismo are still underdeveloped, contrary to what routinization would predict (Aponte 2014; Machado 2009).

From the perspective of the leadership, Chávez's successor, Nicolás Maduro, has made little effort to routinize the movement. Instead, he has focused relentlessly on Chávez's mission to transform society and vanquish the movement's enemies. He has also stressed his spiritual connection to the founder to keep citizens' affective attachments alive and vicariously garner support. For example, shortly after his election in 2013, he claimed that Chávez had returned to Earth reincarnated as a bird to offer a personal blessing to Maduro (Scharfenberg 2013). In 2016, he developed a hologram of Chávez that walked the streets of Caracas to celebrate the "Day of Loyalty and Love for our Commander Hugo Chávez Frías" (@VTVcanal8 2016). By symbolically reconstructing the founder's image, Maduro has attempted to leverage citizens' personalistic bonds to defend the contemporary regime and decry all who oppose it as traitors to Chávez's legacy. Consequently, he has sustained crucial support for a remarkably long time, given the deplorable performance of his regime (GBAO Strategies 2019).

To recapitulate, citizens' deep, emotional ties to the charismatic founders of Peronism and Chavismo, respectively, have remained profoundly affective in nature. Moreover, subsequent leaders of these movements have governed using a direct, charismatic style rather than dispersing power and responsibility to intermediaries in their respective parties. These outcomes contradict the routinization thesis, which emphasizes the depersonalization of citizens' attachments and the dispersion of leaders' power as necessary conditions for the survival of charismatic movements. In light of this puzzle, I develop an alternative theory according to which these movements can survive by sustaining their original personalistic nature.

2.3 A NEW THEORY OF CHARISMATIC MOVEMENT REVIVAL

In light of the limitations of routinization studies, I theorize a different pathway through which charismatic movements can persist and reemerge as powerful political forces. To begin, I describe an important conjunctural condition that generates overwhelming popular demand for charisma and thus allows for the establishment of a charismatic movement: the presence of a crisis that places people in a position of suffering and compels them to look for a savior. Next, I explain how the founder emerges in this context and utilizes both contextual circumstances and personal resources to exercise charisma and form deeply affective bonds with the suffering citizens. I then indicate how these bonds tend to overpower alternative types of political attachments and lend coherence to the movement.

Subsequently, I illustrate the mechanism through which the followers' bonds can turn into an enduring identity that continues to shape their political perceptions, attitudes, and behaviors after the founder disappears. I also indicate how this identity leads to the formation of a resilient cleavage that polarizes both politics and society based on emotional allegiances and aversions to charismatic figures rather than substantive programs and left–right ideologies. While the political relevance of the identity and corresponding cleavage fluctuates over time, I underscore the resilience of their emotional and personalistic core. When adverse conditions cause intense suffering, it is the enduring charismatic nature of followers' attachments that causes these individuals to look for a new hero to rescue them. Politicians who understand this longing and rise under particular conditions have the potential to strategically exert their own charisma to reactivate the followers' attachments, reinvigorate the cleavage, and become the movement's new standard-bearer.

The second portion of my theory moves from demand to supply by focusing on the leaders who seek to revive the movement and consolidate power. In particular, I specify the conditions that facilitate or undermine successors' attempts to signal their charisma and reactivate the followers' emotional bonds to reclaim the founder's authority. As with my study of the followers, I examine the role of conjunctural conditions, including the presence of a crisis, as well the leader's traits, such as personal appeal and political skill. Finally, I weave together my analyses of demand and supply of charisma to shed light on the trajectories of charismatic movements and their detrimental impact on democratic party systems.

2.3.1 The Demand Side: Formation, Survival, and Reactivation of Followers' Charismatic Attachments to the Leader

2.3.1.1 *Formation*

To begin, the revival of charismatic movements depends on the initial formation of the unmediated emotional attachments between a leader and his followers. A crucial condition that enables this process is the presence of a crisis overseen by a low-performing government. The reason is that a widespread and severe crisis places many people in a difficult situation they cannot resolve by themselves, which makes many of them feel desperate for an outside source of relief. As the theory of "proxy control" developed in social psychology suggests, many people who experience crisis and corresponding feelings of exclusion, desperation, and hopelessness seek out a savior to recognize their suffering, take control of their seemingly unmanageable situation, and combat the "evil" forces blamed for their problems (Madsen and Snow 1991, 12–15). When political incumbents confront such crises using bold leadership, they can appear more charismatic to these people (Merolla, Ramos, and Zechmeister 2007). Yet politicians who poorly manage the situation can cause desperate voters to look elsewhere for a hero to rescue them (Madsen and Snow 1991,

143; Weyland 2003, 843). These circumstances provide an important opportunity for ambitious new leaders to rise up and forge powerful attachments
with the suffering people.

I argue that leaders who emerge under these conditions have the potential to
cultivate direct and deeply affective bonds by exercising charisma. Importantly,
crisis does not *produce* a charismatic leader; rather, it provides the *opportunity*
for ambitious individuals who seek power to step forward, exert charisma, and
form attachments with the suffering citizens. The process of cultivating charismatic attachments includes three components. First, the leader appeals to
citizens by directly recognizing their genuine and unwarranted suffering.
Crucially, this recognition results in an asymmetrical relationship: The leader
directly grants recognition to the followers, such that the latter feel indebted to,
rather than empowered by, the former. Using the crisis, the leader calls out the
failures of the established regime, recognizes the people's suffering and perceived exclusion, and vows to personally resolve their misery.

Second, to prove his extraordinary ability to "save" the people, the leader
aggressively attacks the "enemies" held responsible for their misery and implements bold, *initially* successful reforms to improve their condition (Pappas
2012, 4–5; Roberts 2014, 29; Weber 1922/1978, 242). This impressive performance confirms the followers' exalted perceptions of their leader but lacks
programmatic coherence and sustainability. Instead, the leader's early success is
greatly facilitated by his emergence following the eruption of the crisis, which
helps make the leader's bold countermeasures appear particularly heroic
(Weyland 2003, 825). Being at the cusp of favorable economic conditions, such
as rising oil prices or a commodity boom, can further facilitate the leader's
enactment of sensational, though short-lived, reforms. And while the audacious
character of these policies eventually produces their own decline, the swift,
tangible relief they initially provide causes many voters to perceive the leader as
extraordinary, if not miraculous.

The third factor required for the cultivation of charismatic attachments is the
construction of an emotional, symbol-laden narrative that glorifies the leader
alongside other historical protagonists as a hero, vilifies opponents as enemies,
and stresses the leader's mission to rescue and fundamentally transform society.
Discourse that frames politics as an existential struggle between good and evil is
essential to convert strong popular support into an intensely personal form of
"political religion" (Zúquete 2008, 91). Indeed, the narrative unites the followers against the allegedly malevolent opposition and solidifies their identification
with the leader's redemptive mission. To spin a compelling narrative, the leader
draws on personal appeal; achieves constant, direct contact with voters; and
ties himself to "sacred figures, divine beings, or heroes" that already form part
of the voters' cultural identity (Willner and Willner 1965, 82). Additionally, the
leader dominates public spaces with images, words, music, and other symbols
to help reinforce the power and moral superiority of him and his movement
(Plotkin 2002, 24; Zúquete 2008, 93–103).

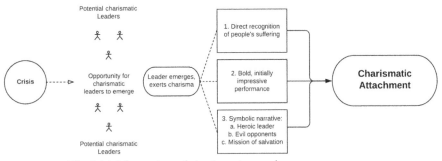

FIGURE 2.1. The initial formation of charismatic attachments

Together, these factors consolidate the suffering citizens' perceptions of the leader's charisma and foster powerful, unmediated bonds between the leader and his followers. Direct recognition of people's exclusion and suffering makes followers feel indebted to the leader; bold reforms deliver tangible improvements to the followers' lives and appear to substantiate the leader's exceptional capacities; and the symbolic narrative solidifies the leader's role as the ultimate savior. Figure 2.1 summarizes the factors involved in the initial formation of charismatic attachments. At the outset, a crisis creates favorable conditions for charismatic leaders to seek power. In turn, if one such leader comes forth and recognizes the people's crisis-induced misery, vows to resolve it through heroic performance, and cultivates a compelling symbolic narrative, the leader can form powerful, long-lasting charismatic attachments with the people.

Although various studies acknowledge the importance of one or more of the abovementioned characteristics for the initial formation of charismatic bonds, I go a step further to identify two ways in which these factors help perpetuate the bonds when the founder disappears. First, I argue that charismatic attachments do not merely establish an emotional connection between the founder and his followers, but that they also undermine the influence of alternative types of political linkages. For one, charismatic attachments provide the leader with a "Teflon shield" that weakens linkages rooted in the substantive coherence and steady performance of the programs and policies (Merolla and Zechmeister 2009a, 33). Indeed, the founder's early, seemingly heroic acts cause the followers to shower him with far more praise than would result from rational evaluations of his performance. Moreover, the followers' perceptions of his performance as miraculous prevents them from "updating" their beliefs and withdrawing their support when the leader's unsustainable initiatives begin their inevitable decline, as would occur with programmatic attachments (Achen 1992, 2002; Downs 1957; Fiorina 1981). Instead, the followers double down on their devotion to the founder, whom they believe will resolve their suffering once again with his superhuman power.

In addition to undermining programmatic attachments, charismatic bonds undercut linkages that develop based on citizens' participation in organizations affiliated with the movement. In particular, the charismatic leader hinders "horizontal forms of association either in civic or partisan areas" for fear that these grassroots activities will distract from his personalistic authority (Roberts 2014, 27–28). Though the founder may create base-level organizations at the outset to mobilize supporters, these clubs actually serve as centers in which to worship the founder rather than vehicles for grassroots empowerment and citizen participation (Hawkins, Rosas, and Johnson 2011, 186–87). Furthermore, these organizations serve to generate "a strong top-down quality in the relationship between citizens and politicians" (ibid.). This contrasts markedly with the notion of grassroots empowerment typically engendered by participatory associations (Ellner 2011, 430–31; Samuels and Zucco 2015, 758–59). The underdeveloped state of programmatic and organizational attachments significantly increases the difficulty of routinizing followers' charismatic bonds upon the founder's death.

Second, I claim that the symbolic narrative initially crafted by the founder plays a crucial role in establishing the followers' attachments as a stable, enduring, and inherently personalistic identification with the movement. Each component of the narrative – the sanctification of the founder, the demonization of opponents, and the cultivation of a mission of salvation – solidifies the followers' charismatic identity and shapes their worldview. The symbolic narrative's quasi-deification of the founder after his death elevates the followers' exalted perceptions of him and sustains their hope that a protégé will eventually pick up his mission to rescue them, thereby reinforcing their personalistic relationship with the movement (Steffens et al. 2017, 531). The demonization of the movement's opponents also imbues the followers with the perception that their livelihood is perpetually under attack, "sharply cleaving the electorate along a personality-based axis of competition" (Roberts 2014, 29). In turn, this crystallization of "in" and "out" groups increases the movement's cohesion and reinforces followers' perceptions of the founder's charismatic appeal (Huddy 2013, 44; Tajfel 1974, 66–67). Lastly, the promise of salvation outlined in the founder's mission increases feelings of solidarity among the followers and provides their righteous community with a profound sense of purpose that goes beyond a superficial connection with a popular leader. In short, by glorifying the founder, demarcating the movement's enemies, and emphasizing this mission to transform society, the symbolic narrative offers the followers "a comprehensive view of the world ... [that] aims to shape and purify the collective consciousness, thus bringing a new society and a new humanity here on earth" (Zúquete 2008, 96).

2.3.1.2 Survival

The personalistic worldview shaped by the founder's symbolic narrative provides the foundation for the perpetuation of citizens' charismatic attachments to the movement. As I will demonstrate in Chapter 4, the followers maintain the founder's perception of reality after his disappearance by retelling cherished, intimate accounts of their life-altering experiences during his rule and by preserving cultural symbols such as portraits of the founder and material objects that commemorate his largesse. Like a religious scripture, these stories and symbols uphold the central components of the overarching symbolic narrative: the heroic status of the founder, the cleavage between the followers and their enemies, and the promise of salvation. Through this mechanism, the narrative cultivates a "strong, internalized subjective identity" that transcends "simple group membership" and profoundly shapes citizens' understanding of the world (Huddy 2001, 149).

In addition to solidifying the followers' positive identification with the founder and his redemptive mission, the narrative demarcates these individuals from their out-group: all nonbelievers, who are framed by the narrative as enemies of the movement. The sharp delineation between followers and non-followers leads to the development of a strong "anti-identity" among the movement's opponents (Cyr and Meléndez 2015). Often remarkably diverse in other respects (e.g., ideological preferences and social backgrounds), the members of this group share only their rejection of the movement, its leaders, and its overarching mission. The solidification of strong, opposing identities centered around allegiance or opposition to a charismatic movement further legitimates the movement's presence and generates a strong, personalistic political cleavage that can overwhelm programmatic and social cleavages (Meléndez 2019; Ostiguy 2009, 4; Roberts 2014, 32). In short, the symbolic narrative, which prizes loyalty to the movement and demonizes opponents, deepens the affective polarization of society, driven by each group's profound "animosity toward the other side" (Iyengar et al. 2019, 129).

Yet, while the preservation of the symbolic narrative helps sustain the charismatic nature of the followers' identification with the movement and strengthens the personalistic cleavage, the prolonged absence of the founder can cause citizens' attachments to become depoliticized over time. Indeed, without a hero to rescue them, the followers may grow disenchanted with politics. Existing studies interpret the waning political relevance of followers' attachments as the first step toward the routinization into programmatic or organizational linkages. Conversely, I contend that the decline in acute intensity is temporary and that the personalistic cleavage endures. Consequently, the founder's absence does not necessarily lead to the transformation of citizens' emotional bonds.

Instead, subsequent politicians have the potential to reactivate the followers' bonds in their original, deeply affective form and thus repoliticize the personalistic cleavage established by the charismatic founder. Precisely because it is difficult for leaders to change the fundamental *nature* of the followers' attachments, "it is much easier to shift [the] salience" of those bonds (Huddy 2001, 49). In particular, the followers' latent desire for a legitimate successor to replace the founder and pick up his mission to transform society remains intact even in the absence of strong leaders. This hope, combined with followers' ongoing distrust of the movement's opponents, creates the potential for their attachments to be strategically reactivated by new leaders. Thus, politicians who convincingly portray themselves as genuine heirs of the founder can appeal to the followers and restore the movement to power by exercising their own personalistic authority.

2.3.1.3 Reactivation

Insights from political psychology support the notion that new leaders who appear as the symbolic archetype with which the followers identify – that is, with the charismatic founder – can resurrect the political significance of the followers' attachments and take ownership of those ties (Haslam, Reicher, and Platow 2011; Hogg 2001; Huddy 2001, 2013; Meléndez and Rovira Kaltwasser 2019). Specifically, new leaders who "craft and shape" different components of the symbolic narrative can enhance its relevance under new circumstances and thus politically reanimate citizens' identification with the movement (Meléndez and Rovira Kaltwasser 2019, 3). By signaling their likeness with the founder and promising to save the community of followers from new threats, new leaders can reactivate the followers' charismatic attachments and mobilize support.

To achieve this ambitious task, I argue that new leaders must communicate a specific set of material and symbolic cues to the followers. The material cue substantiates successors' charismatic authority, while the symbolic cue depicts that authority as though directly reincarnated from the founder. Materially, like the founder, successors must demonstrate extraordinary abilities through impressive performance.[2] They achieve this performance by promising and enacting audacious policies that demonstrate their capacity to rescue the historically marginalized followers. Crucially, the policies must favor grandeur and alacrity over ideological consistency (Weber 1922/1978, 242). Indeed, successors must embrace opportunism through enacting policies that prioritize swift relief rather than sustainability – even if those policies contradict the substance of the founder's original programs. In addition, the policies must deliver tangible benefits to the followers to prove successors' superhuman capacities.

More than cold, rational evaluations of the successors' performance, I argue that this material cue signals to movement followers the new leaders' capacity to fulfill the founder's mission by miraculously resolving the people's urgent problems. Thus, in addition to eliciting positive performance evaluations, the material cue should reinvigorate followers' enthusiasm for and *affective*

---

[2] I do not consider the first condition for the *formation* of personalistic attachments – the leader's direct recognition of a historically excluded group of citizens – to be a separate condition for the *reactivation* of those attachments. Whereas the founder must establish a group of followers from scratch, this group already has a preexisting identification with the movement when successors seek power. Additionally, the symbolic narrative incorporates the followers' sentiment of perpetual exclusion; successors' symbolic ties to the founder and associated narrative are therefore sufficient to reactivate this sentiment among the followers.

attachments to the movement. Furthermore, it should cause the followers to view the successors as more *charismatic* – as noble, selfless heroes capable of providing redemption and a more prosperous future (Pappas 2012, 3).

Second, in symbolic terms, new leaders must depict themselves as reincarnations of the founder committed to resuming his mission of salvation. Specifically, successors must craft and disseminate verbal, auditory, and visual signals that associate themselves with the founder's heroic project and tap into the followers' quest for redemption (Abdelal et al. 2009; Klar 2013; Vavreck 2009). These cues serve as a form of "aesthetic politics" that revive the founder's mission in a contemporary light and mobilize followers to politically reengage with it (Haslam, Reicher, and Platow 2011, 180). For example, successors might reference the founder's name, use a similar tone of voice, play music associated with the founder, adopt similar dress, make personal contact with the followers as the founder did, or incorporate colors associated with the founder's movement to demonstrate their likeness. These signals, spread through the successor's speech, gestures, and symbols, not only remind followers of their beloved founder, but also reenergize their enthusiasm for his transformative mission. Therefore, the cues can reactivate the followers' identity as part of the founder's "moral community" (Zúquete 2008, 104), distinguish them from the movement's out-group – their (real and imagined) enemies – and confirm the successor as the movement's new champion (Tajfel 1974, 66–67).

In sum, a theoretical examination of charismatic attachments from the perspective of the followers underscores the impressive power of these bonds as well as their potential to endure in personalistic form. The factors involved in the initial formation of these bonds – including the founder's direct recognition of the people's suffering and perceived exclusion, the achievement of bold and initially impressive performance, and the cultivation of a powerful symbolic narrative – overpower programmatic and organizational linkages and provide a firm foundation on which to perpetuate charismatic politics. In particular, the narrative, which celebrates the founder, demonizes opponents, and stresses the mission of redemption, transforms the followers' attachments into an enduring identity that shapes their worldview, informs their expectations of future politicians, and establishes a profound cleavage that divides followers from nonbelievers. In turn, successors who replicate the founder's heroic performance and symbolically associate themselves with the founder's mission to transform society can politically reactivate followers' ties and reclaim the founder's personalistic authority. The following section examines the conditions under which successors can fulfill these conditions to return the movement to power in their own name.

2.3.2 The Supply Side: Conditions for New Leaders' Revival of Charismatic Movements

How can new leaders successfully employ the material and symbolic strategies required to reactivate followers' emotional attachments, revive charismatic movements, and establish independent authority? I argue that three conditions related to both structure and agency shape successors' ability to achieve this feat: their mode of selection, the presence of a crisis, and the style of leadership they adopt to consolidate power.

To begin, I clarify the theoretical criteria that constitute the "successful" revival of charismatic movements and outline the corresponding observable implications. Theoretically, success entails three factors: The new leader must openly identify himself as the heir of the charismatic founder, rise to the position of chief executive, and achieve widespread popularity. Three observable implications should follow the new leader's successful revival of the movement: he publicly associates himself with the movement and its founder, becomes the nation's chief executive through legitimate means, and achieves an approval rating that exceeds 50 percent for a period of at least one year. The third and final implication is important because it suggests that, like the founder, the successor has the capacity to establish and maintain impressive, widespread appeal that reaches beyond the movement's core base of supporters.

The first condition that facilitates the successful revival of charismatic movements concerns the way in which successors emerge. I distinguish between two types of successors based on this condition: anointed successors and self-starters. Anointed successors, who are often directly handpicked by the founder and immediately take over, seek legitimacy based on the founder's explicit endorsement. Rather than boasting independent skill and experience, these successors showcase their submissive loyalty to the founder as their most compelling attribute, openly embracing the position of second fiddle. By contrast, self-starters seek power on their own terms, whenever they feel conditions are favorable. Unlike anointed successors, these leaders do not seek the direct endorsement of the founder; instead, they rely on their own resources to leverage the founder's legacy, depict themselves as true heirs, and revive the movement in their own name.

While the direct endorsement of the beloved founder would appear to advantage anointed successors over self-starters, this bequest of charisma makes it exceedingly difficult for such handpicked disciples to successfully revive the movement. Conversely, self-starter status creates a much more favorable window of opportunity for new leaders to revive charismatic movements under their own authority.

Anointed successors' struggles to reactivate the followers' attachments begin with the reluctance of charismatic founders to share power. Because the founders perceive themselves as unparalleled heroes, they hesitate to groom strong deputies and prospective successors (Weber 1922/1978, 241–46). To guarantee their predominance and legacy of unmatched power, these leaders tend to treat everyone else in the movement as an underling and surround themselves with sycophants who pose little threat to their "divine" authority. Charismatic leaders also marginalize skilled politicians, who present potential threats to their unmatched superiority (Lasswell 1948, 101–3). The refusal to nourish a worthy replacement, combined with the determination to eliminate skilled competitors, helps founders consolidate their status as supreme protectors. However, it also results in a scarcity of talented heirs. Indeed, when forced to face their mortality, these leaders are much more likely to select a replacement based on allegiance than skill. Having been followers for years, anointed successors face an uphill battle to become respected leaders in their own right. As fervent disciples, they are likely to demonstrate devout loyalty to the founder but are unlikely to possess the independent strength, self-confidence, and personal appeal to tap into the founder's deep bonds with the followers.

Compounding the problem of anointed successors' inadequacy is the time-bound nature of their bid for power. Because they are typically positioned to immediately replace their charismatic predecessors, these new leaders are forced to inherit the founders' bold policies. While the founder may have used such programs to prove his heroic capacities, the programs are likely to be on the verge of collapse by the time anointed successors take power. The reason is that, for these policies to make a truly remarkable impact, the founder uses resources unsustainably, often draining them. Such behavior makes the founder appear extraordinary (Merolla and Zechmeister 2011, 30). Yet, due to the rushed, haphazard, and weakly institutionalized nature of the founder's programs, they are prone to eventual failure. Crucially, the founder delays this outcome by seeking new ways to impress the followers rather than adapting the policies to achieve more sustainable, if modest, progress. This protects the founder's image, yet it leaves anointed successors – who must also demonstrate extraordinary performance to appear worthy of the founder's mantle – in a precarious position.

On the one hand, the initial benefits generated by the founder's actions profoundly shape the followers' loyalty to the movement in the first place. Thus, any attempt by anointed successors to change these revered policies would appear to betray the founder. Fearing reprisal from the followers, these new leaders therefore tend to be excessively risk-averse, strongly preferring to maintain the status quo rather than enacting a change that could frame them as traitors (Weyland 2002, 5). On the other hand, by the time these successors take power, the early success of the founder's programs has long waned. Because these leaders struggle to demonstrate their independent abilities, followers are likely to blame them, rather than the beloved founder, for these failures. Moreover, anointed successors typically have no scapegoat to target for the resulting problems (Loxton and Levitsky 2018, 120). They cannot blame the founder, who represents their sole source of legitimacy and the object of the followers' adoration. Yet, by directly succeeding the founder, there are few, if any, alternative targets to convincingly accuse. Consequently, anointed successors struggle to demonstrate promising potential. In fact, their loyalty to the founder typically constitutes their *only* redeeming quality in the eyes of the followers.

Scholars of routinization agree that anointed successors face an exceedingly high probability of failure (Kostadinova and Levitt 2014, 500–1; Madsen and Snow 1991, 25–28). However, this fact leads the scholars to conclude that the followers' charismatic attachments inevitably disintegrate. In contrast, I contend that the disappointing leadership of anointed successors has a minimal effect on the profound, affective nature of the followers' bonds with the founder – a point that I will highlight in the case of Venezuela in Chapter 4. Moreover, due to this resilience, I argue that it is possible for subsequent leaders to reactivate the followers' attachments, revive the founder's transformative mission, and consolidate independent authority.

Self-starters have greater potential to revive charismatic movements because they can avoid two key problems impeding anointed successors. Crucially, because self-starters seek power on their own terms rather than requiring the explicit endorsement of the founder, they need not rise immediately after the founder's disappearance. Instead, they often choose to bide their time and seek power several years later. This allows the implosion of the founder's policies and the associated image of inadequacy to fall on someone else, making it easier for self-starters to step out of the founder's overbearing shadow. Furthermore, the ambitious nature of self-starters makes them more likely to exercise the individual agency necessary to adopt a personalistic style reminiscent of the founder. By rising on their own and harnessing independent ambition, skill, and personal charisma, these successors have the capacity to emerge not as subservient followers, but as leaders in their own right who demonstrate their personal talents and attract the movement's supporters.

Even so, the success of self-starters is anything but guaranteed. In fact, most of these aspirational leaders fall short of establishing themselves as powerful heirs of the charismatic founder. Two additional conditions greatly facilitate self-starters' efforts to revive the movement and become its preeminent leader. First, as with the initial formation of charismatic attachments, an exogenous condition – the eruption of an acute crisis – provides an important opportunity for self-starters to reactivate these bonds. Under such circumstances, which are similar to those in which the founder sought power, many people lose their sense of self-efficacy: citizens feel they are unable to control their lives (Madsen and Snow 1991, 14–19; Merolla and Zechmeister 2009a, 27–28; Weyland 2003, 825–26). This is especially true of the followers who, as traditionally marginalized people, are likely to suffer disproportionately. A crisis places these individuals – who are adherents of the founder with great faith in his mission of salvation – in a desperate situation that, once again, causes them to look for a leader capable of rescuing them. It also produces excessive optimism in the followers, increasing their willingness to interpret any indication of positive material performance as evidence of the leader's miraculous powers (Weyland 2003, 825–26). Finally, because a crisis can threaten the livelihood of the followers, it can intensify their identification with the movement and their distrust of outsiders, fostering group cohesion (Huddy 2013, 761; Tajfel 1974, 66–67).

The renewed strength of this identity, combined with feelings of low self-efficacy, intensifies followers' hope for a new hero to save them in a manner reminiscent of the founder and renders it more likely that they see an appealing candidate as the savior they have been waiting for. This condition provides a crucial opportunity for successors to enact the *material* cue necessary for reactivating the followers' charismatic attachments: achieving bold performance to demonstrate heroic capacities.

By itself, however, the existence of a crisis is insufficient to reactivate citizens' charismatic attachments. Self-starters are much more likely to become the movement's new leader if they also fulfill a second, more subjective condition that depends on their individual agency: using their own skill, ambition, and charisma to "perform" as the people's savior by adopting and embodying the founder's personalistic leadership style (Moffitt 2015, 190). In contrast to organization-building and programmatic development – leadership tactics associated with routinization – this strategy better corresponds to the movement's preexisting nature and fulfills most followers' hopes for a new savior. Because it showcases self-starters' charismatic appeal, it resonates deeply with supporters, who desire a new leader to fill the void left by their beloved founder.

To foster their own affectionate bonds with the followers, self-starters draw on supreme communication skills to bypass intermediary institutions and establish frequent, direct contact with the followers (Burns 1978, 20). These politicians also incorporate symbols associated with the founder into their speech, dress, and gestures to appear as genuine heirs (Haslam, Reicher, and Platow 2011, 137). Finally, they frame their actions as crucial steps for fulfilling the founder's mission of transformation and claim personal credit for any shred of success. By adopting a personalistic leadership style reminiscent of the founder, self-starters can effectively implement the second, *symbolic* cue required for reactivating followers' attachments.

In combination with the impressive impact of their heroic accomplishments amid crisis conditions, self-starters' symbolic gestures can persuade followers to view them as contemporary heroes of the movement. The material and symbolic accomplishments also attract new followers (e.g., from newly marginalized groups or younger generations), expanding self-starters' support base and consolidating their image as truly paradigm-shifting leaders – veritable reincarnations of the charismatic founder.

In sum, new leaders are most likely to successfully revive the movement in their own name by fulfilling three conditions: coming to power as self-starters rather than as anointed successors; taking advantage of a crisis, which primes citizens to look for a savior; and tapping into the followers' attachments by using their own skill and charisma to adopt the founder's personalistic leadership style. These conditions provide successors with the opportunity to enact daring policies to "prove" their superhuman potential while co-opting the founder's legacy to reinvigorate the movement and consolidate follower support. Figure 2.2 illustrates these three conditions.

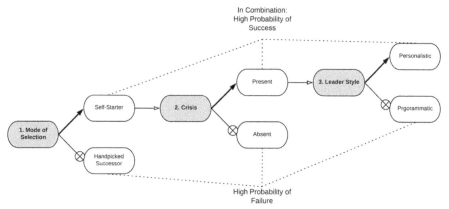

FIGURE 2.2. Flowchart: Conditions for the successful revival of charismatic movements

2.3.3 Integrating Perspectives: The Spasmodic Trajectories of Charismatic Movements

Existing studies suggest that the personalistic nature of charismatic movements has little enduring impact on political systems. In many cases, charismatic leaders arise during extraordinary crises, accumulate impressive but short-lived power, and disappear just as quickly, as society returns to its former routine (Weber 1968, 22). Even if a charismatic movement survives, the routinization thesis indicates that the original leader's charisma has little influence on the movement's subsequent trajectory, as his magnetic appeal transforms into a depersonalized form of authority. If anything, routinized movements are thought to have a *stabilizing* impact on political systems, as the movements discard their charismatic nature and become institutionalized parties, gradually accumulating programmatic strength over time (Converse 1969; Madsen and Snow 1991, 25–29). In this sense, while charisma acts as a "fulcrum" that facilitates the transition to a new institutionalized system, the system soon becomes autonomous (Tucker 1968, 734).

My theory challenges both of these arguments, contending instead that charismatic movements can dramatically shape the political system for decades after the founder disappears. Integrating the perspectives of followers and leaders, I demonstrate that these movements establish a tumultuous cycle of politics in which periods of intense personalistic leadership, when the movement is *revived*, alternate with periods of leaderless fragmentation, in which the movement is *latent*. Thus, unlike routinized parties, which strengthen party institutions over time, I show that charismatic movements repeatedly undermine those institutions.

On the demand side, followers' affective attachments lay the foundation for the fitful trajectories of charismatic movements. Because these attachments develop into a resilient political identity that coincides with a prominent personalistic cleavage, they provide subsequent leaders with the opportunity to win a stable base of support when conditions are ripe. This base may not constitute a majority of voters (often, it encompasses about one-third of the population), but it sustains the movement during latent periods in which the political environment is not receptive to strong, charismatic leadership and the movement is out of power (Taylor 1989, 761). During such periods, followers' attachments to the movement may be "dormant" and the corresponding cleavage depoliticized; in other words, the followers remain passionately devoted to the founder and his mission of salvation, but they feel that there is no current leader who embodies the founder and therefore feel unrepresented in the political arena. Then, when conditions become more conducive to charismatic revival, this reservoir of support provides an important "reserve army" waiting to be mobilized by self-starters who rise up and associate themselves with the founder and movement in their quest for power.[3]

In addition to the resilience of charismatic attachments, their profoundly emotional nature – which remains intact over time, even when the attachments are dormant – entices self-starters to adopt personalistic, rather than programmatic or organizational strategies to secure the followers' loyalty. Thus, whereas extant studies argue that the "rootedness" of citizens' loyalty facilitates the development of an institutionalized party (Levitsky 2003; Loxton and Levitsky 2018; Madsen and Snow 1991, 24; Panebianco 1988), I argue precisely the opposite: paradoxically, citizens' resilient attachments can serve to perpetuate the charismatic and volatile character of the movement.

This is because, while citizens' attachments to the movement persevere, leaders who succeed the founder can only revive charismatic movements in an intermittent and temporary manner. Similar to the founder, successors seek power under conditions that occur sporadically. For example, they tend to emerge after the eruption of serious crises, when the followers feel desperate for a hero to pick up the founder's baton. These new leaders are also more likely to succeed when they can take advantage of favorable political and socioeconomic circumstances to enact bold, initially impressive reforms that "prove" their worthiness to the followers. Since such conditions do not occur regularly, charismatic movements cannot unfold in the stable, linear manner of routinized parties.

Furthermore, while the bold performance of self-starters helps secure their place as charismatic heirs of the founder, it also plants the seeds for the eventual decline of their leadership. Symbolically, while portraying themselves as saviors initially resonates with the followers, these leaders struggle to maintain their heroic image for long – especially as the crisis they valiantly promise to resolve begins to subside, along with the followers' acute desire to be rescued (Madsen and Snow 1991, 22–23; Weyland 2002, 44). More importantly, the successors'

[3] I am grateful to Kurt Weyland for suggesting this term.

seemingly extraordinary "reform packages," though crucial for proving their charismatic power at the outset, undermine the institutions responsible for ensuring that the policies are enforced over time (Bersch 2016, 207; Levitsky and Murillo 2013, 100). In short, the same strategies that enable self-starters to revive the movement also bring about their political demise.

In sum, the dramatic but unsustainable rise of new leaders, made possible by the followers' enduring affective loyalty, causes charismatic movements to develop spasmodic trajectories. Thus, whereas existing studies view charismatic leadership as a temporary disruption of "politics as usual," I argue that the volatility caused by charismatic movements is self-reinforcing. Due to the founder's charismatic prowess, the followers' personalistic attachments solidify into a powerful and enduring political identity that divides society along a cleavage based on citizens' allegiance to or rejection of the charismatic founder. While anointed successors who immediately replace the founder cannot fill his shoes, their poor leadership generates a crisis that causes the followers to search for another savior – a charismatic self-starter – to revive the founder's mission of salvation and provide them with much-needed relief. Under these conditions, self-starters are well positioned to fulfill the followers' expectations by embodying the founder's charismatic authority and implementing audacious policies.

Initially, the policies proposed and implemented by self-starters appear to obliterate the crisis. This reinvigorates citizens' profound reverence for the movement – deepening the stability of their attachments – reenergizes the personalistic cleavage, and bestows a charismatic sheen on the new leader. Yet, because these policies trade long-term sustainability for early success, they are eventually bound to fail and bring the self-starter down with them. Under these circumstances, many followers become disillusioned with the once-impressive self-starter, their attachments temporarily lose their political intensity, and the movement recedes again. The political system then experiences another power vacuum with no leader to guide the way. Nevertheless, citizens' quasi-religious devotion to the charismatic founder and his transformative mission persists – as does the aversion of non-followers to the movement. Moreover, the crisis generated by each new successor's decline generates suffering among the followers that, once again, compels them to look for a new and more convincing replacement to embody the founder's heroic leadership. This process produces a cycle of deeply entrenched political and economic volatility.

Figure 2.3 illustrates the emergence and revival of charismatic movements. As demonstrated in the figure, the movement emerges after the eruption of a crisis with the ascension of the founder. In this context, the leader exerts charisma by recognizing the suffering of individuals who feel they have been marginalized, vowing to resolve their suffering through the enactment of bold and seemingly miraculous policies, and crafting a symbolic narrative that promotes a quasi-religious mission of salvation. The leader's charismatic signals resonate deeply with the suffering people, who crave a savior to resolve

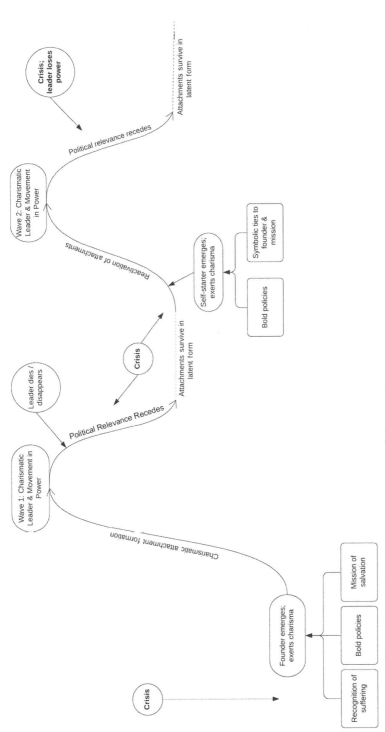

FIGURE 2.3. Illustration of the emergence and revival of charismatic movements

their distress. This results in the establishment of deep, charismatic bonds that catapult the founder and his movement into power. The founder enjoys highly concentrated and personalistic authority until he is unceremoniously removed – either by death (e.g., Juan Perón and Hugo Chávez), force (e.g., Thaksin Shinawatra), or strong pressure (e.g., Alberto Fujimori).

With the founder's disappearance, many followers feel "leaderless," and the political relevance of their attachments declines. Crucially, however, the followers' deeply emotional identification with the movement and founder does not disappear; instead, it persists while becoming politically dormant. During this leaderless period, the movement endures, sustained by followers' resilient identity.

Finally, in the midst of a crisis (whether it is the same crisis that erupted upon the founder's disappearance or a new crisis), an ambitious self-starter rises and depicts himself as a virtual reincarnation of the founder. The self-starter achieves this by expressing her own charisma through promising similarly daring policies and weaving herself into the movement's symbolic narrative as the founder's true heir. This reactivates citizens' charismatic attachments, which enables the self-starter to revive the movement and consolidate power as its new leader. Eventually, the daring yet unsustainable policies of the successor collapse, leading to her demise, and causing the cycle of charismatic movement recession and resurgence to repeat.

2.4 THE CONSEQUENCES OF CHARISMATIC MOVEMENT REVIVAL FOR DEMOCRACY

The resurrection of charismatic movements and their spasmodic trajectories have major repercussions for democratic regimes and the party systems that are supposed to sustain them. My emphasis on the persistence of citizens' deeply emotional attachments to these movements, the incentives of new politicians to exploit those bonds, and the dramatic ups and downs that result suggest that the consequences are mainly negative. Thus, the theory developed in this book yields implications and predictions that diverge starkly from the prevailing routinization arguments.

The logic of routinization suggests that the survival – and hence, the institutionalization – of charismatic movements can strengthen democracy in two ways. First, at the individual level, the transformation of charismatic attachments into programmatic or organizational linkages can improve citizens' political representation. Programmatic linkages induce politicians to respond to and advocate for citizens' substantive policy preferences; in turn, citizens hold their politicians accountable based on the leaders' performance with respect to those policies (Kitschelt 2000, 846). Organizational linkages also enhance citizens' representation by mobilizing voters to participate in the political process, become more politically informed, and feel empowered to defend their interests and preferences (Huckfeldt 2001, 425; López Maya and Lander 2011, 59–60).

Second, routinization improves democracy by replacing the founder's concentrated authority with a depersonalized party organization. Scholars have long argued that institutionalized parties strengthen democracy (Aldrich 1995; Campbell et al. 1960; Converse 1969; Fiorina 1981; Lipset and Rokkan 1967; Mainwaring 2018; Mainwaring and Scully 1995; Roberts 2014; Schattschneider 1942; Ware 1996). Parties aggregate and represent voters' complex interests more effectively than a domineering leader (Aldrich 1995, 18; Kitschelt 2000, 847–48). Moreover, whereas charismatic leaders enact sweeping reforms that attack the status quo, parties tend to embrace a gradual style of reform that better copes with the complexity of social problems and works within the existing institutional framework (Aldrich 1995, 18–27; Bersch 2016, 209–11). This "problem-solving" approach results in more prudent, sustainable policies that reflect constituents' long-term interests (Bersch 2016, 207). Finally, unlike charismatic movements, programmatic parties' entrenched institutional roots and their incremental approach to policymaking enhance the stability of the political system, limit the outbreak of severe political and economic crises, and minimize the likelihood that a hegemonic leader will return to power (Levitsky and Murillo 2013, 99; Mainwaring 2018, 90).

In contrast to the routinization thesis, I argue that the fitful trajectories of charismatic movements infuse democracies with illiberal tendencies and expose them to serious authoritarian threats. At the individual level, the episodic appearance of strong, personalistic leaders reinforces, rather than weakens, the charismatic nature of followers' attachments. In particular, the impressive but short-lived and irresponsible policies of charismatic successors reinvigorate followers' emotional fervor for the movement and cause them to pledge unquestioning devotion to the successor, whom they view as the founder's true heir. Even though the successor's policies eventually collapse, this initial, seemingly miraculous impact lingers with the followers, confirms their perceptions of the successor as extraordinary, and reinforces their personalistic relationship with the movement. As a Peronist disciple explained to me, "I am Peronist because Perón gave my grandfather his first home, Menem gave my father his first car, and [Néstor] Kirchner gave me my first job." Others claimed, "Cristina gave me everything"; "Cristina loved all of Argentina; like Eva, she gave to the poor." Notably, these individuals said nothing of the crises that ultimately unfolded due to each of these Peronist leaders' actions. Instead, they stressed that the leaders single-handedly provided them and their loved ones – the virtuous "people" – with unprecedented benefits. This perception emphasizes the unmediated, asymmetrical, and emotional nature of the attachments between charismatic leaders and their followers.

The resilient charismatic nature of citizens' attachments to the movement erodes their democratic representation in several ways. The attachments urge followers to express loyalty to the leader in the form of unconditional love and compliance. Correspondingly, followers view the act of questioning the leader's behaviors and performance – even when such actions are, in fact, questionable – as a form of betrayal (Fierman 2020, 106). Not only does this undermine these citizens' right to think critically and speak freely, but it also erodes vertical accountability by minimizing the capacity of the electorate to punish the leader for unfavorable policies and/or poor performance (Love and Windsor 2018, 532).

The reactivation of charismatic attachments by new leaders is also detrimental to citizens because it periodically inhibits the development of programmatic and organizational linkages. Programmatically, because successors are judged based on the immediate, tangible impact of their policies, they implement shortsighted reforms without concern for substantive consistency or sustainability. This opportunistic approach makes for an unstable and unpredictable programmatic trademark that further impedes citizens' capacity to hold their politicians accountable (Flores-Macías 2012, 5; Lupu 2014, 568). As I will detail in subsequent chapters, Carlos Menem's popularity among Peronist followers, despite extreme policy reversals, exemplifies this problem.

In addition to the slippery and unpredictable nature of the policies implemented by successors, their inevitable implosion unleashes frequent crises, driving followers to look for new saviors who can implement similarly audacious reforms to provide some relief. Not only does this recurrent suffering and desperation deepen the cycle of charismatic leadership by making citizens crave another redeemer, but it also undermines the potential for organizational ties to develop among the followers. Organizational ties are important because they make voters feel closer to their party and empowered to defend their interests by participating in the political process and/or electing public servants to represent them (Roberts 2014, 27; Samuels and Zucco 2015, 759). The regular collapse of leaders' bold policies in charismatic movements hinders this type of linkage and thus undercuts the quality of citizens' democratic representation. In sum, charismatic movements promote a "disfigured" form of democratic representation that rests on unfaltering devotion to beloved and overbearing leaders rather than the welfare and interests of the people (Urbinati 2019, 3).

At the system level, charismatic movements divide societies along a political cleavage that prioritizes personalism while undermining programmatic competition and democratic pluralism. In doing so, these movements promote authoritarian leader tendencies, perpetuate institutional weakness, and generate tremendous political and economic volatility. Much literature has identified these problems as common in developing democracies in Latin America and throughout the world (e.g., Bersch 2016; Levitsky and Murillo 2013; Mainwaring 2018; Mainwaring and Scully 1995; O'Donnell 1996; Riedl 2014; Roberts 2014). In countries where charismatic movements have emerged, scholars have even acknowledged the notable pattern of "hyperpresidentialism," institutional weakness, and volatility. For example, various authors refer to the "de facto weakness of institutional veto players" and "serial replacement" of institutions (Levitsky and Murillo 2013, 95, 100), the "bipolar" character of society (Mora y Araujo

2011), the "vicious cycle" of bold and irresponsible policymaking (Bersch 2016, 215), and the "ebb and flow" of populism (Roberts 2007, 3).

My theory of charismatic movement revival provides a novel explanation for the episodic cycle described by these authors. To begin, the recurrent emergence of personalistic successors also perpetuates the extreme concentration of executive authority. To establish a heroic image and ensure their personal grip on power, these leaders manipulate rules and procedures that threaten their almighty authority, declare states of emergency, and rule by decree whenever they can. Successors also strangle voices of dissent by appointing loyal family members and friends as key advisors, marginalizing experienced public servants who might question or usurp the leaders' authority, and stacking courts and other political institutions with sycophants – a phenomenon I will reveal in detail in the Argentine case in Chapter 7. Finally, to revive the founder's mission of profound transformation, successors antagonize actors who question their extreme policy agendas. In short, the periodic rise of charismatic successors establishes a political climate marked by hyperpresidentialism, corruption, scant horizontal accountability, extreme polarization, and low tolerance.

Because charismatic movements are revived in this irresponsible fashion, they also hinder institutional development in several ways. First, successive leaders wipe out organizational party structures to ensure programmatic flexibility and secure their personal predominance. Thus, while charismatic movements become all-powerful with the rise of each new leader, their fragile structures decay precipitously when the leader meets his inevitable downfall. Second, successors' compulsion to declare states of emergency, rule by decree, overpower institutions, and eliminate opposing voices undermines crucial institutional checks on executive power by compromising the independence of the legislative and judicial branches of government. These actions, as well as the construction of loyal ruling coalitions, also cause corruption, inefficiency, and disorganization to proliferate across government agencies. Notably, important studies have highlighted that political outsiders have a similar, deleterious impact on party organization and democracy (e.g., Flores-Macías 2012, 5; Mainwaring 2018, 78; Roberts 2014, 37). My analysis extends these authors' findings to argue that such organizationally destructive behaviors apply not only to political outsiders, but also to leaders who revive charismatic movements.

In addition to the extreme concentration of executive power and persistent institutional weakness, I contend that charismatic movements generate enduring political and economic volatility. Scholars of Latin America have long recognized the positive relationship between institutional weakness and this type of volatility (Bersch 2016; Flores-Macías 2012; Levitsky and Murillo 2013; Mainwaring 2018; Mainwaring and Scully 1995; O'Donnell 1996; Riedl 2014; Roberts 2014). I go a step further to argue that charismatic movements turn this relationship into a self-reinforcing cycle. During each wave of charismatic leadership, a successor rises and implements irresponsible policies that are not designed to last. When these sweeping policies reach exhaustion, there is no infrastructure or institutional foundation on which to rebuild. In combination with disastrous policies, the absence of a strong institutional base unleashes political and economic collapse. The fragile structure propping up the leader's party deteriorates, the movement retreats into a state of leaderless fragmentation, and society is left to suffer the consequences. Crucially, while followers may become disenchanted with particular successors when these crises expose the unsustainability of the successors' actions, this disappointment targets the individual leader rather than the overarching movement. In fact, because conditions of crisis intensify the followers' thirst for a savior, the failures of one successor open up the possibility for future self-starters to rise. Over time, the recurrent pattern of personalism and crisis amplifies the damage to citizens' representation, democratic institutions, and societal stability. It is this self-reinforcing nature of charismatic movements that makes them so pernicious.

In conclusion, this book challenges the conventional wisdom that charismatic movements must routinize in order to survive. Instead, I argue that charismatic movements can persist by sustaining their original, personalistic core. However, they do so in a spasmodic fashion that damages the quality of citizens' substantive representation, undermines the development of strong and enduring democratic institutions, and exposes societies to frequent and serious crises. In the chapters that follow, I illustrate how the revival of charismatic movements unfolds by focusing on the prominent cases of Peronism and Chavismo.

PART II

THE DEMAND SIDE

Charisma from the Followers' Perspective

3

The Formation of Charismatic Attachments

This chapter examines the process through which charismatic attachments between leaders and followers develop in the first place. The process deserves careful investigation because it influences how charismatic leaders establish a loyal following and consolidate paradigm-shifting political movements. Moreover, it lays the foundation for the trajectories of charismatic movements after the deaths of their founders. As I will demonstrate, the factors involved in the creation of charismatic attachments undermine the mechanisms required for the depersonalization of those bonds while setting up the possibility for their reactivation in personalistic form.

This chapter focuses on analyzing Venezuela due to the relatively recent emergence of Chavismo. Whereas Perón first governed Argentina over sixty years ago, from 1946 until 1955, Chávez ruled Venezuela from 1999 until 2013, just seven years before the time of writing. I leverage the contemporary nature of Chavismo to investigate firsthand the conditions under which charismatic attachments form and to illustrate the mechanisms at work. This analysis provides two key advantages over existing studies, which tend to examine the charismatic bonds in a strictly theoretical or historical context (e.g., Eatwell 2006; Eisenstadt 1968; Jowitt 1992; Madsen and Snow 1991; Pappas 2012; Weber 1922/1978). First, it reveals fresh insights from a diverse range of voters and elites tied to the regime who remember their personal experiences during the founder's rule. Second, it provides access to relevant, high-quality public opinion data as well as ample primary sources from the period under examination, which are crucial for discerning between the relative influence of

This chapter is based on an article the author originally published in 2020 in the *Journal of Politics in Latin America* (Caitlin Andrews-Lee. 2019a. "The Power of Charisma: Investigating the Neglected Citizen-Politician Linkage in Hugo Chávez's Venezuela." *Journal of Politics in Latin America* 11(3): 298–322, DOI: 10.1177/1866802X19891472). Reprinted with permission.

programmatic, organizational, and personalistic influences on citizens' relationship to the founder and his movement.

The chapter begins with a review of the three characteristics involved in the cultivation of deep, unmediated, and emotional ties between charismatic leaders and their followers. I then illustrate how Chávez took advantage of contextual circumstances and his own alluring traits to fulfill these conditions and establish powerful, resilient bonds with his supporters. Next, I contrast the charismatic mechanism of attachment with programmatic and organizational mechanisms, indicating how the former overpowered the latter two to shape citizens' attachments to Chavismo. To carry out this analysis, I rely on secondary research as well as information from elite interviews, direct observation, and archival research that I conducted during a total of four months of fieldwork in Caracas, Venezuela, in 2014 and 2015.

I complement this qualitative examination with a quantitative analysis of the competing factors involved in citizens' attachments to the movement. Using an important survey conducted by the Latin American Public Opinion Project (LAPOP) in 2007, at the height of Chávez's rule, I demonstrate the overwhelming influence of personalistic rather than programmatic or organizational factors on citizens' ties to the movement. Building on these findings, Chapter 4 uses evidence from focus groups I conducted with followers to assess how their charismatic attachments develop into a resilient identity rather than transform into routinized political linkages. This analysis sheds light on why many remain loyal to the movement *after* the death of the founder.

3.1 ESTABLISHING CHARISMATIC ATTACHMENTS

How do leaders foster direct, deeply affective attachments with voters to generate loyalty to their movements? As outlined in the previous chapter, I argue that leaders achieve this by fulfilling three conditions. For each condition, contextual factors interact with subjective leader traits to shape citizens' attraction to the leader and cultivate fervent ties to his movement. While citizens' initial attraction to the leader helps form these ties, I argue that it is the latter outcome – the process of bonding with the leader's *movement* – that is especially important for shaping the trajectory of the movement and its impact on democratic development.

To begin, I argue that the leader must reach out directly to citizens who feel that mainstream society has forgotten them. Due to feelings of suffering and perceived exclusion, these individuals become convinced that the political establishment has no interest in them. Thus, they look for a distinct and impressive political outsider who recognizes their misfortune and appears willing and able to address their long-neglected needs (Madsen and Snow 1991, 12–15). A crisis that causes disproportionate misery often accentuates these citizens' thirst for a savior; a cunning leader, in turn, can take advantage of this opportunity to portray himself as the hero that people crave (Weyland 2003, 843).

Importantly, to cultivate charismatic attachments, the leader does not only recognize and promise to resolve the people's suffering. Rather, he must fulfill a second condition: He must demonstrate his ability to resolve their misery and defend them against the "evil" forces blamed for their distress. To do so, the leader enacts bold policies that quickly produce tangible, impressive results (Pappas 2012, 4–5; Weber 1922/1978, 242). Whereas direct recognition provides marginalized citizens with hope for a more dignified life, the leader's daring performance convinces them that he is capable of delivering on this promise. Importantly, the perception of the leader's performance as "miraculous" exceeds the positive outcome that would result from voters' rational performance evaluations; instead, the leader's performance produces an emotionally intense and unquestioning devotion in the followers that endures even after the leader's performance declines.

Finally, the leader cements his charismatic image and consolidates a loyal following by crafting a narrative that reinforces his superhuman power, intrepid quest to vanquish the people's enemies, and commitment to transforming society. To ensure that the narrative resonates with his followers, the leader ties it to relevant cultural figures and symbols with whom his followers already identify (Willner and Willner 1965, 82). Likewise, the leader associates his opponents with familiar, epic foes. By integrating these commonly understood prototypes of good and evil, his narrative reframes well-known historical events "within a salvation framework" that reinforces the legendary character of his leadership (Smith 2000, 103–4). To ensure widespread dissemination of the narrative, the leader infuses public spaces with the movement's symbols and emphasizes key components of the narrative via frequent, unmediated interactions with his followers (Plotkin 2002, 24; Zúquete 2008, 93–103). Together, these actions shape the leader's capacity to establish direct, profoundly emotional connections with his followers.

3.2 CHARISMATIC ATTACHMENTS IN CHÁVEZ'S VENEZUELA

Hugo Chávez's meteoric rise to power and his fourteen-year rule over Venezuela clearly illustrate the process through which leaders exert charisma to form steadfast attachments and establish powerful movements. Chávez made his political debut in the early 1990s as a military officer amid the collapse of Venezuela's *Punto Fijo* (PF) regime. The regime, which was born out of a 1958 political pact between two major, centrist political parties that sought to secure democratization, achieved uniquely high levels of political stability and economic growth compared to its Latin American neighbors for several decades (Smilde 2011, 4; Weyland 2003, 826).[1] However, when the

---

[1] The Punto Fijo pact established a well-institutionalized, democratic, and moderate political system that consisted primarily of a center-right party (the Christian Democrats – COPEI) and a center-left party (Democratic Action – AD) (Smilde 2011, 3).

country faced a protracted economic downturn starting in the 1980s, establishment politicians from the two main parties undermined their own legitimacy in several ways. First, they enacted a series of deeply unpopular and ultimately ineffective economic reforms in an attempt to address the worsening crisis, causing citizens prolonged suffering (Weyland 2003, 826–27). Second, while ideologically distinct in name, the two parties became virtually indistinguishable due to their shared commitment to a neoliberal approach (Morgan 2007, 83–84). Third, as establishment politicians clung to power, massive corruption scandals implicating both parties surfaced, proving to citizens that writ large the system no longer represented their interests (Seawright 2012, 90).

In February 1992, during this party-system breakdown, Chávez led a clandestine group of officers called the Revolutionary Bolivarian Movement-200 (MBR-200) in an attempted coup against President Carlos Andrés Pérez (Smilde 2011, 487). Although the coup failed and Chávez served the next two years in prison, his defeat earned him national notoriety as an honorable young man determined to rescue Venezuelans from the grips of the selfish "partyarchy" (Coppedge 1997). By 1998, another failed round of neoliberal policies enacted by President Rafael Caldera sealed the fate of the PF regime. Out of its ashes, Chávez – who promised a radical departure from the outgoing regime's corruption and incompetence – took the country by storm, winning the presidential election with 56 percent of the vote (Weyland 2003, 828).

3.2.1 Direct Recognition of Marginalized Citizens

Over the course of his rise and rule, Chávez exerted all three of the above-described components of charisma, resulting in the formation of steadfast bonds with millions of Venezuelans. First, he directly recognized and politically incorporated masses of impoverished citizens who had suffered terribly during the 1980s and 1990s, during which Venezuela experienced a sustained economic decline and the PF regime disintegrated (Lupu 2014; Maingon 2004; Mainwaring 2014; Morgan 2011; Seawright 2012; Weyland 2003). Specifically, in the years leading up to his first presidential candidacy in 1998, Chávez recognized that Venezuelans' widespread feelings of exclusion and suffering presented an important opportunity. Unlike politicians from across the ideological spectrum who came to support the PF regime's widely unpopular neoliberal policies, Chávez publicly empathized with the people's intense frustration and misery – as demonstrated through his attempted coup in 1992 (Roberts 2013, 1434–40). As a result, poor citizens came to see Chávez as the *only* leader capable of understanding and resolving their suffering. A Chavista activist illustrated this sentiment in an interview with the author. Unlike politicians from the PF regime who remained preoccupied with their "elite intellectualism ... Chávez made the poor and invisible people visible."[2] Similarly, a prominent opposition politician stated that Chávez's open recognition of people's feelings of suffering and marginalization resonated deeply with them. The politician said, "Chávez understood the people's accumulated frustration. The people didn't feel valued [by other politicians]; Chávez made them feel recognized."[3]

Throughout his presidency, Chávez publicly acknowledged his followers' suffering and reinforced his role as their savior. A speech he gave on January 10, 2003, illustrates how he claimed personal responsibility for poor and excluded groups:

> Make no mistake about Hugo Chávez ... in accordance with the Constitution of the Republic and my powers as Chief of State and my responsibilities as President of the Republic, I cannot permit that people die of hunger; I cannot permit that children die because there isn't medicine or there isn't milk; I cannot permit that the people drown of hunger and death. Above all things it is my responsibility in front of God and the flag to defend the Venezuelan people, above all things and as dictated by the Bolivarian Constitution! (Chávez 2003c)

By promising to single-handedly protect his people from hunger, disease, and death – maladies they suffered at the hand of his predecessors – Chávez illustrated how he sought to personally acknowledge and incorporate excluded sectors of the population into the center of political life. This recognition proved tremendously successful in laying the foundation for many poor citizens' devotion to Chávez. Indeed, it consolidated their "powerful belief in the ability of the leader to provide transcendence and moral-political renewal" (Hawkins, Rosas, and Johnson 2011, 187).

3.2.2 Approbation of Heroic Powers through Bold Reforms

To substantiate his claim to rescue the people from their misery, Chávez implemented a series of daring reforms that promised to sweep away the malevolent "political class" and bring peace and prosperity to the masses. He established what would become the cornerstone for all of these ambitious reforms – a new, hyperpresidential constitution that granted him hegemonic control over politics – immediately after assuming the presidency (Corrales and Penfold 2015, 19–20; Ellner 2011, 435; Stoyan 2020, 99–100). During his 1998 presidential campaign, Chávez vowed to enact this constitution to break away from the corrupt PF regime, personally restore and protect Venezuelans' socioeconomic rights, and enhance their direct participation in politics. After

---

[2] Author interview with a Chavista activist and journalist, October 24, 2015. Due to the dangerous political climate in Venezuela, all interviews conducted in the country have been anonymized to protect the interviewees.

[3] Author interview with a National Deputy and member of the political party *Voluntad Popular*, September 25, 2015.

his victory, in his February 1999 inaugural speech, the new president declared what would become a celebrated refrain among his followers: "I swear before God, before the Country, before my people that over this moribund Constitution, I will enact the democratic transformations necessary for the Republic to have a Magna Carta that fits with the new times. I swear" (Chávez 1999). On December 15, 1999, the referendum on the new constitution passed with 72 percent support.

The swiftness and thoroughness with which Chávez oversaw the construction of a new, far-reaching, and overwhelmingly popular constitution made him appear truly heroic in the eyes of his supporters. Several prior leaders, including Jaime Lusinchi (1984–89) and Rafael Caldera (1994–99), who had promised similar constitutional reforms, had failed to follow through (López Maya and Lander 2011, 58). In contrast, Chávez made good on his vow by installing a new and transformative Magna Carta immediately after assuming office. This act – which, among other things, renamed Venezuela "The Bolivarian Republic of Venezuela" – confirmed Chávez's position in the eyes of his marginalized followers as their liberator and the symbolic reincarnation of national independence hero Simón Bolívar (López Maya and Lander 2000, 8–10).

The new constitution outlined a series of ambitious and unprecedented objectives, further demonstrating Chávez's extraordinary capacities to provide the suffering followers with material prosperity and spiritual transcendence (Hawkins 2010, 35; Stoyan 2020, 105). For instance, in addition to representative democratic institutions, it created new participatory institutions, including electoral and civil branches to be overseen by the National Electoral Council and the Defender of the People, respectively. The constitution also moved beyond basic political and civil rights to proclaim economic and social inclusion for all citizens. To achieve this vision of inclusion and equality, Chávez endeavored not only to redistribute wealth, but also to fundamentally transform society – to "reestablish the human condition" (López Maya and Lander 2011, 63). By ratifying his new constitution in the first year of his presidency, Chávez boldly signaled his intention to fundamentally transform Venezuela – a proposition that the poor masses embraced with fervor.

Inspired by the success of his new constitution, Chávez implemented several programs that achieved impressive initial results and thus further demonstrated his extraordinary capacities to his supporters. For example, starting in November 2001, he enacted an unprecedented program of land reform through the Law of Land and Agricultural Development and Decree 1.666. This program established a series of Rural and Urban Land Committees through which poor citizens could "exercise their right of property" and thus achieve socioeconomic inclusion, as envisioned by the new constitution (López Maya and Lander 2011, 65). By 2005, 6,000 Urban Land Committees incorporating nearly one quarter of poor Venezuelans had been established (ibid., 66).

Despite the early success of the new constitution and the policies it inspired, however, several problems emerged that went unaddressed. Consequently, the striking initial impact of these reforms began to deteriorate just a few years after their implementation. For example, the new participatory institutions, purportedly designed to empower ordinary citizens, leaned heavily on Chávez's personal leadership and thus served to concentrate his executive authority rather than provide the citizens with a direct and independent role in the political process (Ellner 2011, 431–32; López Maya and Lander 2011, 60). Similarly, the land reform policies lacked regulation and enforcement mechanisms, resulting in violent conflict between landowners and peasants after the establishment of Rural Land Committees (ibid., 65–66). Additionally, Urban Land Committees, while initially successful in mobilizing the urban poor, became increasingly dependent on the Chávez regime for resources, resulting in a hierarchical structure that undermined the autonomy of local committee members (ibid., 67). Notably, in spite of these clear shortcomings, followers continued to view Chávez as their savior.

As these examples indicate, though Chávez's constitution made sweeping promises to promote participatory democracy and social justice, the programs allegedly designed to achieve these objectives fell short and even contradicted values of political participation and social inclusion. Yet, rather than acknowledging these shortcomings, Chávez continually papered over them with new, equally bold and unrealistic measures, which he delivered through spontaneous executive decrees and "organic laws" rushed through the National Assembly (López Maya 2016, 211). The audacity and seemingly direct delivery of these gestures only reinforced Chávez's valiant image in the eyes of his supporters. As a policy coordinator from the Central Bank of Venezuela described, "Chávez was a magician who created the illusion of progress."[4] While unrealistic and irresponsible, the initial, tangible effects of his daring policies – embodied by his ambitious new constitution – "proved" his extraordinariness in the eyes of the followers, thereby making him worthy of their devotion.

3.2.3 Construction of a Symbolic Narrative

To solidify his charismatic bonds with the people and consolidate the transformative power of his movement, Chávez cultivated a vivid narrative with three key characteristics. First, the narrative employed "missionary" rhetoric that glorified his image and tied him to classic heroes embedded in Venezuelan culture, including Simón Bolívar, Venezuela's nineteenth-century liberator; Ezequiel Zamora, the hero of Venezuela's Federal War; Guicaipuro, an indigenous Venezuelan chief who fought against the Spanish Conquest; and even

---

[4] Author interview with an economic policy coordinator from the Central Bank of Venezuela, October 22, 2015.

Jesus Christ (Martínez Meucci and de Lustgarten 2014, 19–21; Michelutti 2017, 237–38; Zúquete 2008, 97). The comparison with familiar, beloved heroes cast a saintly glow on Chávez's figure and imbued his mission with profound historical importance. In fact, the very labeling of his movement as "Bolivarian" suggested to his followers that Chávez did not merely seek to improve their lives, but that he also sought to "reclaim the dignity of the people, of the country, and of the supposedly better past, the mystical, glorious and heroic path that Venezuela always associated with the figure of Bolívar" (Martínez Meucci and de Lustgarten 2014, 23). By depicting Chávez as the true son of Venezuela's most celebrated and tragic hero, his narrative tapped into several preexisting identities relevant to his followers, ranging from popular Christianity to mestizaje to Santería, and caused Chávez's followers to worship him like a deity (Michelutti 2017, 234–36). As a professor of social and cultural studies at the Bolivarian University of Venezuela passionately proclaimed two years after the leader's death, "Chávez is on the altar with the saints!"[5]

Second, while cultivating his image as a hero of epic proportions, Chávez's narrative also demonized his opponents. In contrast with his followers, whom he affectionately called "patriots" and "soldiers," Chávez referred to his adversaries as "enemies," "coup plotters," "imperialists," and agents of the "extreme right" (Gauna 2018, 47). For example, in 2003 he declared in a speech, "this is not about the pro-Chávez against the anti-Chávez … but … the patriots against the enemies of the homeland" (Zúquete 2008, 105). Further, when opposition citizens protested, he often framed them as enemies of the true "people" and responded with brutal punishment rather than openness to negotiation, as illustrated by his response to the December 2002 strike by workers from the national oil company, Petróleos de Venezuela (PdVSA) (Corrales and Penfold 2015, 24–25).[6] He also routinely marginalized and persecuted opposition judges, leaders, and parties and expelled advisors from within his own ranks whom he accused of betraying him, periodically humiliating these individuals through surprise attacks broadcasted to the public on his weekly television show (Carroll 2013, 64).

The establishment of an all-out war against a "clear-cut enemy" helped promote cohesion and obedience among Chávez's followers by convincing them that their beloved leader's critics posed a grave, even existential, threat (Huddy

---

[5] Author interview with a professor of social and cultural studies at the Bolivarian University of Venezuela, October 14, 2015. In 2003 Chávez established this university by decree as part of the Sucre mission (D'Elia and Maingon 2009, 5). Although its stated mission is to provide free postsecondary education to Venezuelan citizens, Chávez used the university as a vehicle to strengthen his charismatic attachments to his followers. Since his death, the university has devoted itself to commemorating his heroic legacy.

[6] Another reason Chávez responded to this protest with brute force was that opposition forces had recently staged a coup against him (Corrales and Penfold 2015, 24–25).

2001, 150). As explained by the Bolivarian University professor, "Under threats from the 'extreme right,' Chávez would unify the people, so there was not dispersion." In addition to strengthening cohesion among his followers, this strategy made Chávez appear even more charismatic and provided him with convenient scapegoats to blame for drops in performance. By alienating his movement's opponents and attacking "traitors" from within it, the narrative also helped solidify a deep-seated and profoundly personalistic cleavage.

Third, Chávez's symbolic narrative generated a mission that promised not only to vanquish evil opponents but also to emancipate the followers from their suffering by bringing about a holistic transformation of society. In contrast to "small, pragmatic changes to an already existing political system," the mission envisioned a "rebirth" of Venezuela (Zúquete 2008, 112). The urgency of this all-encompassing agenda left no time or space for questions from hesitant observers. Rather, Chávez emphasized that successful transformation demanded the absolute faith of his followers; those who failed to demonstrate this commitment would suffer dire consequences. As Zúquete states, "To stress this need for a radical transformation of the country, Chávez's discourse gain[ed] an apocalyptic dimension in which the survival of the country and even the world seem[ed] to be in question" (ibid.). A Chavista activist and journalist further stressed, "the transformation cannot happen without the followers; we need their faith in Chávez."[7]

To build his symbolic narrative, Chávez established constant, direct communication with his followers through speeches and other performances that dominated media outlets. As the journalist explained, Chávez was a "communicational genius who started a revolution through the media." The star of his own weekly television show, "Aló Presidente," he spoke directly into the camera for hours, giving his followers the impression of having an intimate conversation with their president (Capriles 2012, 60; Carroll 2013, 15–18; Zúquete 2008, 100). He also frequently interrupted radio and television programs to make "emergency" announcements (*cadenas*) and reinforce the perception of his omnipresence in Venezuelans' lives (Carroll 2013, 24). As a palace historian and archivist for Chávez described, the founder also traveled tirelessly around the country to personally connect with his followers, both during and between electoral campaigns.[8]

In addition to ensuring frequent and direct communication with his followers, Chávez strengthened his narrative by tightening his control over the media and saturating public spaces with symbols that glorified him and his movement. For example, Chávez's government purchased or intimidated opposing news outlets by cutting funding, revoking licenses, and constricting the availability of material supplies (Weyland 2013, 19, 23–24). This left the movement with

---

[7] Author interview with journalist at Venezolana de Televisión and former communications official at the Ministry of Tourism, October 2, 2015.

[8] Author interview with palace archivist and historian for Chávez, October 17, 2015.

FIGURE 3.1. Mural of Chávez, Christ, and Bolívar

unencumbered space to project the narrative through media platforms ranging from television to radio to print. Chávez also took literal and symbolic owner-ship of traditional Venezuelan literature, art, and music. His regime sponsored literature, film, art, and music festivals and enjoyed the support of authors, musicians, and artists who fervently dedicated their work to the *Comandante*. Lastly, the movement filled physical spaces with Bolivarian symbols in the form of posters, murals, statues, buildings, colors, and songs that glorified the founder and his heroic predecessors. For example, Figure 3.1 displays a mural depicting Chávez with Bolívar and Christ (Ramirez 2014). When combined with his recognition of previously excluded citizens and his implementation of bold reforms, the omnipresence of Chávez's narrative transformed Chavismo into "a charismatic form of political religion" to which his followers became deeply attached (Zúquete 2008, 92).

In sum, Chávez formed steadfast charismatic bonds with his followers by fulfilling three conditions. First, he directly recognized the suffering of margin-alized citizens and promised to rescue them from their misery. Second, he proved his ability to follow through on this promise by implementing bold reforms that made an impressive initial impact on followers' lives, such as a radical new constitution. Third, he established a compelling narrative that tied his heroic leadership to Venezuelan history, underscored the dangerous threat posed by his opponents, and reinforced his mission to provide transcendence by bringing about a profound transformation of society.

3.3 ASSESSING THE RELEVANCE OF ALTERNATIVE LINKAGE TYPES

The preceding section outlined the conditions under which charismatic attachments form and demonstrated the role of these ties in Chavismo. Yet, evaluating the impact of charisma on citizens' attachments and identification with the movement also requires analysis of competing linkage types. This section assesses the extent to which followers developed alternative forms of attachment to Chavismo rooted in programmatic and organizational mechanisms, and it demonstrates how followers' charismatic bonds overwhelmed these more conventional linkages.

3.3.1 Programmatic Attachments

The programmatic mechanism suggests that citizens' attachments rest on the substantive coherence of the leader's policies. Grounded in long-standing studies of issue preferences, retrospective and prospective economic voting, and partisanship, most scholars assume that this mechanism forms the natural and proper core of party and electoral politics (e.g., Achen 2002; Downs 1957; Fiorina 1981; Key 1966; Roberts 2014). To develop programmatic ties, citizens must have well-formed issue preferences that align with the leader's policies (Key 1966, 7–8). In addition, the leader must *consistently* and *successfully* carry out these policies to earn voters' approval and establish a clear programmatic trademark that is distinct from that of other parties (Fiorina 1981, 66). In contrast to bold, shortsighted reforms, whose initially impressive performance casts the individual leader in a heroic light, the programmatic trademark rests on the substantive content and steady functioning of social and economic policies. Citizens "periodically update" their attachment to the movement based on the leader's adherence to this trademark (Kitschelt 2000, 846). If the leader fails to implement distinctive and effective policies that are consistent with this trademark, citizens punish him and reduce their attachment to the movement (Achen 2002, 151; Lupu 2013, 52).

Several scholars claim that Chávez developed a programmatic trademark that emphasized state-centered economics and redistributive social programs called missions. To begin, Chávez attempted to increase the state's role in the economy. For instance, he tightened government control over the state-run oil company, PdVSA, by ratifying the New Organic Hydrocarbon Law in 2001 (Parker 2005, 44). Shortly thereafter, he nationalized dozens of non-oil companies and implemented a sweeping Land Reform Law. He also eventually imposed strict currency exchange and price controls to counteract inflation and keep consumer goods affordable (Corrales and Penfold 2015, 64).

However, Chávez did not stake out a clear position on economic policy until late 2001, well after he had consolidated widespread popular support. Upon taking office, he confirmed his center-right predecessor's minister of finance,

Maritza Izaguirre, and appeased the International Monetary Fund by cutting the state's budget by 7 percent and strengthening the Investment Fund for Macroeconomic Stabilization (Corrales and Penfold 2015, 48–55). Despite these economically liberal policies, which contrasted sharply with his later turn to "socialism of the 21st century," Chávez's movement cultivated impressive popular support: In 1999 and 2000, between 38 and 41 percent of Venezuelans claimed to identify with the movement and 75 to 84 percent approved of Chávez's performance (Consultores 21 2014).

By late 2001, Chávez began to advertise and implement state-centered policies that were inspired by his new constitution. While many of these programs achieved impressive results at the outset, their performance soon dropped, providing little foundation for sustained programmatic support. For example, though booming oil prices from late 2003 to 2008 facilitated substantial economic growth, Chávez's protectionist policies failed to stimulate investment and instead invited rampant corruption (Ellner 2010, 88–91; Corrales and Penfold 2015, 70). Thus, production in non-oil sectors declined, leading to sharp rises in the number of imported goods; investment in infrastructure lagged, generating electricity and water shortages; and price and exchange controls caused increasing inflation, a rising black market exchange rate, consumer goods shortages, and capital flight. The economy contracted by 3.3 percent of GDP when oil prices fell in 2009, and in 2010, Chávez was forced to sharply devalue the local currency (Corrales and Penfold 2015, 63–70). The ultimate failure of these policies and the resulting inflation and shortages disproportionately affected low-income citizens, many of whom were strong supporters of Chavismo.

Nevertheless, the substantial decline in Chávez's economic performance did not temper his followers' praise. Instead, his policy failures provided an opportunity for the charismatic leader to strengthen his symbolic narrative by blaming opposition actors whom he labeled as enemies of his revolution, including "imperial powers" like the United States and local agents of the "extreme right" (Zúquete 2008, 104–7). For instance, as Chávez's economic performance declined over the course of his rule, his anti-US rhetoric steadily increased – even as the US tempered its critiques of Venezuela (Corrales and Penfold 2015, 113). Similarly, on the domestic front, Chávez accused his opponents of plotting "conspiracies against and betrayals of the homeland," thereby undermining the success of his policies (Gauna 2018, 54–55). The success of this rhetorical strategy demonstrates citizens' willingness to shield their beloved leader from criticism and suggests that their loyalty to his movement was not rooted in the substantive content and consistent performance of his economic programs.

In addition to state-centered economics, Chávez implemented dozens of redistributive social "missions." Beginning with their launch in 2003, Chávez poured billions of petro-dollars into these programs in areas ranging from health care to information technology (Maingon 2016, 20). The most prominent missions sought to reduce poverty and inequality through better provision of food, health care, education, and housing. Through these programs, Chávez appeared to prioritize the objectives of equality and social justice showcased in his new constitution.

Yet, like his economic policies, Chávez's social missions suffered from serious problems. The missions sprang up via presidential decree in a rapid, improvisational, and politicized manner that undercut their sustainability. Consequently, while they improved poor Venezuelans' quality of life at the outset, the missions failed to perform favorably after their first few years of operation (Corrales and Penfold 2015, 61; España 2014). In fact, by 2007, Chávez's most popular social program – the healthcare mission *Barrio Adentro* – was considered deeply flawed and largely inoperational (Aponte 2014, 128, 165). While poverty declined from 2003 to 2006, it stagnated from 2007 to 2012 and began to reverse thereafter (Ellner 2011, 433–38; Aponte 2014, 153; Maingon 2016, 119–20). By 2014, poverty had risen to 48.4 percent, surpassing 1998 levels by over 3 percentage points (España 2014, 4). Finally, despite the missions' rapid initial growth, a 2014 survey indicates that a mere 10 percent of citizens report having benefited from them, suggesting a failure to sustainably reduce poverty and protect Venezuelans' socioeconomic rights (Aponte 2014, 168; España 2014, 8). Thus, it is more likely that followers' fervent approval of Chávez's programs throughout this period arose from "lingering beliefs in [his] charisma" than from the substantive integrity of his policies (Merolla and Zechmeister 2011, 29).

In short, the superficial nature and volatile performance of Chávez's economic and social policies indicates his preference for dramatic reform over programmatic development. Though he promised to establish economic and social inclusion in Venezuela, the delayed implementation of his policies and, ultimately, their negative performance made for a weak programmatic trademark. Most importantly, the bold, hasty application and short-lived success of these policies prioritized the establishment of Chávez's savior-like image at the expense of medium- and long-term effectiveness. Consequently, while deepening followers' affective ties to Chávez, these policies held little appeal for programmatically principled voters. Moreover, the delayed application of Chávez's policies cannot account for the movement's widespread support during his first three years in office. These factors demonstrate how personalism infused Chávez's policy agenda and compromised the development of programmatic linkages.

3.3.2 Organizational Attachments

The organizational mechanism suggests that political attachments rest on the ties people cultivate with each other through local involvement in movement-affiliated activities and groups. Through these ties, citizens foster an enduring group identity that is maintained via involvement in the movement's social clubs, neighborhood associations, and political organizations (Granovetter 1973; Green, Palmquist, and Schickler 2002). Building this type of bond requires the followers' *widespread* and *regular* participation. The movement's organizations must also be sustained and strengthened over time and must maintain a "horizontal" rather than hierarchical character to inspire group members' feelings of efficacy (Ellner 2011, 430–31; Rhodes-Purdy 2015, 423–24). Unlike charismatic attachments, in which followers' sense of belonging comes directly from the leader, the organizational mechanism suggests that the followers ease their feelings of exclusion in a bottom-up fashion by interacting with each other.

Chávez promoted the organizational dynamic of his movement and even enshrined citizen participation in the 1999 constitution as a necessary condition for democracy (García-Guadilla 2012, 220). Early in his presidency, he launched several community-based organizations aimed at placing governance into the hands of the people, including Urban Land Committees, Health Committees, Technical Roundtables for Water, and Bolivarian Circles (Aponte 2014; López Maya and Lander 2011). In 2006, he appeared to strengthen this initiative by establishing the Communal Councils (CCs). Officially registered, neighborhood-level groups consisting of 200 to 400 families, the CCs were intended to be self-governing: They would elect representatives, run their own meetings, and solicit funds directly from the government to resolve problems (Aponte 2014, 264).

In practice, however, this network failed to cultivate genuine organizational ties to the movement. First, citizen participation in the CCs was neither widespread nor regular. A 2005–2007 survey of poor Venezuelans by Universidad Católica Andrés Bello (UCAB) suggests that only 29 percent had ever participated in a community event, while only 7 percent had participated in a CC (Aponte 2014, 260). Among the few citizens who participated in CCs, a 2008 survey by Centro Gumilla indicates that less than 50 percent regularly attended meetings (Machado 2009, 48–49). Second, the poor infrastructure of these groups compromised followers' ability to develop a strong grassroots network. Chávez's sluggish and haphazard institutionalization of the CCs reflects this weakness: He did not legally recognize them through the Law of Communal Councils until 2006, and he neglected to establish a government ministry to oversee them until 2010 (Aponte 2014, 264). By 2012, in a famous speech titled "Changing Course" (*Golpe de Timón*), Chávez angrily acknowledged the weakness of his movement's grassroots spirit (Chávez 2012). Third, much evidence indicates that the CCs functioned in a hierarchical fashion. In many CCs, a mere handful of members remained active, and leaders often served as party bosses rather than local representatives, usurping control over projects and funds at the expense of other residents (García-Guadilla 2012, 227–35). Perhaps as a result, a 2009 survey by Centro Gumilla suggests 76 percent of Venezuelans perceived CCs as corrupt, while 77 percent agreed that CCs did not involve most members of their community (Machado 2009, 37; Aponte 2014, 271).

Ultimately, the evidence suggests that the CCs did not foster genuine grass-roots empowerment. While Chávez extolled the virtues of participatory democracy and made dramatic (if irregular) efforts to establish community organizations, these groups suffered from low participation rates and severe institutional weaknesses. Outspoken leaders dominated many CCs and bred distrust rather than a genuine participatory spirit. Moreover, citizens' feelings of recognition and inclusion depended more on their devotion to Chávez than their involvement in community affairs. Indeed, while followers praised Chávez for giving them a voice in politics, they did not exercise that voice in practice through involvement in the movement's participatory organizations. Instead, Chávez imposed cohesion over his movement in a top-down fashion, preventing "formal collective decision-making" and suppressing "the emergence of a second-in-command" (Ellner 2011, 434). Therefore, it is unlikely that swaths of followers developed strong attachments to Chavismo based on an organizational mechanism.

3.4 A QUANTITATIVE ANALYSIS OF COMPETING ATTACHMENT MECHANISMS

I draw from a nationally representative 2007 survey by LAPOP to quantitatively investigate the impact of charisma on citizens' attachments to Chavismo relative to programmatic and organizational factors. The survey contains relevant questions for all aspects of my analysis, including attachment to the movement (dependent variable); evaluation of economic and social policies (programmatic independent variables); participation in the CCs (organizational independent variable); and perceptions of Chávez's charisma (personalistic independent variable). In addition, the survey was fielded in August and September of 2007, shortly after Chávez's second reelection. By that time, voters had several years to experience and evaluate both programmatic and grassroots components of Chávez's movement, including the social missions and CCs. Thus, the survey allows for an important analysis of the personalistic mechanism's relative strength at a crucial point during Chávez's rule.

3.4.1 The Dependent Variable

I construct the dependent variable – attachment to Chavismo – using a question on respondents' party identification. Political scientists have long understood party identification as a genuine expression of membership in or attachment to a political group (Campbell et al. 1960; Green et al. 2002; Lupu 2013). Venezuelans' identification with Chavista-affiliated parties, therefore, captures their self-perceived political ties more adequately than vote choice, which can result from a range of factors extending beyond attachment to the movement. I create a dichotomous measure of attachment where citizens who identify with one of three party labels connected to Chávez's movement – Movement of the

Fifth Republic (MVR), Fatherland for All (PPT), or the United Socialist Party of Venezuela (PSUV) – are considered "attached" while citizens who do not are considered "not attached."[9] Twenty-three percent of all respondents express attachment to these parties, while just fewer than 9 percent identify with non-Chavista parties. Due to the weakly institutionalized nature of Chavismo, measuring identification with associated parties likely underestimates the number of Venezuelans attached to the broader movement. Nevertheless, I use this measure because the survey does not ask about attachment to the movement per se – and I assume that citizens who identify with affiliated parties also have genuine attachments to the movement.[10]

3.4.2 The Independent Variables

I select several survey items as independent variables to represent the three attachment mechanisms. For the charismatic mechanism, I incorporate a five-question battery on perceptions of Chávez's charisma developed by Merolla and Zechmeister (2011).[11] This focus on citizens' perceptions of the leader, rather than "objective" personality traits, captures the subjective dynamic of charismatic authority (Weber 1922/1978, 242). As shown previously in this chapter, the factors underlying the charismatic mechanism – direct recognition, bold reforms, and the symbolic narrative – also serve to increase perceptions of the leader's charisma, suggesting the validity of the measure. Though many successful leaders are perceived as charismatic, scholars have stressed that, relative to other Latin American presidents, perceptions of Chávez's charisma were uniquely high throughout his tenure (Weyland 2003, 822; Zúquete 2008, 91; Hawkins 2010, 37–38; Merolla and Zechmeister 2011, 37–38). Furthermore, while related to party attachment, leader approval, and vote choice, charismatic perceptions remain a theoretically and empirically distinct concept.[12]

---

[9] The Fatherland for All party was not explicitly part of Chavismo, but was allied with the movement during Chávez's rule.

[10] See Merolla and Zechmeister (2011, 40) for a similar coding strategy.

[11] Merolla and Zechmeister (2011) developed the charisma battery based on a larger set of questions from the Multifactor Leadership Questionnaire – 5X Long Form, which was first introduced in the United States, and they have used the battery to assess citizens' perceptions of charisma in Mexico and Venezuela.

[12] To validate charisma's conceptual distinctiveness, Merolla and Zechmeister use the 2007 LAPOP survey to predict presidential approval with charisma, party identification, ideology, and performance evaluations (2011, 51). Though charisma has a strong, significant effect on presidential approval, "these effects do not drown out the influence of other key factors." Moreover, while the correlation between charisma, presidential approval, and vote choice are moderately high, they are "far from perfect," indicating the empirical distinctiveness of the charisma battery.

The questions in the LAPOP charisma battery ask respondents to report on a four-point scale the extent to which they agree about five statements: (1) Chávez articulates a compelling vision of the future, (2) Chávez instills pride in being associated with him, (3) Chávez's actions build my respect for him, (4) Chávez considers the moral and ethical consequences of his decisions, and (5) Chávez goes beyond his own self-interest for the good of the group (Merolla and Zechmeister 2011, 37). I add and rescale these items to create a continuous score of Chávez's charisma ranging from zero (not at all charismatic) to one (very charismatic).[13]

For the programmatic mechanism, I first include survey items that gauge respondents' perceptions of Chávez's economic performance. Following Merolla and Zechmeister (2011), I combine four questions – on current and retrospective evaluations of the economy at the national and personal levels – into a single variable using factor analysis, then rescale the variable to range from zero (bad) to one (good). It is important to note that this indicator does not exclusively reflect the programmatic mechanism. Indeed, citizens could give positive evaluations because they approve of the regime's economic programs *or* because they perceive Chávez as a savior who makes good on his promise to rescue the people. As Merolla and Zechmeister suggest, "individuals who perceive Chávez as highly charismatic see Venezuela's economy ... through rose-colored glasses" (2011, 31). In other words, charismatic perceptions of Chávez may cause respondents to evaluate the economy more favorably. To examine this possibility, I run one set of models in which economic evaluations and charismatic perceptions are independent and a second set of models in which they are interacted. The interaction term will shed light on whether and how charismatic perceptions impact the effect of economic evaluations on citizens' attachments to Chavismo.

In addition to economic performance, I incorporate two questions on respondents' assessments of Chávez's two largest social missions to measure the strength of the programmatic mechanism – the health mission (*Barrio Adentro*) and the food mission (*Mercal*). I add these evaluations and rescale the sum to range from zero (bad) to one (good). Incorporating these variables cuts the sample size by over half (N = 641) because only about 50 and 70 percent of respondents report having used the health and food missions, respectively. To address this issue, one set of models examines whether respondents accessed these missions in the first place, while a second set

---

[13] Eighty-four percent of respondents answered all five questions in the battery while 11 percent only answered some of the questions. To include these respondents, I impute the mean of the items in the battery they answered onto the items they did not answer. The five items are highly correlated (Cronbach's alpha = 0.953), and the imputation does not produce significant differences in the mean charisma score for the entire sample (mean = .57, SE = .37 before imputation; mean = .55, SE = .36 after imputation).

TABLE 3.1. *Descriptive statistics for dependent and independent variables*

Variable	Scale	N	Mean	Std. Dev.
Attachment to Chavismo*	0–1	1510	0.23	0.42
Charismatic perceptions	0–1	1438	0.55	0.36
Economic evaluations	0–1	1474	0.50	0.22
Mission recipient	0–1	1510	0.60	0.39
Evaluation of missions	0–1	641	0.84	0.21
Communal Council participation	0–1	1495	0.25	0.36
Socioeconomic status	0–1	1510	0.58	0.24
Education (years)	0–20	1509	10.50	4.45
Age	18–89	1510	36.27	14.06
Female*	0–1	1510	0.50	0.50
Urban*	0–1	1510	0.95	0.21

* The proportion rather than the mean is given for dichotomous variables.

explores the subsample of respondents who report having used both missions. Whereas the former variable measures access to the missions, which tends to be restricted based on partisanship (Hawkins et al. 2011), the latter more closely reflects citizens' substantive evaluation of those programs.

To measure the influence of participation in movement-affiliated organizations on attachment to Chavismo, I incorporate a question about respondents' involvement in the CCs. Because the CCs represent the movement's central network of participatory organizations, respondents with organizational ties should report extensive involvement in these groups. I rescale a four-point scale in which one is "never" and four is "every week" to range from zero (low) to one (high).

Finally, I incorporate four control variables thought to influence citizens' identification with Chavismo: socioeconomic status, education, age, and gender.[14] Table 3.1 displays descriptive statistics for the key dependent and independent variables for both surveys. Additional information on the survey can be found in the online Appendix A.

In total, I analyze four binary logistic regression models. Models A and C include the variable on access to the missions and thus include most respondents ($N = 1326$). Models B and D replace this variable with one on substantive evaluation of the missions among those who accessed them ($N = 579$). Finally, Models A and B treat charismatic perceptions and economic evaluations independently, whereas Models C and D interact with the two variables. The next section discusses the results based on these four models.

---

[14] I construct a weighted index of household assets to measure socioeconomic status to reduce the nonresponse bias associated with questions on respondents' income (Córdova 2009).

3.4.3 Results

The results (Table 3.2) suggest the uniquely strong influence of charisma on citizens' attachments to Chavismo. Models A and B indicate that charismatic perceptions have a statistically significant and substantively large impact on citizens' ties to the movement. In the unrestricted sample (Model A), respondents who perceive Chávez as extremely charismatic (score of one) are 47 percentage points more likely to express attachment than those who find Chávez extremely uncharismatic (score of zero), holding the remaining independent variables constant at their means. Among mission users (Model B), this figure rises to 58 percentage points (Figure 3.2).

In contrast, the programmatic and organizational variables are only weakly associated with attachments to the movement. Models A and B suggest that

TABLE 3.2. *Binary logistic regression results*

	Model A	Model B	Model C	Model D
Charismatic perceptions	4.06***	3.74***	6.32***	6.65***
	(0.36)	(0.49)	(1.04)	(1.51)
Economic evaluations	0.79	0.52	4.26**	4.85*
	(0.41)	(0.52)	(1.50)	(2.11)
Charismatic perceptions *	–	–	−4.32*	−5.30*
Econ. evaluations			(1.77)	(2.49)
Mission recipient	1.26***	–	1.25***	–
	(0.23)		(0.23)	
Evaluation of missions	–	0.48	–	0.42
		(0.53)		(0.53)
CC participation	0.17	0.29	0.20	0.32
	(0.20)	(0.25)	(0.20)	(0.25)
Socioeconomic status	0.18	0.02	0.20	0.04
	(0.33)	(0.43)	(0.33)	(0.43)
Education	0.05**	0.07**	0.05**	0.07**
	(0.02)	(0.03)	(0.02)	(0.03)
Age	0.02**	0.02**	0.02**	0.02**
	(0.01)	(0.01)	(0.01)	(0.01)
Female	−0.19	−0.20	−0.19	−0.20
	(0.15)	(0.19)	(0.15)	(0.19)
Urban	0.22	0.59	0.24	0.63
	(0.35)	(0.47)	(0.35)	(0.47)
Intercept	−6.65***	−6.11***	−8.52***	−7.92***
	(0.55)	(0.84)	(0.99)	(1.38)
N	1390	607	1390	607
Pseudo-r^2	0.29	0.20	0.29	0.20

Standard errors shown in parentheses.
*$p<.05$; **$p<.01$; ***$p<.001$

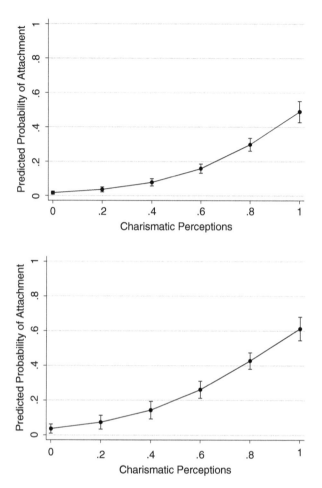

FIGURE 3.2. Predicted probability of attachment at different levels of charismatic perceptions

economic performance does not have a significant, independent impact on Bolivarian attachment. Models C and D examine the potential interactive effect of charismatic perceptions and economic evaluations on attachment. Interpreting this effect requires visual examination of predicted probabilities (Figure 3.3), as the statistical significance of interactions in nonlinear regression does not necessarily indicate a substantively meaningful effect (Brambor, Clark, and Golder 2006, 73–74). Model C suggests that there is no meaningful interactive effect: At different levels of charismatic perceptions, the influence of economic performance evaluations on attachment does not change significantly. However, Model D suggests that the interactive effect may have a small,

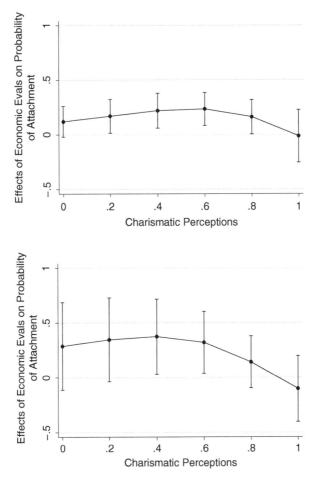

FIGURE 3.3. Effect of economic evaluations on probability of attachment at different levels of charismatic perceptions: Interactive models

negative effect among mission users: As charismatic perceptions of Chávez increase, the effect of performance evaluations on Bolivarian attachment decreases slightly. While this interaction appears significant, its negative sign suggests that higher charismatic perceptions dampen the influence of perform-ance evaluations. The evidence therefore underscores the "Teflon" effect of Chávez's charisma (Merolla and Zechmeister 2011, 30), which protects him from the negative consequences of poor performance.

In terms of social programs, accessing benefits from one or both missions significantly increases the probability of expressing attachment to the move-ment. However, as discussed earlier, this does not necessarily suggest that the programmatic mechanism is at work. In fact, among mission users (Model B), substantive assessments of the missions have no significant effect, suggesting that the quality of these programs does not influence respondents' attachments. Finally, across all four models, participation in the CCs has no significant association with attachment. These data indicate the relative weakness of the programmatic and grassroots mechanisms while further highlighting the strong effects of personalism on loyalty to the movement. Taken together, the four models suggest the relative insignificance of programmatic and organizational factors on Bolivarian attachments while highlighting the disproportionate influence of charismatic perceptions of Chávez.

To ensure the validity of the results, I explore two alternative explanations for the underwhelming effects of programmatic and organizational factors. First, in the additive models (A and B), multicollinearity between charismatic perceptions and the other independent variables could artificially inflate the significance of the former and depress that of the latter. However, the variance inflation factor (VIF) for charisma for both models is low (1.66 and 1.48, respectively), suggesting that multicollinearity does not account for the results.[15] Second, preference falsification may explain the insignificance of these variables. Specifically, respondents could feel pressured to evaluate Chávez's charisma more highly than they otherwise might. Yet, citizens generally do not hesitate to express dissatisfaction with Chávez's regime. In fact, 17 percent of respondents perceive Chávez as completely uncharismatic and 56 percent rate his performance as mediocre, poor, or very poor. One would expect substantially higher approval ratings if preference falsification were at play. The remaining explanation suggests that citizens' intense perceptions of Chávez's charisma are intimately linked with their attachment to his movement, while programmatic and organizational factors have notably weaker effects.

3.5 CONCLUSION

This chapter has investigated the mechanisms through which charismatic attachments form and overpower alternative forms of citizen–politician linkages. Recognition of historically marginalized citizens, daring yet short-lived policies, and a captivating symbolic narrative of redemption cause citizens to perceive the leader as intensely charismatic and solidify their deep, emotional attachments to the leader's movement. Moreover, the formation of such quasi-religious attachments undermines the development of programmatic and grassroots linkages. Charismatic leaders' need to demonstrate impressive performance compromises the effectiveness and sustainability of their policies, which weakens the programmatic mechanism of attachment. Additionally, the

---

[15] Scholars suggest multicollinearity issues emerge when the VIF ranges from 2.5 (conservative) to 10 (lenient) (Allison 2012).

leaders' unmediated, top-down recognition of excluded sectors concentrates their personalistic authority and therefore undermines genuine grassroots participation.

I illustrate this argument focusing on the formation of citizens' attachments to Chavismo in Venezuela. Drawing on qualitative insights from secondary research and three months of fieldwork that I conducted in 2015, I demonstrate that Chávez expertly fulfilled the three conditions necessary for cultivating strong, charismatic attachments with his followers. Subsequently, using data from the 2007 LAPOP survey, I show that voters' perceptions of Chávez's charisma provided a stronger, more consistent foundation for their attachment to his movement than factors based on programmatic evaluation and participation in Chavista organizations. Though Chávez proclaimed state-centered economics, redistributive social programs, and grassroots organizations as central to his movement, the results suggest his personal appeal eclipsed these factors. Indeed, most programmatic and organizational elements of Chavismo had no significant relationship with attachment to the movement; in contrast, citizens' perceptions of Chávez's charisma were strongly associated with their loyalty to the movement.

I contend that the process through which citizens' charismatic attachments form is crucial for understanding the resilience of those ties. The three conditions that help form those attachments do not only serve to establish the leader's initial popularity, but they also make it difficult for subsequent politicians to depersonalize those attachments when the founder disappears. The subsequent chapter draws on focus groups conducted with followers of Peronism and Chavismo to investigate how charismatic attachments, once formed, can develop into a resilient political identity that undermines efforts at routinization while setting the stage for the revival of the movement in personalistic form.

4

The Survival of Charismatic Attachments

The previous chapter demonstrated the process through which the founder of a charismatic movement fosters powerful, direct, and emotional attachments with his followers. To so demonstrate, I indicated that the leader fulfills three conditions: He directly recognizes the people's suffering, implements bold policies to demonstrate his ability to resolve their suffering, and crafts a symbolic narrative that praises his leadership as heroic, portrays opponents as malevolent, and proclaims his sacred mission to transform society.

Existing studies confirm the importance of these conditions for the initial cultivation of charismatic attachments (e.g., Eisenstadt 1968; Madsen and Snow 1991; Pappas 2012; Shils 1965; Weber 1922/1978; Willner and Willner 1965). Yet, in line with the routinization thesis, these studies claim that the *survival* of the attachments depends on the physical presence of the leader. Consequently, when charismatic leaders die, the literature concludes that citizens' attachments fade away. Studies of Peronism and Chavismo reflect this assumption. In Argentina, scholars and strategists from across the political spectrum argue that citizens' affective attachments to Peronism have long since vanished.[1] In Venezuela, though Chávez died much more recently, scholars – citing the disastrous performance of Chávez's hand-picked successor, Nicolás Maduro – have concluded that citizens' deep, emotional ties to Chavismo are fading away (López Maya 2014, 2016; Denis 2015).[2]

In contrast, this chapter argues that citizens' charismatic attachments can outlive the founder by *sustaining*, rather than discarding, their affective nature.

---

[1] Several academics and political advisers voiced this opinion in interviews with the author, including three advisers from the Cristina Kirchner administration, two Peronist analysts unaffiliated with Kirchner, and one adviser from the Mauricio Macri administration.

[2] See Cyr (2013) for an important exception.

The symbolic narrative underlying charismatic bonds causes the followers to develop a resilient political identity that shapes their worldview, perpetuates the cleavage between the followers and their opponents, and reaffirms the followers' faith in the founder's mission of transcendence. When the leader dies and can no longer physically maintain his personal connection with the followers, this narrative serves as a scripture, which, like the New Testament for many Christians, upholds the followers' identification with the movement. Whereas routinization scholars would suggest that the emotional power of this narrative grows weaker over time, I contend that the followers keep the narrative alive by recounting their cherished, personal experiences living under the founder's rule, passing those stories to younger generations, and preserving symbols that commemorate the founder's valiant leadership.

The followers' stories and symbols safeguard their emotional connections to the movement and its righteous community of followers by reinforcing the key elements of the founder's narrative: a worldview that worships the founder as their ultimate savior, a stark pro/anti-movement cleavage, and a profound faith in the founder's mission of salvation. Consequently, the movement can persist in a leaderless state for a strikingly long period of time without undergoing routinization. Moreover, because the personalistic nature of the followers' attachments shapes their expectations of future politicians, it incentivizes future leaders to portray themselves as new saviors capable of picking up the founder's baton and resuming his mission to rescue society. As I will demonstrate in Chapters 5 and 6, leaders who respond to these incentives when conditions are favorable can reactivate citizens' attachments and restore the movement to power under their own charismatic authority.

The present chapter investigates the survival of charismatic attachments in two stages. I begin by analyzing how the founder's narrative helps the attachments develop into an enduring political identity. Next, I explore the mechanism through which the followers perpetuate this identity after the founder's death. I illustrate this process using evidence from focus groups conducted with the followers of Peronism and Chavismo after the deaths of Juan Perón and Hugo Chávez, respectively.[3] In both cases, the findings reveal that the followers' deeply personal, affective identification with the movement and its founder persists. Furthermore, the focus group discussions illustrate how the preservation of cherished stories and symbols at the level of the individual follower has sustained the narrative and, by extension, the followers' personalistic attachments to the movement. These results underscore the resilience and centrality of the followers' attachments for upholding the charismatic nature of the movement after the founder's death.

---

[3] Internal Review Board Approval was obtained from the University of Texas at Austin to conduct these focus groups (IRB 2013-03-0046).

4.1 A THEORY OF CHARISMATIC MOVEMENT SURVIVAL

4.1.1 The Symbolic Narrative and the Establishment of a Resilient Political Identity

I claim that the followers' charismatic attachments help perpetuate the movement by cultivating an enduring political identity. This identity is important because, as suggested by political psychologists, it influences citizens' attitudes, behaviors, and sense of purpose in several ways. For one, it provides citizens with a "lens to interpret their world" (Cramer 2016, 6, 20). This "worldview" shapes identifiers' understanding of their surroundings, including the mundane activities of daily life, major events, and the motives and behaviors of other people. Second, the identity causes the followers, who are members of the "in-group," to distinguish themselves from non-identifiers, the "out-group." This division is important because in-group members often struggle to sympathize with and can even alienate their out-group counterparts, who maintain a fundamentally different worldview (Tajfel 1974). Likewise, members of the out-group develop an "anti-identity" and corresponding feelings of aversion toward the followers, thereby increasing the affective polarization of society and strengthening the personalistic cleavage (Cyr and Meléndez 2015; Iyengar et al. 2019; Meléndez 2019). Third, while generating antipathy between in- and out-groups, the identity increases cohesion among fellow in-group members by providing them with a shared sense of meaning in their lives and faith in a common purpose (Huddy 2013, 18; Zúquete 2013, 266–67). In short, citizens' identity can influence politics by shaping their worldview, antagonizing outsiders, and infusing the followers with a shared sense of purpose.

The charismatic founder's symbolic narrative plays a crucial role in the construction of the followers' identification with the movement because it reinforces each of the abovementioned elements. First, the narrative's glorification of the founder forms the basis of the followers' worldview. More than merely viewing the founder as an inspirational leader, the narrative endows him with "quasi-divine status," such that the followers feel his symbolic presence in their daily lives (Zúquete 2008, 107). Even after the founder has died or disappeared, the followers continue to praise him in a Christ-like fashion and even search for manifestations of the founder's spirit in their world. This ongoing hero worship impacts the followers' understanding of politics. In particular, it sustains their collective faith in the leader's mission to provide the followers with salvation. Moreover, the followers come to believe that the mission cannot succeed without a heroic leader at the helm. This, in turn, shapes their expectations of future politicians: Who, they ask, will embody the spirit of the founder and revive his quest to rescue the people?

In addition to anchoring the followers' understanding of the world in the immortal and heroic vision of the founder, the narrative's portrayal of opponents as threats to the people's well-being strengthens the followers' identity. The perception that followers are constantly under attack generates feelings of fear and anxiety, which bolsters "in-group unity" while "inflaming out-group hostilities" (Huddy 2013, 44). Additionally, the narrative causes supporters to feel resentful toward those who oppose the movement. This makes reconciliation between the two groups more difficult after the founder has gone, and it incentivizes subsequent leaders to deepen, rather than soften, the divide between the followers for political gain (Cramer 2016, 14–15).

Third, the narrative helps turn charismatic attachments into a resilient identity by upholding the founder's mission of societal transformation and spiritual transcendence. Whereas the attacks on opponents distinguish the followers from their "enemies," this mission provides the followers with a *positive* reason for belonging to the group: the promise of societal transformation and, ultimately, salvation (Zúquete 2013, 267). Even after the death of the founder, their continued faith in his mission strengthens feelings of warmth, pride, and closeness with one another, as it reaffirms their sense of purpose and provides "a sense of symbolic common fate" (Huddy 2013, 24).

Together, the three abovementioned elements contribute to the persistence of the followers' attachments and corresponding identity by strengthening the "simultaneously individual and social" nature of the identity (Huddy 2001, 146). At the individual level, the followers perceive themselves as having unmediated, personal connections to the founder. This perception holds tremendous emotional significance for the followers and impacts their attitudes and behaviors. At the group level, the followers' shared belief in and commitment to the founder's mission to transform society makes them part of a "moral community," which transcends the individual level by providing the followers with the powerful feeling that they belong to the group (Zúquete 2013, 263–34). This collective dimension of the followers' identity gives them a common purpose and holds the movement together over time, lending it coherence despite ideological heterogeneity, programmatic volatility, and factionalism.

In sum, the charismatic founder's symbolic narrative plays a crucial role in constructing a stable, deeply personalistic identity among the followers that has strong individual and collective dimensions. First, the narrative's sanctification of the founder perpetuates his symbolic influence in the followers' lives and establishes an enduring worldview. Second, the portrayal of opponents as enemies strengthens the identity by deepening the cleavage between the founder's disciples and opponents, generating affective polarization, and promoting cohesion among the followers. Third, faith in the founder's mission of holistic transformation provides the followers with positive affirmation and a deep sense of purpose that transcends the self. The combination of these aspects of the symbolic narrative turns citizens' attachments to the leader into a profound, quasi-spiritual identity that cannot be easily transformed when the founder disappears.

4.1.2 The Perpetuation of the Charismatic Identity after the Death of the Founder

As described earlier, the cultivation of a charismatic identity helps solidify citizens' attachments to the founder during his lifetime. Even so, his death generates a crisis because he can no longer personally sustain his deep, emotional bonds with the followers. To recover from this situation, the routinization thesis indicates that, similar to more conventional parties, the movement must develop an organizational network through which to reach supporters and maintain their loyalty (Madsen and Snow 1991). Samuels and Zucco's important study of the Workers' Party in Brazil illustrates this mechanism of creating and sustaining attachments. As the authors state, the party mobilizes "pre-existing organizational networks" and sets up local offices to "cultivate extensive and lasting affective partisan attachments" (Samuels and Zucco 2015, 755).

In contrast, I argue that, in charismatic movements, it is the followers' personal preservation of their identity, rather than the mobilization of an organizational network, that sustains the movement in the wake of the founder's death. The followers, who are distraught due to their founder's departure, cling to his symbolic narrative to preserve their sense of identity and reassure themselves of his ongoing spiritual presence. This sentiment carries the movement forward until a new leader rises and assumes the founder's mantle.

During such leaderless periods, I claim that the followers engage in two activities to sustain the founder's narrative and, by extension, their affective identification with the movement. First, the followers preserve and recount cherished memories of their personal experiences, or their loved ones' personal experiences, during the founder's rule. These stories describe the followers' interactions with the founder and depict how he single-handedly improved the lives of the followers and their loved ones. The focus of these stories on the relationship between individual followers and the founder, as well as on the leader's heroic gestures, reflect and sustain the unmediated emotional nature of the followers' relationship to the movement. Moreover, as parents and grandparents regale their children with these stories, younger generations of the followers develop their own affective ties to the movement, even without personally experiencing the founder's rule. The retelling of these stories, thus, establishes a pattern of "continuous ritualization and symbolism" that helps preserve the identity over time (Zúquete 2013, 267).

In addition to these stories, the followers save physical objects and other symbols that memorialize the founder and his mission of transcendence. For example, some keep items such as clothing, flags, and "gifts" from the founder ranging from marbles to books to sewing machines. They also bequeath these sacred objects to their children, helping perpetuate the identity over time. Other supporters change their physical appearance, donning tattoos of the founder's face or changing their hairstyle to mimic the founder's (e.g., Auyero 2001, 120).

These symbols maintain the followers' sentimental connections to the movement because, as suggested by political psychologists, they evoke overwhelming, positive emotions among members of the group (Citrin and Sears 2009, 162; Huddy 2013, 19; Sears 2001, 14). The symbols also provide physical markers that differentiate members of the group from outsiders, reinforcing the cleavage between the followers and their opponents (Sears 2001, 15). Finally, similar to the crucifix in Christianity, the symbols remind the followers of the reason they belong to the movement: namely, their belief in the founder's mission of salvation (ibid., 16).

4.1.3 Charismatic Movements "In Abeyance"

To recapitulate, the symbolic narrative is crucial for the survival of citizens' charismatic attachments to the movement after the death of the founder. The followers sustain the narrative through individual-level stories and symbols, which reinforce their attachments and solidify their personalistic identification with the movement. Importantly, the personalistic nature of the followers' identity becomes remarkably stable (Huddy 2001, 131; Meléndez and Rovira Kaltwasser 2019, 3). Thus, even as the political relevance of the identity rises and falls over time, its charismatic core resists change (Huddy 2001, 149).

This deeply entrenched identity forms the foundation for the survival of charismatic movements. Its role is especially important when the movement finds itself in leaderless situations. During such junctures, the symbolic image of the founder and his promise to deliver salvation maintain the followers' feelings of hope and loyalty which, in turn, preserve the movement "in abeyance,"[4] helping it cohere for a significant period of time (Taylor 1989).[5] Although the absence of a strong leader during these stretches of time can cause citizens to become politically disengaged, the personalistic nature of their identity sustains their sense of belonging to the founder's righteous community and provides them with hope that a new leader will eventually rise and take the founder's place. Thus, when conditions become more favorable, a new leader can politically *reactivate* the followers' identity and restore the movement to power (Cramer 2016, 15; Huddy 2001, 148; Huddy 2013, 12; Klar 2013, 1108; Meléndez and Rovira Kaltwasser 2019, 3). The next section turns to focus groups with the followers of Peronism and Chavismo to illustrate the process through which citizens' charismatic attachments to the founder develop into a resilient identity that sustains the movement after the founder's death.

---

[4] This phrase is adopted from Taylor's article, "Social movement continuity: the women's movement in abeyance" (1989). I am grateful to Cathy Schneider for suggesting this reference.

[5] Specifically, a charismatic movement can survive in the absence of a leader as long as the generations of followers who personally experienced the founder's rule, and who sustain a powerful identification with the movement, remain alive.

4.2 RESILIENT IDENTITIES AND THE SURVIVAL OF CHARISMATIC MOVEMENTS: EVIDENCE FROM FOCUS GROUPS

4.2.1 Research Design

To investigate the survival of charismatic movements from the followers' perspective, I conducted thirteen focus groups – six in Venezuela and seven in Argentina – with self-identified the followers of Chavismo and Peronism, respectively.[6] In both countries, the focus groups took place in 2016 – 3 years after the death of Hugo Chávez and 42 years after the death of Juan Perón. This timing allowed me to assess the extent to which the followers have maintained charismatic attachments during two important junctures after the disappearance of the founders: in the direct aftermath of the founder's death, in Venezuela, and decades later, in Argentina. In both cases, the results demonstrate that the founder and his narrative remain central to the followers' loyalty to the movement. In addition, the Argentine case reveals how the followers can update and even strengthen their personalistic identity based on positive experiences under subsequent movement leaders, whom the followers view as genuine heirs of the founder.

I designed the focus groups with two objectives in mind. First, I sought to probe the nature of the followers' identification with the movement. Therefore, participants discussed why they considered themselves to be "Chavista" or "Peronist"; what, if anything, continued to inspire them about the movement's founder; and what characteristics they generally looked for in political leaders. Considering the collective and subjectively understood nature of identities, this portion of the analysis focused on the *group* as the unit of analysis (Cyr 2016, 234–35; Huddy 2001, 131). Unlike in-depth interviews or surveys, which investigate individual perspectives, the social environment of focus groups enabled participants to collectively contemplate the nature of their shared identity. This approach also revealed key insights about how participants "piece the world together for themselves," considering not only *what* constitutes their identity, but also *why* the identity matters to them (Cramer 2016, 20). A third advantage of the focus group method was that it encouraged participants to reflect on the complex and nuanced nature of their shared identity in a relaxed setting, with the help of fellow group members and the guidance of an expert moderator, rather than undertaking this cognitively difficult task alone (Cyr 2016, 235).

My second reason for conducting focus groups was to explore how followers sustain their identity to the movement in the absence of the founder.

---

[6] Because my study focuses on the survival of followers' preexisting attachments to the movement, I narrowed the scope of this analysis to self-identified followers of the movement rather than recruiting subjects from the general population.

I gathered participants' accounts of their experiences under the founder as well as under subsequent leaders. I also listened to participants describe the symbols they had preserved over the years to commemorate the movement's leaders and mission of transcendence. This portion of the study focused on the *individual* followers as the unit of analysis rather than the group. As Cyr indicates, focus groups can be useful for gathering "rapid, individual-level feedback" from a relatively large number of individuals – a larger number than can be achieved through in-depth interviews (Cyr 2016, 234). By capturing group dynamics as well as participants' individual perspectives, I assessed both the individual and collective aspects of followers' identification with the movement (Huddy 2001, 146).

To carry out the focus groups, I recruited self-identified followers of the movement from the lower and lower-middle classes in both countries. I selected these citizens as participants because my theory suggests that, having experienced greater socioeconomic marginalization, these individuals constitute the most crucial and consistent support base for both movements.[7] To obtain a range of perspectives, the focus groups were divided between followers who do and do not support the most recent leader of the movement (Cristina Kirchner in Argentina and Nicolás Maduro in Venezuela). To the extent possible, focus groups were also divided by age to explore how different generations of followers perceive their attachments to the movement, its founder(s), and subsequent successor(s). All groups were balanced in terms of gender.

I partnered with professional public opinion firms in each country to conduct the focus groups. Trained staff members recruited participants using a quota sampling method and contact lists from each firm's database. Participants who met the criteria for age, gender, socioeconomic status, movement identification, and geographical location were included.[8] The latter criterion required that participants come from a range of neighborhoods in each city where the focus groups were held. (See more detailed information in the country-specific descriptions presented subsequently.) In selecting participants, the staff ensured that the subjects did not know each other prior to participating in the focus group. Given the non-random method of recruiting participants, the sample cannot be considered as representative of the broader population of followers in either country. Nevertheless, the focus groups revealed valuable information from the perspective of the followers regarding

[7] Because I focus on the survival of pre-existing followers' attachments to the movement, only self-identified followers – as opposed to non-identifiers or opponents of the movement – were recruited as participants. In both countries, public opinion specialists estimate that self-identified followers constituted about one-third of the population at the time the focus groups were conducted, in 2016.
[8] Per the suggestions of public opinion specialists in both countries, education was used as a proxy for socioeconomic status. The highest education level for all participants was less than a college degree.

the nature of their identity with the movement, their personal experiences as movement followers, and their impressions of the founder and subsequent leaders.

Experienced local moderators led all focus group discussions. Participants were served light refreshments and received modest monetary compensation for their time. The moderator reassured participants of the confidentiality of the session, encouraged them to express their honest opinions, and guided conversation based on a predesigned script. The scripts for both countries asked participants to reflect on and share why they identify with the movement; specific experiences that drew them toward the movement; positive and negative feelings toward the movement and its different leaders, both past and present; feelings toward the movement's opponents; thoughts and feelings about the movement's future; and what activities, objects, or events, if any, have made them feel closer to the movement since the founder's death (sample questions from each script are listed in online Appendix B).[9]

In Venezuela, six focus groups with eight to ten participants each were conducted in partnership with Consultores 21, a renowned, local public opinion firm with ample experience. Due to logistical limitations, participants in all groups were recruited from the capital city of Caracas and its outskirts. Two groups were conducted with adults aged 18 to 25, two groups were conducted with adults aged 26 to 40, and two groups were conducted with adults aged 41 to 55. Participants in three groups (one from each age range) were supportive of Chávez's current successor, Nicolás Maduro, while participants in the three remaining groups were opposed to Maduro.

In Argentina, seven focus groups with seven to ten participants each were conducted in partnership with Trespuntozero, a local public opinion firm that specializes in political campaigns throughout the country. The focus groups were conducted in three different provinces to obtain a more geographically diverse sample of followers than if the focus groups had been conducted exclusively in the Federal Capital of Buenos Aires. Three groups were held in the Federal Capital, incorporating participants from the city and its outskirts, where many popular sector Peronists reside; two groups were held in Córdoba, the country's second largest city and a traditionally anti-Peronist stronghold; and two groups were held in La Rioja, a rural, traditionally Peronist region and Menem's home base, which shares a border with Chile. Six of the seven groups were conducted with adults aged 25 to 55, while one (the third held in Buenos Aires) was conducted with young adults aged 18 to 24.[10] Four groups (one per

---

[9] All focus groups were conducted in Spanish. I analyzed and translated excerpts from the focus group discussions into English using audio and video recordings and transcripts. Original wording in Spanish is available upon request.

[10] The seventh group was conducted with youth in Argentina to explore how the Peronist identity transfers to new generations decades after the disappearance of the founder. This seventh group was excluded from the design in Venezuela due to the recent nature of Hugo Chávez's death.

region plus the young adult group in Buenos Aires) were sympathetic to the current Peronist leader, Cristina Kirchner, while three groups (one per region) were opposed to Kirchner.

4.2.2 Results: The Establishment of a Resilient Charismatic Identity

4.2.2.1 *Venezuela*

GLORIFICATION OF THE FOUNDER. The focus group discussions in Venezuela underscored the central role of the symbolic narrative in solidifying citizens' charismatic identification with the movement. First, consistent with the narrative, participants praised Chávez not simply as a past leader, but as an immortal hero whose spirit continues to watch over them and offer them protection. One participant stated, "What we have is an affective connection. What other leaders could have done will stay in the past. But with Chávez the connection will live on in each person." A second proclaimed:

For me, Chávez was, and will always be, my hero. Not because he fought for one person, but because he fought for an entire nation. He was the hero of all those who needed him and even those who didn't, because for him there was no distinction. He didn't see who was rich and who was poor, he helped everyone ... for me he was a hero, everything about him. He gave all of himself to the country, he died for the country. Because even in his sickness he continued to fight for us. For me, that's what a hero is.

A third stated, "I am Chavista because I believe in Chávez. Because I believe in what he says ... that's the way it is and the way it will be. I believe in him and that's why I'm Chavista." A fourth participant noted, "I am Chavista because I am committed to the revolution, Chávez and Bolívar." Speaking about the future, another participant said, "I am Chavista because I am convinced that, in every way, we are going to move forward." Another replied, "I am with the future, and it's with Chavismo that we're going to get it." As illustrated by these statements, participants demonstrated an understanding of the world that revolved around Chávez. Their perception of the founder as an everlasting savior also indicates that he remains the central protagonist of the movement, even in death. The participants' use of the present and future tenses to describe Chávez further attest to his ongoing influence on their worldview and suggest the potential of their personalistic identity to survive in the future.

Interestingly, participants shielded Chávez's sanctified image from the regime's poor performance under his handpicked successor, Nicolás Maduro. For example, participants critical of Maduro isolated the successor from Chávez's heroic reputation. As one stated, "When you heard [Chávez] speak, at least when he gave announcements, you always stopped everything to watch his announcement. Maduro, in contrast ... I don't agree with him, it's a shame that he's the one that represents Chavismo now." Another participant sadly expressed, "Maduro hasn't followed Chávez's legacy, he hasn't been able to." Additionally, while praising Chávez as a beloved hero, participants did not hesitate to disparage Maduro with titles such as "donkey," "rag doll," and "puppet."[11]

Crucially, these participants clarified that their disappointment in Maduro did not compromise their commitment to the movement or their faith in the founder. One said, "Like I told you, I am Chavista, I was Chavista, and I will continue being Chavista but I am not with Maduro." Two participants further explained, "Maduro is a bad Chavista"; "we are more Chavista than Maduro is." Participants across the three anti-Maduro focus groups agreed with this phrasing, as reflected in the following exchange:

MODERATOR: Just so I can understand, let me be the devil's advocate. Maduro is Chavista. Is he a bad Chavista?
ALL: He's a bad Chavista.
MODERATOR: He is the son of Chávez, I recall. Didn't Chávez say that?
PARTICIPANT 1: All of us are children of Chávez. Here, we are all children of Chávez.

While claiming ongoing attachments to Chávez, these participants denied that Maduro held a special place as Chávez's successor.

In contrast to anti-Maduro participants, their pro-Maduro counterparts did not openly decry the successor's performance. Nevertheless, participants supportive of Maduro acknowledged his weaknesses and admitted he was incapable of replacing the founder. For example, when the moderator asked what participants thought about the popular refrain, "Maduro isn't Chávez," one participant responded, "Well, it's the truth. He isn't Chávez but, I'm telling you, he's following [Chávez's] legacy. Obviously, he's a different person and he's not going to be equal to Chávez, because nobody ever will." A second stated, "I feel that something is lacking [in Maduro], he lacks that extra urge to make things advance, the capacity that [Chávez] had ... it's one of the things that has emboldened the opposition, that Maduro isn't Chávez, nobody will be like Chávez, it will be difficult for anyone to equal him." A third explained, "[Maduro] isn't a leader as such. But he was the person that Chávez confided in enough to leave in his place, and that gives [Maduro] a vote of confidence above and beyond. He's charismatic, not as much as Chávez obviously, but then again, there is no comparison." A fourth declared, "Maduro, as president, I don't see him ... not like Chávez, because he's never going to be like Chávez. But he's learned some things from Chávez. What I see is that he wants to be strong but he has a heart that's too soft. He isn't like Chávez." While these participants spoke of Maduro in more favorable terms, they struggled to compare him to Chávez and, to varying degrees, also expressed disappointment with his leadership.

Most importantly, regardless of their feelings toward Maduro, all participants stressed that their loyalty to the movement remains rooted in Chávez.

---

[11] Several participants called the successor "Maburro," which is an insult commonly used by Maduro's critics that combines his name with the Spanish word for "donkey" (*burro*).

As one stated, "There is a misunderstanding. You know that when Maduro comes to power ... he comes to power with Chávez, as the son of Chávez, and that's why we call him Chavista ... I defend [Maduro] but we aren't Maduristas ... we are Chavistas." Another declared, "It's like this. If we are waiting in line to buy food or medicine ... the name you hear is Chávez, not Maduro. Of course, if I had to vote another time, I would vote for Maduro, [but it would be] a vote of faith because Chávez supported him. When we're in the street, we speak in terms of Chávez." These individuals' resolute defense of the founder demonstrates that his charisma continues to protect him from the decline of his own performance during his lifetime as well as the disastrous performance of his successor, whom he personally entrusted with the people's well-being. Moreover, the followers' ongoing support for the movement, independent of their feelings toward Maduro, underscores the resilience of their devotion and suggests the capacity of the movement to sustain itself during periods of weakness.

THE CLEAVAGE BETWEEN CHAVISTAS AND ANTI-CHAVISTAS. In addition to declaring their commitment to the everlasting spirit of Chávez, participants across the six focus groups expressed strong aversion toward opponents of Chavismo, revealing the continued importance of the second aspect of the symbolic narrative: the demarcation of in- and out-groups. Indeed, participants depicted the world as divided into two discrete categories: the poor, virtuous people of Chávez, on the one hand, and the privileged, selfish enemies of his movement, on the other. To illustrate this divide, the participants referred to the former group (with which they all identified) using labels such as "poor," "people," and "family." In contrast, they used terms including "rich," "squalid ones," "liars," and "agents of the right," to describe Chávez's critics.[12]

Furthermore, participants in all focus groups – including those critical of Maduro – viewed the opposition as complicit in the economic crisis, which many referred to as an "economic war." For example, in one focus group, participants discussed how "private companies and the opposition" intentionally hoard products in order to undermine Chavismo's mission to help the people:

PARTICIPANT 1: [The private companies and the opposition] have the products, but they hoard them.

PARTICIPANT 2: I don't know how they do it. I bought baby formula last Wednesday and already there isn't any more.

PARTICIPANT 1: Well, they've hoarded it. That's the economic war.

PARTICIPANT 3: In a video clip, I don't know if you all saw it on channel 8, it lasted about 5 or 10 minutes ... it showed a label in the background, "Empresas Polar, Secretary," and I don't know what else. It turns out that the company lowers its

---

[12] "Escuálidos," or "squalid ones," is a term that Chávez frequently invoked in reference to members of the opposition. Similarly, he used the term "right" in reference to the political right – the group he accused of conspiring to sabotage his mission to rescue the people.

production levels on important dates, like when there are protests and elections. Why? So that people think [the scarcity of goods] is the government's fault and the people suffer more.[13]

A participant from a different focus group depicted a similar understanding of the world as divided into two groups waging an all-out battle: victimized Chavistas versus greedy, powerful enemies:

Well, at work I know a lot of people with money, with resources, and even they say that the big companies are part of this economic war. Those same people with money, they are the ones who run things and it's always going to be like that, that's why they've gotten together to form a group. Very powerful people that want to oust Maduro, they got together and they're going to try to do away with him.

In addition to large companies and their executives, participants described members of the opposition in daily, personal interactions as selfish and hostile. To illustrate the difference between the two groups, one participant explained, "If you are rich and I am poor, who says that you should be able to have air conditioning, but not me? That's what Chávez was about." A second described the ongoing division between Chavistas and anti-Chavistas in her neighborhood. She said, "I used to live in Llanito, where they were very Chavista and spontaneous. Where I moved, everyone is squalid. I keep quiet but you know, because they are suspicious."

Interestingly, a set of pro-Maduro participants spoke bitterly of self-proclaimed Chavistas who had abandoned Maduro, accusing these individuals of being opposition members who were "disguised as Chavistas." One such participant stated, "These [disguised Chavistas] are the ones who have the most." Another condemned this group for "going down the path of the [political] Right." As these statements suggest, the stark division between virtuous followers and selfish opponents emphasized by Chávez's narrative became an intrinsic component of the followers' identification with his movement.

FAITH IN THE MISSION OF TRANSCENDENCE. Finally, participants exuberantly proclaimed their commitment to Chávez's mission to "free" his righteous community of followers from the malevolent opposition. One participant stated, "Chávez awakened his people, who were in darkness and gloom." Another said, "Chávez gifted us a country that he wanted to be free. Where am I? I am here with him and his people. We are the country, we are his people." Another declared, "As the people, we have to awaken and we have to maintain a vision of everything Hugo Chávez Frías did ... He was a national leader, a global leader. And why do I say he is still a leader today? Because even though he isn't with us physically, his legacy continues, just like he thought it would, with us as his people giving the movement continuity."

---

[13] Channel 8, "Venezolana de Televisión," is a television channel with state-run programming. Empresas Polar is the largest brewery and food processing plant in Venezuela.

Participants further expressed their belief in Chávez's mission of salvation when asked to draw a picture of what Chavismo meant to them. In fact, in all focus groups, participants drew images to express their love for the movement and their sincere belief that Chávez would bring them a better future. As one participant described, "I drew a map of Venezuela covered in a heart, which represents the unity of all of us. For me Chávez is the country, all of us, with health, family, independence, [and] riches." Another drew a staircase climbing toward paradise. Describing her illustration, she claimed, "We are advancing, although the other side doesn't want to see it, we are advancing." The participants' effusiveness toward Chávez and his community of followers show that in-group cohesion remains strong even in his absence. Moreover, the drawings depicting a transcendent future suggested that the followers remain committed to Chávez's mission of transcendence and are optimistic that a new leader – one who is "charismatic," "strong," "extraordinarily capable," "incorruptible," and "100 percent Chavista" – will eventually take his place.

4.2.2.2 *Argentina*

In Argentina, focus group discussions with self-identified Peronists suggested that the symbolic narrative underlying these citizens' charismatic attachments continues to uphold their identification with the movement. Indeed, despite the passage of more than four decades since Perón's death, the focus group participants indicated that they sustain genuine, emotional attachments to the founder and his movement. Furthermore, regardless of whether or not participants supported Néstor and Cristina Kirchner, the most recent leaders of Peronism, they expressed their relationship to the movement in terms consistent with the founder's narrative, indicating its central role in the perpetuation of their attachments and identity.

THE GLORIFICATION OF THE FOUNDER. To begin, participants praised the charismatic founder and his captivating second wife, Eva, as archetypal leaders. When asked to describe ideal characteristics of a leader, participants in all seven focus groups quickly referenced (Juan) Perón – and often Eva – by name. Moreover, when asked to evaluate contemporary leaders, participants consistently categorized the leaders from best to worst on a scale from "most" to "least" Peronist, always placing Perón and Eva at the top. These gestures indicate that participants' understanding of politics and, in particular, their evaluations of politicians, remained anchored in the glorified image of the charismatic founders.

In addition, while acknowledging that Perón ruled long ago, participants insisted that his heroic legacy remained fundamental to the movement's contemporary identity. For instance, when asked to explain what Peronism is, one stated, "Everything is Perón, Perón, Perón … the point is Perón, always reflecting all [socioeconomic] classes. Perón is immense." Another said, "The first thing that comes to mind is Perón and Evita." A third answered, "Peronism refers to Perón." A fourth declared, "Let's get to the point, we are talking about

Perón." When the moderator prompted, "Is Peronism alive today?" another participant explained that, even when Argentina is governed by non-Peronists (such as Mauricio Macri, the President of Argentina at the time the focus groups were conducted), "Perón is there. He's dormant, but he's out there." In short, regardless of participants' opinions of subsequent leaders of the movement, an enthusiastic consensus emerged across the focus groups regarding the sacred status of Perón and Eva, suggesting that the followers' identity remains anchored in the sanctified image of the founding couple.

Notably, disagreements emerged between pro- and anti-Kirchner participants regarding whether different successors of Perón qualified as "true Peronists." Pro-Kirchner participants perceived Néstor and Cristina Kirchner as heroes and genuine successors of Perón and Eva, and thus claimed fervent attachments to the contemporary leading couple. As one pro-Kirchner participant stated, "Néstor embodies Perón and Cristina embodies Evita." Another described, "To this very day, Perón and Eva are present, Cristina [and Néstor] too." When the moderator asked if Cristina tried to copy Eva, one group of pro-Kirchner participants responded:

PARTICIPANT 1: Yes, but [Eva and Cristina] are part of the same base.

PARTICIPANT 2: I think Eva and Perón were the masters, and through that [the Kirchners] made their own project, but using the same base, in different time periods and with a different situation for the people.

PARTICIPANT 3: I think that Cristina, being a woman, followed Evita as an example. But Evita always had Perón at her side; Perón was in politics and Evita was with the people. Cristina had to do it all by herself [after Néstor died], at one time she did it all with Néstor, but then she had to go it alone.[14]

Participants in other pro-Kirchner focus groups echoed these sentiments, stating that the Kirchners "represented a new expression of Peronism," "drew inspiration" from Peronism, and "wrote another chapter of the same [Peronist] guidebook."

Remarkably, the pro-Kirchner youth, who had only inherited memories of Juan and Eva Perón indirectly from older generations, also described the founders as directly influencing the Kirchners' leadership. One youth stated, "The two leading couples that are here for the youth and the adults today are Perón and Evita, Néstor and Cristina." Another explained, "The thing is, we grew up with the [Kirchner] model. We know that Kirchnerismo comes from Peronism, but it is an updated Peronism, one that is with the people, that is more combative." A third replied, "We are living Peronism through Kirchnerismo."

Conversely, anti-Kirchner participants expressed disappointment in Cristina and her husband and thus felt no attachment to these successors. These

---

[14] Néstor died of a heart attack in October 2010, during the third year of Cristina's first presidential term.

participants felt deeply offended that the Kirchners had the nerve to call themselves "Peronist." Referring to the Kirchners, one such participant stated, "there are many fake Peronists, who hang onto the Peronist label, who carry the Peronist flag." Another explained:

I think that [the legacy of Perón and Eva] ... is a virtuous path and that it could come to manifest itself once again. But what makes me furious is ... seeing pictures where Perón and Evita are next to Néstor and Cristina (whom I hate), comparing the pictures ... crazy, no, why would you dirty [the founders' image] like that?

Likewise, when asked what Kirchnerismo and Peronism have in common, another group of anti-Kirchner participants responded as follows:

PARTICIPANT 1: Nothing
PARTICIPANT 2: Nothing
PARTICIPANT 3: The little picture [of Juan and Eva] in the background
PARTICIPANT 4: There are a lot of thieves in Kirchnerismo
PARTICIPANT 5: They take advantage of Peronism and the ideal of social equality to make themselves look good, but the way they operate is very different. Peronism prioritized the worker's rights. Kirchnerismo only takes money away from the worker.

Furthermore, whereas pro-Kirchner participants applauded Cristina for drawing inspiration from Eva, anti-Kirchner participants viewed this behavior as a horrific and unsuccessful attempt to mimic their beloved Eva. Indeed, when asked if Cristina attempted to copy Eva, participants replied, "Yeah, she tried, but she didn't succeed by a long shot"; "She tried to dress and speak like [Eva], but she didn't actually imitate her"; "Cristina wanted to be like Eva, but she doesn't have a single hair in common with Eva. [Cristina] is an old walking idiot."

Due to their extreme disappointment in contemporary, "so-called" Peronist leaders, many anti-Kirchner participants referred to themselves as "Peronists of Perón," emphasizing that they drew inspiration from and claimed attachments to the movement's founders rather than from subsequent leaders, whom they labeled "false," "fraudulent," and "disguised" Peronists. For example, one participant stated, "Perón is the motor that keeps the country going." Another said, "I feel Peronist, of the *original* Peronism. If I had been born earlier [during Perón's era], I would be ultra-Peronist." Crucially, these disillusioned participants sustained their personal identification with Peronism in spite of their disappointment with the movement's subsequent leaders. Thus, while describing themselves as genuine Peronists, the participants referred to successors – including Carlos Menem and the Kirchners – as traitors of the movement.

However, despite disagreements between pro- and anti-Kirchner Peronists regarding the status of Peronist successors, similarities across the two sets of participants prevailed. For example, both sets of participants labeled leaders with no claim to Peronism, such as Elisa Carrió and Mauricio Macri, as anti-Peronist and expressed uniform disgust toward such politicians. As described earlier, pro- and anti-Kirchner participants also held the original founders – Juan and Eva – in the highest regard, demonstrating that the charismatic duo continues to serve as a moral compass and a lens through which to interpret politics for pro- and anti-Kirchner followers alike.

THE CLEAVAGE BETWEEN PERONISTS AND ANTI-PERONISTS. Next, similar to Chavistas in Venezuela, participants across the seven focus groups described their world as divided into two categories: the virtuous yet excluded "people" (*pueblo*) whom Peronism defends, on the one hand, and the enemies of the people, on the other. Participants, who all identified themselves as part of the former group, referred to fellow Peronists as "comrades" (*compañeros*).[15] In contrast, they associated non-Peronist sectors with conspiratorial elites seeking to further marginalize the poor, and frequently referred to opposition members as "gorillas" (*gorilas*), "rich," and "oligarchs."[16] As one group of participants said:

MODERATOR: If I say "gorillas," whom am I talking about?
PARTICIPANT 1: Anti-Peronism
PARTICIPANT 2: The Right
PARTICIPANT 3: Gorilla is like River if Peronist is Boca.[17]
PARTICIPANT 4: It reminds me of something that affected me deeply, what happened with the cadaver of Eva Perón. I never understood why [the opposition] would be so bitter about a woman who did so much good for the country.[18]

In addition to ordinary citizens, participants in several focus groups demonized leaders whom they felt had directly attacked or betrayed the legacy of Perón. For example, several participants referred to leaders whom they disliked – ranging from Menem and the Kirchners to Macri, the current president – as "unmentionables," "weaklings," and "puppets." When asked what feelings these leaders evoked, participants offered labels including "darkness," "horror," "poverty," and "shame." As described earlier, anti-Kirchner Peronists described Néstor and Cristina using these terms. But even pro-Kirchner Peronists categorized "good" (Peronist) and "bad" (anti-Peronist) leaders in similarly polarized terms. For example, pro-Kirchner participants depicted Cristina (like Eva) as a hero and defender of "true Argentines" fighting against selfish, anti-patriotic elites. These participants further applauded

---

[15] In the Peronist tradition, the term "compañero," which originates from the Communist term "comrade," refers to fellow movement supporters.

[16] The term "gorilla" (*gorila*) is a traditional, pejorative term referring to anti-Peronists.

[17] River and Boca are historic rival soccer teams; the former is associated with anti-Peronists, while the latter is the team of Peronism.

[18] In 1955, three years after her death, the Argentine military removed Eva's embalmed corpse from the country, quietly interring it in a crypt under a different name in Milan. Her husband recovered her corpse in Spain in 1971, and it was finally returned to Argentina and housed in its final resting place, the Recoleta Cemetery of Buenos Aires, in 1976 (Page 1981).

"Cristina's confrontation" with her critics, whom they perceived as existential threats to the well-being of the people. In short, regardless of their opinions about the Kirchners, all focus group participants described their world as divided into two groups – Peronists and anti-Peronists – suggesting that this cleavage continues to drive their identification with the movement.

FAITH IN THE MISSION OF TRANSCENDENCE. Finally, consistent with the symbolic narrative, focus group participants described Peronist leaders as responsible for transforming society and delivering a prosperous future. This sentiment was particularly fresh for pro-Kirchner participants, who felt that Néstor and Cristina, with Perón and Eva's blessing, were fulfilling this redemptive mission. "With Néstor and Cristina, we had a future!" cried one participant. While anti-Kirchner individuals had a more cynical view of contemporary politics, they described the period when Perón and Eva governed as a golden age. "Perón kept this country afloat," one participant remarked; another explained that, under Perón, the people had "food and options. The people always had something to eat, and if you wanted to work, you could do it, you had the possibility of becoming something more." While both sets of participants felt that Argentina had fallen from grace – either long ago (for anti-Kirchner groups) or recently with Macri's electoral victory (for pro-Kirchner groups) – they expressed the common belief that *true* leaders are devoted to carrying out the mission of Perón: to rescue the followers from their misery and provide material and spiritual transcendence. One pro-Kirchner participant even said, in earnest, "the other day I ran into to a girl at church, and she said a prophet had told her that a new Néstor was going to come save the country." And although participants agreed that no such leader was in power during the time that the focus groups were conducted, they expressed hope that such a leader would eventually appear, reunite the movement, and don their beloved founder's mantle.

In sum, the focus group conversations in both Venezuela and Argentina revealed that the symbolic narrative cultivated by Perón and Chávez, respectively, has continued to shape citizens' identification with the movement. First, in both countries, participants indicated that they still claim attachments to the founder and worship him as their ultimate savior. Though opinions of subsequent leaders of the movement varied – especially in Argentina, where Cristina Kirchner has had a particularly polarizing effect – participants across the board agreed that the founder represents the archetypal charismatic leader and savior of the people. Second, participants in both countries described the world as separated into two groups: one consisting of virtuous movement supporters and a second made up of privileged, out-of-touch, and nefarious opponents. Participants consistently identified with the former group while expressing distrust of the latter, indicating that these in- and out-groups remain intrinsic to their identity. Third, participants expressed faith in the founder's mission of societal transformation and hoped that a new leader would rise and pick up the founder's mantle. Importantly, even anti-Kirchner participants, who expressed disillusionment with contemporary politics

and politicians, expressed longing for a new leader to appear and carry out the
founder's mission to provide a better future.

4.3 RESULTS: THE PERSONALISTIC MECHANISM
OF IDENTITY PERPETUATION

The previous section described the crucial role of the symbolic narrative for
turning citizens' deep, emotional attachments to the charismatic founder into a
resilient political identity. The present section uses evidence from participants'
individual accounts to illustrate the mechanism through which the followers
perpetuate this narrative and identity once the founder has died. Specifically,
I show that, by retelling stories about personal experiences under the founder's
rule (and, in some cases, telling stories about experiences under the rule of
successors) and preserving sacred objects to commemorate the founder's heroic
leadership, the followers sustain direct ties to the founder and maintain their
faith in his redemptive mission.

4.3.1 Venezuela

Participants in the Venezuelan focus groups shared cherished memories of their
lives during Chávez's presidency. In particular, their accounts highlighted the
deeply personal and unmediated nature of their connections to the leader. For
example, one participant recounted:

When I was little, I remember in my house they always spoke a lot about Chávez, and
I remember when I was 5 or 6 years old, he was in the neighborhood where I lived, out
on the soccer field ... I said, "I want you to take me, I want you to take me," until my
family took me and I had the honor of holding Chávez's hand. I was so little and I gave
him my hand ... I remember clearly, I was little and they held me up and I had Chávez in
front of me and he gave me a bag of toys and I will never forget it.

A second participant recalled meeting Chávez in similar circumstances, when
the founder passed through the participant's neighborhood. Describing the
encounter, the participant said:

I liked having him in front of me, I admired him as a person, for everything he was and
for everything he had become. And really, when I see him it makes me proud, to know
Chávez ... he is the one supporting me in practically everything, he is the one who is
lifting my foot out of the mud.

Notably, this participant switched to present tense when talking about Chávez,
suggesting the ongoing spiritual presence of the leader in his life.

Several other participants across the six focus groups shared stories about
their personal encounters with Chávez. They consistently reported these
events as sentimental and even transformative experiences, as reflected in
the following exchange:

PARTICIPANT 1: When I saw Chávez for the first time, I was an opponent of his movement, 100%. But I happened to go to an event … and people said, "Here comes Chávez!" and I saw him riding in on a truck. He was already sick at the time, greeting the people, and it gave me goose bumps. It was really something … I mean, he was such an extraordinary human being, and when he passed in front of you, your hair stood on end … it was something strange.

MODERATOR: Is that the moment when you became Chavista?

PARTICIPANT 1: Listen. In that moment he got my attention … He stepped out of the presidential protocol, came to the streets and put himself in a poor neighborhood. There, he spoke with the little old ladies and the people … so he got my attention and I said, "this guy is a leader, that is how you govern!" And from that moment on I have been Chavista.

PARTICIPANT 2: The same thing happened to me. He came to my neighborhood and I got goose bumps. He came really close to me because I was pressed up against the railings. He was so close … I felt a really good vibe and my hair stood on end.

In addition to stressing their personal closeness with Chávez, the participants' stories also emphasized the founder's extraordinary capacity to resolve their suffering. For example, two participants in separate focus groups said they had written letters to Chávez pleading him to help their sick family members. Both participants claimed that Chávez personally returned their phone calls to arrange treatments for their loved ones. Several others discussed receiving health, nutritional, and educational benefits *directly* from Chávez, as illustrated in the following conversation:

MODERATOR: Did you know anyone that Chávez helped directly?

ALL: Yes.

MODERATOR: Tell me, whom did you know, whom Chávez helped directly?

PARTICIPANT 1: The pensioners, my grandma. He gave her a pension even though she never worked. That was direct assistance.

PARTICIPANT 2: He gave spine surgery to an aunt of mine. He gave her money for the operation.

PARTICIPANT 3: He gave to my sister, thank God. Today she has a home, thanks to the housing mission. And my brother-in-law is in the army and has a job.

PARTICIPANT 4: One of my neighbors too, she has a daughter who is special needs and he helped her directly, taking her out of the society we lived in, and he gave her another house and medical services that she needed.

PARTICIPANT 5: My godfather, for example, he had cancer and there was a time when he was very delicate and he got a wheelchair, a stretcher and all kinds of things, through a mission.

MODERATOR: And did Chávez give these things, or did he simply establish the mission, which made it possible for your godfather to exercise his right to get the things?

PARTICIPANT 5: Well, ok, healthcare is a right, but my mom tells me that before [Chávez] the government didn't do that kind of thing for the needy, even though it was a right … no other president would go through the trouble of helping you, unlike Chávez. For Chávez, it was a duty, and he followed through with that duty.

These statements show that participants perceived Chávez as single-handedly responsible for tangibly improving their loved ones' lives. Even if their family members received help from missions he established rather than from Chávez himself, the participants viewed the assistance as a personal gift from their beloved leader.

As the participants told these stories, their deep affection for Chávez seemed to reignite itself. Indeed, as described earlier, many spoke of "getting goose bumps" and "good vibes." Some participants even began to cry as they expressed their love for Chávez, especially when sharing stories about his death. One emotionally described, "It's incredible, because when he died ... it was awe-inspiring to see how the people cried. And when his body passed by [during the funeral procession] I also cried. And you saw all the people there, so many people, and it's not like the opposition says, that they were paid. They never gave me anything." Another said, "When Chávez died ... you asked how Chávez's death affected the people ... I felt it in my heart. I cried." Though Chávez died several years before the focus groups were conducted, these sentimental expressions made clear that the participants' cherished memories of the founder perpetuated their unmediated, personalistic, and profoundly affective bonds with the leader and his movement.

In addition to personal stories, the Venezuelan participants mentioned keeping various objects that symbolized their personal connections to Chávez. Several claimed to own T-shirts embossed with an image of the founder. One explained that wearing the shirt made her feel "a respect, an admiration ... he is like a brand, for me. Instead of saying Adidas or Columbia, it says Chávez." Others described hanging up photographs and posters to commemorate the founder. Still others claimed to keep maps and flags of Venezuela as a reminder of how Chávez had liberated the country. In each of these cases, participants reported displaying the objects with great pride – especially in the face of the movement's critics – as symbols of their continued loyalty to Chávez's movement.

4.3.2 Argentina

In contrast to Venezuela, where Chávez recently passed away, the focus groups in Argentina were conducted decades after Perón's death. Nevertheless, the resulting discussions suggested that, as in Venezuela, personal stories and symbols play an essential role in the perpetuation of followers' personalistic identification with Peronism.

Crucially, Argentine participants' stories emphasized personal interactions that their loved ones – namely, parents and grandparents – had had with Perón and Eva during Perón's original rule, suggesting those individuals had profound attachments to the founder and his wife. In particular, participants highlighted the direct, miraculous impact of the founders' deeds on their relatives' lives. One participant described, "I have been Peronist since I was in my mother's belly. My grandmother was a cook for Perón." For this participant, the grandmother's role as a cook for Perón seemed reason enough to justify his own loyalty to the movement decades later. Another participant explained, "Ever since I met my spouse, Perón was burned onto my brain; I listened to all of Evita's speeches." Another told a heartfelt story of how she became Peronist through her parents' experience:

I am Peronist because ... I came from working parents, they built their house themselves and had six daughters ... I am Peronist because of all of the benefits my father had. We were born in private clinics, like it should be – born in private clinics and not [public] maternity wards. We studied. The benefits my father had, for example, to be able to go on vacations during the summer, to go camping ... my father was Peronist, my mother even more so. She told us about different things, about neighbors who received sewing machines and other things from Evita. Even if my parents didn't receive a house paid for by the government, [Perón and Eva] made it possible for them to build a house for themselves. So, when you have grown up with that kind of foundation, at least for me, I am Peronist.

Another participant explained:

I am Peronist because my grandma and my mom lived during that time [of Perón and Eva] and they speak to me of miracles. I decided to investigate for myself in books and I concluded that I agreed with the social and economic ideals of Peronism. For example, in the economic sphere, they took care of the peon, let's call it. And in the social sphere, because Perón was a very charismatic leader and his charisma brought him closer to the people.

While this participant claimed to be Peronist due to "social and economic ideals," his description of those ideals reflected Perón's unmediated, charismatic – rather than programmatic – relationship with the poor. Several other participants told similarly vivid, emotional stories of grandparents who personally met and received things from Perón and Eva, such as a small toy "that had been made for the rich," a sewing machine, and a job as a nurse in Eva's first hospital. While they did not directly experience the founders' heroic acts, the participants appeared to cultivate affectionate connections to Perón and Eva vicariously, through stories passed down by their loved ones.

In addition to celebrating the founders as saviors, participants told stories of their interactions with subsequent leaders whom they considered to be genuine heirs of Perón and Eva. These participants noted that they personally benefited from the successors, and therefore considered the leaders to be "true Peronists." For example, one participant stated, "I am Peronist because Perón gave my grandfather his first job, Menem gave my father his first car, and Néstor gave me my first job." Another participant claimed to be Peronist because of the benefits she received from Menem and Cristina:

PARTICIPANT: I am Kirchnerista, but I think that you can't separate Kirchernismo and Peronism. It's just that I am living today and Peronism ... when I was a child ...

MODERATOR: You weren't even alive yet ... you must have been born the year that Perón died.

PARTICIPANT: I got married when I was young, so we experienced Peronism with Menem. During those years we were doing really well. And with Cristina too ... My husband collects bicycles, and in the age of Menem we had five bicycles, with Cristina we had three, and now [under Macri] we don't have any.

Another participant who prospered during Menem's presidency painted a romantic vision of Menem riding on horseback to save the country during the 1988 electoral campaign – an image not unlike those described by Venezuelan participants of Chávez riding into their neighborhoods atop a truck. Similarly, a third participant shed tears when he recalled how he got a job that saved him after the 2001 crisis "thanks to Néstor." A fourth emotionally exclaimed that she supported the Kirchners due to their similarities with Perón and Eva. After listing various material goods that she and her family had received "thanks to Cristina," ranging from medicine to food to DVD players, she stated, "I am Kirchnerista because [Néstor and Cristina] help the people from below, the poor people, and this is very similar to what my mother experienced in the time of Perón and Evita."

In short, though participants disagreed with each other regarding whether Menem, Néstor Kirchner, and Cristina Kirchner deserved the label of "true Peronist," they appeared to judge the three successors based on the same criterion: the leader's personal provision of material benefits to the participants (or their relatives). The participants suggested that stories of each leader's largesse served as proof of the leader's love for the people and, correspondingly, his/her ability to fulfill the Peróns' legacy. These cherished memories of the leaders – which, notably, were shared after all three successors had fallen from power – clearly played a central role in sustaining the participants' identification with the movement.[19]

In addition to recounting stories of their interactions with the movement's heroic leaders, many participants reported safekeeping symbols that reminded them of these leaders and their mission of salvation. One participant proudly declared that he still had the sewing machine that Eva gave to his grandmother. Another claimed she saved the toy scale – a "rich people's toy" – that Perón had given to her grandfather during a campaign visit to La Rioja. Other participants saved objects in homage to subsequent movement leaders. For example, several kept T-shirts they had worn when attending rallies with Cristina Kirchner. Some participants in every focus group also reported that they kept photographs of

---

[19] The following Peronist successors governed Argentina: Carlos Menem (1989–99), Néstor Kirchner (2003–7), Cristina Kirchner (2007–15), and Alberto Fernández (2019–present). The focus groups took place in 2016, less than two years after Cristina Kirchner stepped down from power and was replaced by Mauricio Macri, a non-Peronist.

movement leaders – from Juan and Eva Perón to Néstor and Cristina Kirchner – in their homes. The participants noted that they kept these pictures in important places, such as beside their beds or on shelves with portraits of their family members. As indicated in the subsequent discussion, participants suggested that they cherished their photographs of Peronist leaders and considered the leaders to be members of their inner circles:

PARTICIPANT 1: I have a photograph of Perón and Eva that was given to me. It's in my bedroom.
MODERATOR: Do you keep the photo with other pictures? If so, of whom?
PARTICIPANT 1: I keep it with pictures of my kids and grandparents, my parents, and my godchildren. That's where I keep a picture of Perón and Eva, together.
MODERATOR: Who gave the photo to you?
PARTICIPANT 1: My grandfather, just before he died.
PARTICIPANT 2: In my house, my parents live upstairs and they have a big picture of Perón. It's been there for as long as I can remember … it's next to the image of Christ in my mom's room.

In a different focus group, a participant further explained the perceived connection between Peronist leaders and family members as follows:

The leader loves his people. He isn't going to rob them; he is going to work for his people so that they're ok. It's like family. One loves his family and does everything to make sure his family is ok. The same thing happens with the government. If the leader loves his people and wants his people to be well, if he values and respects them, he is going to give them even more than they expect.

For many participants, material objects ranging from toys to T-shirts to portraits symbolized the powerful, emotional, and intimate connections they – and, importantly, their parents and grandparents – maintained with their beloved leaders. As indicated by these examples, even decades after Perón's death, symbols have continued to play an important role in perpetuating Peronist followers' affective and unmediated identification with the movement and profound attachments to its leaders.

4.4 CONCLUSION

This chapter has demonstrated that the survival of charismatic attachments depends primarily on the followers' adherence to the symbolic narrative. Specifically, the movement's superhuman portrayal of the founder, demonization of opponents, and mission of societal transformation form the core of followers' resilient identification with the movement. After the founder's death, the followers sustain this identity through stories and symbols that celebrate the narrative and preserve the affective power and directness of the followers' connections to the founder (and, in the case of Argentina, to subsequent leaders). This finding contrasts markedly with the logic of routinization, which suggests that charismatic movements must renounce their personalistic nature and transform into sophisticated party organizations to survive after the death of the founder.

Evidence from thirteen focus groups conducted with the followers of Chavismo and Peronism, respectively, indicate the relevance of the personalistic mechanism to movement survival. In Venezuela, participants enthusiastically demonstrated the vitality and emotional intensity of their attachments to Chávez and his movement three years after the death of the founder. Their ongoing devotion – and their ability to shield it from the deplorable perform-ance of Chávez's handpicked successor, Nicolás Maduro – is a testament to the power and resilience of their loyalty to the movement. In Argentina, partici-pants' profoundly sentimental attachments to Juan and Eva Perón are equally impressive, given that the founding couple has been dead for decades. Participants' tendency to compare subsequent leaders to Juan and Eva Perón – whether to praise the successors or to disparage them – further indicates that these citizens still use their Peronist identity as a lens for under-standing the world and judging politicians.

As suggested by the results in Argentina, while followers' personalistic identification with the movement can survive for years or even decades, the political salience of their identity can fade with the prolonged absence of a charismatic leader. While sustaining loyalty to the movement and founder, followers can become increasingly disillusioned with politics during periods in which no leader seems capable of fulfilling the founder's mission to deliver them prosperity. However, because these individuals continue to interpret the world through the lens of their personalistic identity, they maintain hope that a strong leader will eventually appear, pick up the founder's baton, and rescue society once more. As I will show in the next chapter, leaders who appear to embody the founder's charismatic qualities are capable of reactivating the followers' attachments and restoring the movement to power in their own name.

5

The Reactivation of Charismatic Attachments

Thus far, this book has investigated the revival of charismatic movements from the perspective of the followers. Chapter 3 demonstrated how unmediated, emotional attachments form between the followers and their heroic leader, while Chapter 4 illustrated how these bonds develop into an enduring identity that continues to shape followers' worldview after the leader dies. Because this identity remains anchored in the supporters' direct, emotional connections to the leader, it shapes their understanding of politics and expectations of future politicians in starkly personalistic terms. Thus, rather than viewing their politicians as ordinary public servants, the followers hold politicians to the standard of the charismatic founder. As reflected in the focus groups conducted with followers of Peronism and Chavismo, these individuals expect new leaders to embody the founder by performing heroic feats, providing tangible benefits, and fulfilling the founder's mission of transcendence.

In light of these findings, I argue that successors must demonstrate their worthiness of the founder's mantle in order to satisfy the followers' expectations and win their support. Specifically, politicians who depict themselves as symbolic reincarnations of the founder have the potential to reactivate the political significance of the followers' charismatic identity and garner support as new standard-bearers of the movement. This process of reactivating citizens' attachments, which hinges in large part on the strategies undertaken by new leaders, is essential for the political revival of charismatic movements. Without successors who can harness the emotional power of citizens' preexisting attachments, the movement is unlikely to reclaim its predominant position in politics.

This chapter is based on an article the author originally published in 2019 in *Comparative Political Studies* (Andrews-Lee, Caitlin. 2019b. "The Revival of Charisma: Experimental Evidence from Argentina and Venezuela." *Comparative Political Studies* 52(5): 687–719, DOI: 10.1177/0010414018797952). Reprinted with permission.

This chapter investigates the strategies that new leaders must implement to reinvigorate citizens' deep, affective ties to the movement and garner support. Drawing on insights from studies in political psychology, sociology, leadership, and electoral campaigns, I contend that successors must enact two strategies – one material and one symbolic – to achieve this ambitious task. First, successors must establish their own charisma by proposing and implementing bold policies that translate into tangible benefits for the followers and alleviate widespread suffering. Second, successors must cultivate symbolic ties to the founder to associate their charisma with the founder's glorified legacy and demonstrate their commitment to fulfilling the founder's mission to transform the followers' lives.

To test whether and how new leaders can associate themselves with their charismatic predecessor's legacy to revive citizens' affective ties and win political support, I analyze original, face-to-face survey experiments conducted with 999 movement followers in Argentina and Venezuela.[1] Specifically, I construct a 2×2 experimental design in which a potential successor running for president implements (or does not implement) a set of strategic cues related to bold policies and symbolic ties to the founder.

Contrary to studies of routinization, which suggest that charismatic attachments cannot survive in personalistic form beyond the founder's death, the results indicate that citizens' deep, emotional ties to Peronism and Chavismo endure. These findings corroborate the focus group evidence from the previous chapter regarding the survival of citizens' personalistic identification with the movement.

Moreover, in the context of presidential campaigns, the survey experiment reveals that a new leader's bold, initially successful policies and symbolic ties to the founder can politically reactivate followers' attachments by intensifying the followers' positive feelings toward the movement, enhancing their perceptions of the new leader's charisma, and boosting the leader's support. In short, these results indicate that, while the personalistic *nature* of citizens' attachments remains relatively constant over time, the *intensity* of those attachments can shift based on the coming and going of new leaders who claim to embody the founder.

The remainder of the chapter develops and tests my theory on new leaders' reactivation of the followers' charismatic attachments. In the next section, I briefly review the process through which charismatic attachments between leaders and followers initially develop and explain how new politicians can

---

[1] I refer to the transfer of citizens' charismatic attachments from the founder to the successor as "revival" or "reactivation" regardless of the amount of time that has passed since the founder's death. This is because, as I shall argue later in the chapter, new leaders must actively reinvigorate – rather than passively inherit – the founder's mantle of authority to be considered true heirs by the followers. Thus, even though Chavismo has not lost power in Venezuela since Chávez's death, a new leader's ability to sustain the movement would require that he/she *reactivate* the followers' attachments. Failure to do so might result in the temporary political latency of these attachments, but not necessarily their irreversible disintegration.

reactivate those ties to garner support. I then lay out the hypotheses, design, and results of the survey experiment conducted in Argentina and Venezuela. Finally, I discuss the substantive implications of the findings. In subsequent chapters, I examine the conditions that shape new leaders' capacity to enact these strategies of reactivation and analyze how, together, these strategies and conditions cause charismatic movements to develop fitful trajectories that undermine the development of stable, programmatic party systems.

5.1 A THEORY OF CHARISMATIC ATTACHMENT REACTIVATION

5.1.1 A Review of Attachment Formation

I begin by reviewing the three conditions that the founders must satisfy to initially establish charismatic bonds with their followers. These conditions are important because they inform the strategies that successors use later on to reactivate the attachments. First, the founder directly recognizes the suffering of citizens who feel they have been excluded by mainstream society. The founder focuses on these individuals because their unfavorable circumstances make them more likely to look for a savior to rescue them (Bandura 1982; Madsen and Snow 1991; Merolla and Zechmeister 2011; Spruyt, Keppens, and Van Droogenbroeck 2016; Weyland 2003).

Second, to secure these citizens' devotion, the founder demonstrates the capacity to single-handedly resolve their misery. Specifically, he must provide "proof" of his charismatic power by promising and implementing bold policies that showcase seemingly miraculous abilities (Pappas 2012; Weber 1922/1978, 242). From the followers' perspective, the daring character and capacity of these policies to confer material benefits – rather than programmatic content and long-term sustainability of the policies – are essential for substantiating the leader's extraordinary abilities. Once implemented, these policies confirm the founder's superhuman image and can temporarily protect him from subsequent drops in performance (Merolla and Zechmeister 2011, 30).

Third, the leader cultivates a narrative that glorifies his position as the people's savior, demonizes opposing groups as enemies blocking the people's path to salvation, and stresses the founder's promise to transform the society and deliver prosperity to the followers. This narrative, which frames the leader's mission as an all-out battle against evil forces, infuses followers' attachments with a profound moral intensity. Thus, the followers' support for the leader rests not just on much-needed recognition and tangible goods, but also on a deep sense of righteousness that inspires religious devotion to the leader, whom the followers come to view as brave and selfless (Zúquete 2008, 106).

As shown in Chapter 4, the founder's narrative is especially important for the survival of charismatic movements because it develops citizens' initial attachments into an enduring and deeply personalistic identity. This identity, in turn, shapes the followers' worldview, reinforces their belief in the founder's mission of ultimate salvation, and thus influences their political preferences and expectations even after the founder has disappeared. In particular, the identity provides citizens with a "framework that allows [them] ... to make sense of social, political, and economic conditions" that occurred in the past, are unfolding in the present, or are yet to occur (Abdelal et al. 2009, 24–25). It also gives these individuals "ways of recognizing, identifying, and classifying other people, of constructing sameness and difference, and of 'coding' and making sense of their actions" (Abdelal et al. 2009, 25; Brubaker, Loveman, and Stamatov 2004, 47). As a worldview, then, the followers' identification with a charismatic leader can shape their perceptions and evaluations of future politicians.

5.1.2 Strategies of Attachment Reactivation

Political psychologists suggest that, over time, various factors can shift the political intensity of a preexisting identity. In other words, the identity can be politically deflated or recharged depending on the circumstances. In the context of charismatic movements, as described in Chapter 4, the prolonged absence of the leader can cause the emotional charge of citizens' identification with the leader's charismatic movement to fade. While remaining profoundly attached to the charismatic founder and his redemptive mission, identifiers can become disillusioned with the current political landscape. However, a change in circumstances – specifically, the eruption of a crisis – can make the followers feel threatened and cause them to look for a new savior to rescue them from the situation, which creates the potential for new leaders to reactivate the followers' attachments to the founder and movement (Huddy 2013, 15, 44; Merolla and Zechmeister 2009a, 27–28; Weyland 2003, 839).

Once a crisis occurs, causing widespread feelings of anxiety and desperation, politicians can strategically manipulate the intensity of citizens' attachments by portraying themselves as model, "prototypical" members of the group (Huddy 2013, 12, 18). Potential successors have several incentives to engage this strategy. Namely, doing so can strengthen the impact of citizens' attachments on their political preferences and increase political engagement – the combination of which can mobilize a strong base of support for the new leader (Citrin and Sears 2009, 148; Cramer 2016, 12; Klar 2013, 1108). Moreover, research suggests that successors who depict themselves as symbolic archetypes of the identity – that is, the beloved founder – tend to appear more trustworthy and charismatic to fellow identifiers (Huddy 2013, 18; Haslam, Reicher, and Platow 2011, 96, 101–3; Hogg 2001, 190).

To reactivate citizens' attachments, new leaders must disseminate cues through speech, symbolic gestures, and policies that associate the core symbols and values of the identity with the current context and the leader's personal profile (Cramer 2016, 12; Huddy 2013, 12; Klar 2013, 1108; Meléndez and Rovira Kaltwasser 2019, 3). Specifically, I argue that successors who enact two cues – one material and one symbolic – similar to those implemented by the founder can reactivate citizens' deep, unmediated, emotional ties to the movement. If successfully executed, these cues signal to the followers that the leader embodies the founder and is committed to reviving his mission.

In material terms, successors must promise and enact bold, initially successful policies to prove their extraordinary power to rescue the people. This impressive performance signals their potential to fill the founder's shoes and convinces the followers that the new leaders are capable of delivering salvation. To demonstrate herculean abilities, the successors' policies must prioritize the rapid delivery of tangible benefits to the followers over programmatic coherence and sustainability. Though it is difficult for successors to implement this cue at the national level *before* becoming chief executive, past records of bold, impressive performance as subnational executive officeholders – for example, as governors – can provide followers with an initial cue regarding the successors' potential to fulfill their heroic promises.

Once implemented, this material cue should cause followers to evaluate the successors' performance in highly favorable terms. More importantly, however, the cue should reignite the followers' passion for and identification with the movement by convincing them that an authentic savior has emerged to pick up the founder's baton and deliver a prosperous future. In other words, more than simply demonstrating good performance, this cue should enhance the followers' *emotional* attachments to the movement and increase their charismatic perceptions of the successor.

Symbolically, successors must weave themselves into the founder's narrative by depicting themselves as true heirs and demonstrating their commitment to his mission of societal transformation. This requires successors to update the original narrative to fit with their personae and the contemporary circumstances. To do so, the leaders emphasize aspects of the founder that they share – such as tone of voice, word choice, dress, and physical gestures – while deemphasizing aspects they do not have in common. Additionally, successors can frame their opponents as traditional enemies of the movement to strengthen followers' support. They can also portray their policies – whose substantive content may differ from the policies of the founder – as achieving the same end goal: providing the followers with immediate relief and eventual salvation. To enact this set of symbolic cues, successors communicate them through verbal, auditory, and visual channels in order to repeatedly remind the followers of the charismatic founder, reinvigorate the followers' feelings of excitement for the founder's transformative mission, and convince the followers that the successors are worthy of the founder's mantle.

In sum, my theory of charismatic attachment reactivation challenges the logic of routinization, which suggests that these affective bonds must transform into depersonalized linkages to survive and remain politically relevant after the founder disappears. Instead, I contend that the followers sustain a deep, emotional identification with the movement that reinforces their commitment to the founder's heroic mission to transform society, shapes their worldview, and influences their expectations of future politicians. Subsequent leaders can therefore reactivate followers' attachments and gain support by (1) promising and implementing bold policies that deliver tangible benefits to the followers and (2) symbolically linking themselves to the charismatic founder and his transformative project.

5.2 TESTING THE REACTIVATION OF CHARISMATIC ATTACHMENTS: EVIDENCE FROM SURVEY EXPERIMENTS

I adopt an experimental approach to test the individual and combined effects of successors' bold policies and symbolic ties on the followers' expressions of emotional attachment to the movement and support for the heir. In particular, I draw on the priming, cue-taking, and identity literatures from political psychology (Abdelal et al. 2009; Hogg 2001; Klar 2013; Tajfel 1974; Van Vugt and Hart 2004) to design a survey experiment with two manipulations that represent strategic cues enacted by a hypothetical candidate seeking the presidency: *bold policies* and *symbolic ties* to the charismatic founder. The first manipulation corresponds to the material cue: the promise and implementation of bold policies. Because it is ultimately the *fulfillment* of these policies that "proves" the successor's charisma, I manipulate whether or not the candidate has fulfilled his bold, tangible promises to resolve citizens' most pressing problems in the past. The second manipulation, which represents the symbolic cue, incorporates visual and auditory symbols that associate the candidate with the charismatic founder of the movement. I construct a 2x2 design with four conditions such that respondents are randomly assigned to receive both, one, or neither of the two cues. Next, I measure the respondents' expressions of attachment to the movement and support for the successor (see Table 5.1).

5.2.1 Hypotheses

Based on my theory, I develop three sets of hypotheses about the combined and marginal effects of bold policies and symbolic ties on followers' charismatic attachments to the movement and support for the successor.

TABLE 5.1. 2 × 2: *Experimental conditions and summary of hypotheses*

	Presence of Symbolic Ties	Absence of Symbolic Ties
Fulfilled Bold Policies	*Fulfilled/Symbol* (Expect *strong* attachment and support for the successor)	*Fulfilled/No Symbol* (Expect *middling* attachment and support for the successor)
Unfulfilled Bold Policies	*Unfulfilled/Symbol* (Expect *middling* attachment and support for the successor)	*Unfulfilled/No Symbol* (Expect *low* attachment and support for the successor)

HI. Candidates who *combine* the material and symbolic cues can revive citizens' emotional attachments and garner support more effectively than candidates who implement only one or neither of the two cues. Thus:

A. Respondents in the *fulfilled/symbol* condition will express the strongest attachment to the movement. Specifically, they will identify most intensely with the movement and will express the strongest positive feelings and weakest negative feelings toward the movement.

B. Respondents in the *fulfilled/symbol* condition will express the strongest support for the candidate. Specifically, they will perceive the candidate as most charismatic and will express the strongest intentions to vote for the candidate in future elections.

HII. *Both* bold policies and symbolic ties to the founder are necessary for successors to fully reactivate citizens' attachments and garner support. The bold policies demonstrate the successor's charismatic power, while symbolic ties associate the successors' heroic capacity with the founder and his redemptive mission. Correspondingly, each of the two cues should not be as effective when applied in isolation. Nevertheless, candidates who implement *only one* of the two cues should elicit stronger attachment and support than candidates who use *neither* cue. In short:

A. Respondents in the *fulfilled/no symbol* condition and in the *unfulfilled/symbol* condition will express stronger attachment to the movement than respondents in the *unfulfilled/no symbol* condition.

B. Respondents in the *fulfilled/no symbol* condition and in the *unfulfilled/symbol* condition will express stronger support for the candidate than respondents in the *unfulfilled/no symbol* condition.

HIII. Finally, symbolic ties increase followers' support for the candidate because they link the candidate directly to the movement's charismatic founder and thus intensify the followers' deep, emotional identification with the movement. Therefore:

A. Followers' identification with the movement will *mediate* the effect of symbolic ties on support for the candidate.

5.2.2 Participants, Design, and Procedure

In partnership with two local public opinion firms – Trespuntozero in Argentina and Consultores 21 in Venezuela[2] – I conducted face-to-face survey

---

[2] The local public opinion firms that conducted the focus groups discussed in Chapter 4 – Trespuntozero in Argentina and Consultores 21 in Venezuela – also conducted the survey experiments in each country. Trespuntozero conducted the survey in Argentina from October 21 to November 20, 2016. Consultores 21 conducted the survey in Venezuela from February 1 to 18, 2017. The Institutional Review Board at the University of Texas at Austin approved the study (2013-03-0046).

experiments with a sample of each movement's most important and consistent base of followers: self-identified Peronist and Chavista adults (18 and older) from the "popular" (lower- and lower-middle-class) sectors.[3] While it would be interesting to analyze the impact of successors' material and symbolic cues on non-followers as well as middle- and upper-class citizens, I limited the scope of the present study due to theoretical expectations and resource constraints. First, I focused on movement followers rather than all citizens because the experiment aims to test the potential reactivation of *existing* attachments rather than the formation of *new* attachments among previously unaffiliated individuals. Certainly, political candidates should also endeavor to expand their support base by incorporating new voters. Yet, because the movement followers constitute a sizeable proportion of the population – about one-third of the electorate in both Argentina and Venezuela (Briceño 2015a; Calvo and Murillo 2012) – earning their loyalty provides new leaders an enviable "electoral cushion" (Levitsky 2003, 13–14). To narrow the sample in this way, respondents were asked a screening question in which they indicated which of several political traditions they felt closest to. Those who selected "Peronism" or "Chavismo" were included in the study.[4]

Second, I limited the sample to followers from the popular rather than the middle and upper classes because my theory suggests that socioeconomically marginalized citizens are more likely to experience seemingly unmanageable challenges, suffer disproportionately, and develop feelings of low self-efficacy. Popular-sector citizens are therefore more likely to look for and become emotionally attached to a leader whom they perceive as heroic (Burns 1978 Madsen and Snow 1991). Furthermore, in both Argentina and Venezuela, these low-income citizens make up the largest group of movement followers and a vital source of support for political candidates (Briceño 2015a; Calvo and Murillo 2012). As suggested by public opinion specialists in both countries, education

---

[3] In Venezuela, participants were randomly selected from the population of interest in the designated regions of the design. In Argentina, convenience samples were drawn from each region at outdoor shopping malls and plazas due to resource limitations. For the Argentine sample, quotas were used for demographic characteristics including gender, age, and education based on 2010 census data.

[4] This question wording was developed based on extensive interviews, pretests, and consultation with public opinion specialists. It was chosen because it does not indicate the intensity of one's attachments, nor does it imply identification or membership with a formal party. Because of the weakly institutionalized nature of Peronism and Chavismo, many popular-sector citizens identify with them as "movements" or "traditions," but not as official "parties." This and other screening questions were asked of all respondents well before exposure to the experimental manipulation (the material and symbolic cues) to avoid priming respondents to feel more or less identified with the movement. Specific question wording and closed-list response options can be found in Appendix 6.

TABLE 5.2. *Characteristics of selected regions*

Selection Criteria	Argentina	Venezuela
Federal Capital and Outskirts	Lanús, La Matanza (Province of Buenos Aires)	Caracas (State of Miranda)
Urban, Anti-Peronist/ Anti-Chavista Region	Córdoba (Province of Córdoba)	Maracaibo (State of Zulia)
Rural, pro-Peronist/ Pro-Chavista region	La Rioja (Province of La Rioja)	Cumaná (State of Sucre)

was used as a proxy for socioeconomic status; respondents with less than a college degree were included.[5]

In sum, while the population of interest in this study – movement followers from the popular sectors – is limited, it provides a crucial foundation of support for aspiring political candidates. To approximate a nationally representative sample of this population, the experiment was fielded in three diverse regions of each country: the federal capital and its outskirts, an urban and traditionally anti-Peronist/anti-Chavista region, and a rural, traditionally pro-Peronist/pro-Chavista region (see Table 5.2). Many studies of Peronism and Chavismo focus exclusively on the federal capital, which, while populous and politically important, has distinct characteristics compared to the rest of the country. In contrast, this three-region design better captures the followers' attitudes and behaviors at the *national* level, accounting for demographic, cultural, and political variation.

The survey experiment was designed as follows. Respondents were randomly assigned to one of the four experimental conditions, each of which provided information about a hypothetical governor running for president.[6] After a set of filter questions intended to restrict the sample to individuals from the population of interest, enumerators carefully explained the scenario, verified respondents' understanding, and proceeded to one of the four randomly assigned experimental manipulations, described below.

To maximize external validity, the two sets of manipulations – one for fulfillment/un-fulfillment of bold policies and a second for the presence/absence of symbolic ties – imitated stimuli that voters would encounter in a real

---

[5] Because more popular-sector citizens attend local colleges in both countries today than in the past, respondents aged 18 to 25 currently enrolled in college, but whose parents had completed nothing more than a high school degree, were also included in the study.

[6] In Argentina, the survey was administered on digital tablets using Qualtrics, which was set to randomly assign respondents across the four conditions in a balanced fashion. In Venezuela, due to resource constraints and safety concerns, the survey was administered on paper. Equal numbers of all four conditions were printed in advance and were shuffled at random by the supervisor before the enumerators received them. Enumerators were instructed to administer each paper survey as it appeared in the pile without rearranging it. Please see Appendix C for a table with the number of individuals assigned to each group as well as a table with balance checks indicating random assignment was successful.

presidential campaign. I developed each manipulation with the assistance and feedback of local campaign strategists, in-depth interviews and pretests with individuals from the population of interest, and, in Argentina, a pilot survey distributed online via email and Facebook ($N = 239$). To enhance internal validity, the survey was conducted in face-to-face format with local, trained enumerators to ensure that respondents understood the scenario and received the correct manipulations.[7] Manipulation checks (described subsequently) further verified that each stimulus achieved its intended purpose.

For the two conditions in which bold policies were enacted (*fulfilled*), the enumerator described to the respondent the candidate's successful completion of bold policies as governor, emphasizing impressive, tangible benefits he provided to popular-sector citizens in his province/state. For the remaining two conditions (*unfulfilled*), the enumerator indicated the candidate's failure to implement the same policies as governor. To stress the daring character of the candidate's policies, exaggerated wording was used, such as the promise to "end" (rather than reduce) poverty, "eliminate" unemployment, and "combat" crime. The policies also addressed real citizens' most pressing concerns, as indicated by surveys conducted no more than three months prior to fielding the study (economic crisis, unemployment, and poverty in Argentina; economic crisis, crime, and food shortages in Venezuela). Finally, to personalize and enhance the emotional persuasiveness of the scenario, I used an episodic frame (a personal anecdote) rather than a thematic frame (factual information) to depict the candidate's successful/failed implementation of bold policies (Iyengar 1994; Klar 2013). Prioritizing emotional responses to the candidate's policies in this way corresponds to my theory that the implementation of bold, initially impressive policies strengthens followers' *charismatic* – deeply emotional and personalistic – attachments to the movement.

Next, respondents were exposed to auditory and visual cues representing the presence/absence of the candidate's symbolic ties to the founder.[8] First, respondents listened to a 90-second speech by the candidate using headphones

---

[7] Enumerators in both countries were hired from each region where the survey was conducted. Supervisors from the contracted public opinion firms conducted half-day training sessions with the enumerators and continuously monitored their progress. To check validity of survey responses, supervisors called 10 percent of all respondents to ask about the content of the survey. Among this subsample, fewer than 5 percent were invalidated and were thus excluded from the analysis. All interviews produced by enumerators with invalidated responses were also excluded from the analysis.

[8] Leaders in both countries who attempt to reactivate citizens' charismatic attachments use several overlapping cues – such as colors, dress, images, and rhetoric – to signal their symbolic connection to the movement founder. Thus, to enhance external validity, the design incorporated both auditory and visual components into the symbolic cue. To the author's knowledge, this is the first experimental study to test the influence of these types of symbols on citizens' charismatic – rather than programmatic or ideological – attachments. Future studies should separate and test the effects of different symbolic cues in isolation.

provided by the enumerator. The speech was recorded rather than printed because voters tend to listen to, rather than read, candidate speeches in the context of presidential campaigns. Each speech was developed based on several real speeches made by prominent movement leaders including Carlos Menem and Cristina Kirchner in Argentina and Nicolás Maduro and Henri Falcón in Venezuela.[9] In each country, local campaign experts with public speaking experience recorded the speech.

In both versions of the speech, the candidate reflected on the country's current state of affairs and expressed bold promises that he would fulfill if elected. Next, in the two conditions in which symbolic ties were present (*symbol*), the candidate mentioned the founder by name (Perón/Chávez), referred to the followers using a typical in-group label (comrades/the Bolivarian people), and stressed the transformational character of the movement.[10] Conversely, in the two conditions where symbolic ties were absent (*no symbol*), the candidate did not mention the founder's name, used a neutral label for the voters (compatriots/the Venezuelan people), and referred to progress in terms of realistic development rather than using the more grandiose and missionary language of transformation. The remaining content, tone, and length of the speech in each country were held constant across all four conditions.

While listening to the candidate's speech, participants viewed a card with an image of the candidate's campaign poster, which was also designed based on materials from recent presidential campaigns and feedback from local experts.[11] Each version of the poster contained a generic campaign slogan (*Opportunity for All/Together with the People*), a solid color background, an image of children, the candidate's name, the title "President," and a picture of the candidate from the chest up.[12] In the version with symbolic ties, the background color corresponded to the movement (celeste/red) and the image featured the founder among the children. The version without symbolic ties had a generic background color unaffiliated with any major political party in the country, and the image of children did not include the founder.[13]

---

[9] Henri Falcón is one of few opposition politicians in Venezuela who had defected from Chavismo since the time when the experiment was run. Falcón's speeches reference Chávez's symbolic narrative while separating himself from the current regime's failures. For these reasons, I adapted excerpts of his speeches into the experiment.

[10] All comparisons listed in parentheses in this section are separated by country, not by experimental condition. The first term refers to Argentine version while the second term refers to the Venezuelan version.

[11] Though the survey was delivered via digital tablet in Argentina, respondents also viewed a physical, color copy of the campaign poster corresponding to their randomly assigned treatment group. Respondents in Venezuela also viewed a physical, color copy of the campaign poster.

[12] Stock photos for candidate images were purchased based on pretests and advice from local campaign experts.

[13] Because only the symbolic condition featured the founder, distinct images were used for symbolic and control images. The different images were selected based on similar criteria, including general tone, apparent age, and socioeconomic status of the subjects, and number of subjects.

Following exposure to one of the four randomly assigned conditions, respondents answered a range of survey questions regarding their emotional attachment to the movement and support for the candidate – the dependent variables of the study. To measure emotional attachment, respondents were asked how Peronist/Chavista they felt on a scale from 0 to 10. They were also asked to indicate the intensity of their positive and negative feelings toward the movement on four-point scales including pride, excitement, and hope; anger, disappointment, and fear. Due to the high interitem correlation between the three survey items for positive and negative feelings, respectively, I collapsed each set into an additive index and rescaled it to range from 0 to 10.[14] I interpreted statistically significant increases in the former two measures and a significant decrease in the latter as successful *reactivation* of citizens' emotional attachments to the movement.[15]

To measure support for the candidate, respondents were first asked a series of questions regarding their perceptions of the candidate's charisma. Based on my theory, a compelling leader who materially and symbolically embodies the founder's heroic image should appear significantly more charismatic to the followers – especially if the candidate is to consolidate his own personalistic authority.

To operationalize the candidate's charisma, respondents were asked to indicate their level of agreement on a four-point scale with three statements about his selflessness, vision of the future, and capacity to solve the country's problems. While charisma is difficult to measure quantitatively, these items have been validated in previous studies of charisma in Latin America and represent key components of the concept as outlined in my theory. I drew the first two of these statements from a five-question charisma battery developed by Merolla and Zechmeister to assess citizens' perceptions of leaders' charisma in Mexico and Venezuela.[16] I selected the following items: "[Leader's name] articulates a compelling vision of the future," and "[Leader's name] goes

---

The experimental manipulation can be viewed in the online appendix posted on the author's website, www.caitlinandrewslee.com.

[14] The order of these questions was randomized in Argentina, but not in Venezuela due to the use of paper surveys. Cronbach's alpha scores were 0.83 for positive feelings and 0.66 for negative feelings in Argentina, and 0.83 for positive feelings and 0.79 for negative feelings in Venezuela.

[15] I measured statistical significance at the $p = .1$ level due to the directional nature of my hypotheses.

[16] As discussed in Chapter 3, Merolla and Zechmeister (2011, 36–37) developed this five-question battery based on a larger set of questions from the Multifactor Leadership Questionnaire – 5X Long Form, an index that has been widely used to measure charismatic leadership in the United States. The authors selected these questions from the larger survey due to higher loadings on factor analysis from a 2007 survey in the United States. The battery has since been validated by multiple studies in Latin America, including a 2006 survey in Mexico by *Beltrán y Asociados* and a 2007 survey in Venezuela by the Latin American Public Opinion Project.

beyond his own self-interest for the good of the group."[17] The first reflects the leader's enactment of the founder's mission to establish a more prosperous future for the followers; the second relates to the leader's willingness to sacrifice personal goals to fulfill this righteous mission on behalf of the followers. I incorporated the third statement – "[the leader] is capable of resolving [Argentina's / Venezuela's] problems" – to capture respondents' perceptions of the leader's heroic capacity to resolve their misery. Though this statement is not included in Merolla and Zechmeister's battery, it comprises a central component of my definition of charisma that is also stressed by Weber: the leader's extraordinary ability to solve the people's problems. Unlike survey questions in which respondents are prompted to explicitly evaluate the candidate's economic performance (which was also incorporated in the study as a manipulation check, described subsequently), the broader and more prospective nature of this statement better (if imperfectly) captures whether the candidate inspires and convinces the followers of his/her heroic potential – a crucial component of charisma. I collapsed this three-item charisma battery into an additive index and rescaled to range from 0 to 10.[18]

In addition to the charisma battery, I included a survey question to measure respondents' intention to vote for the candidate in future elections. Whereas charismatic perceptions indicate respondents' potential to form emotional ties to the leader, this item provides a more concrete measure of support that is also necessary for the leader's consolidation of power. This item was also rescaled to range from 0 to 10 in both countries. Further details regarding all survey questions, including wording and response options, can be found in online Appendix C.

5.2.3 Manipulation Checks

The survey included additional questions to verify that the experimental manipulations had their intended effects. For bold policies, respondents were asked to evaluate the candidate's performance as governor on a four-point scale. As expected, respondents in the two conditions where the candidate fulfilled bold policies as governor rated his performance significantly higher

---

[17] The remaining items in the Merolla and Zechmeister battery include the following: "the leader instills pride in being associated with him"; "the leader's actions build my respect for him"; and "the leader considers the moral and ethical consequences of his decisions." The former two were not included in the survey experiment because they could have generated confusion due to the hypothetical nature of the design. (In other studies, the charisma battery has been used with *existing* leaders.) The third question was not included because citizens found the question wording confusing in a pretest that was conducted in partnership with the Argentine Panel Election Study in 2015.

[18] As with positive and negative feelings, the order of the charisma battery items was randomized in Argentina, but not in Venezuela due to the use of paper surveys. Cronbach's alpha scores for the charisma battery were 0.82 for Argentina and 0.89 for Venezuela.

than respondents in the two conditions where he failed to implement the policies ($M_{\text{Policies}} = 3.21$ vs. $M_{\text{No Policies}} = 2.19$, $p < .05$ in Argentina; $M_{\text{Policies}} = 3.11$ vs. $M_{\text{No Policies}} = 2.42$, $p < .05$ in Venezuela).

To verify the symbolic manipulation, respondents were asked to evaluate how Peronist/Chavista the candidate appeared on a scale from 0 to 10. On average, respondents in the two conditions with symbolic ties perceived the candidate as more Peronist/Chavista than in the two conditions without symbolic ties ($M_{\text{Symbol}} = 6.98$ vs. $M_{\text{No Symbol}} = 6.46$, $p < .05$ in Argentina; $M_{\text{Symbol}} = 7.56$ vs. $M_{\text{No Symbol}} = 5.63$, $p < .05$ in Venezuela). These data suggest that respondents in both countries received the correct cues for both sets of manipulations.

5.2.4 Results

HI: *The combined effects of bold policies and symbolic ties cause followers to express the strongest (A) attachment to the movement and (B) support for the candidate.*

For the most part, the results support HI, suggesting that the combined effect of bold policies and symbolic ties cause followers to express the most intense emotional attachment to the movement and the greatest support for the candidate. Specifically, in Argentina, respondents who received both cues (*fulfilled/ symbol*) expressed the strongest identification with Peronism, the most intense positive feelings, and the weakest negative feelings toward the movement, providing strong support for HI(A). Pairwise difference-of-means tests demonstrate that, on average, the joint effects of fulfilled bold policies and symbolic ties had a significantly greater, positive impact on followers' expressions of emotional attachment based on these three indicators. The differences were statistically significant ($p \leq .09$) in seven of nine pairwise comparisons between the *fulfilled/symbol* condition and each of the remaining conditions. The two differences that did not reach statistical significance – between *fulfilled/symbol* and *unfulfilled/symbol* for Peronist identification and for positive feelings toward Peronism – were in the hypothesized direction, with larger scores in the *fulfilled/symbol* condition.

Likewise, Argentine respondents exposed to both fulfilled bold policies and symbolic ties endorsed the candidate most enthusiastically, supporting HI(B). On average, respondents in the *fulfilled/symbol* condition perceived the candidate as more charismatic. These respondents also expressed greater willingness to vote for the candidate than respondents in the remaining conditions. All difference-of-means tests between this condition and each remaining condition were positive and significant ($p \leq .076$). Figure 5.1A and B present graphical illustrations of the results and Figure 5.2 shows pairwise *t*-tests between the *fulfilled/symbol* condition and each of the three remaining conditions (full ANOVA results and *p*-values for all pairwise *t*-tests are presented in online Appendix C).

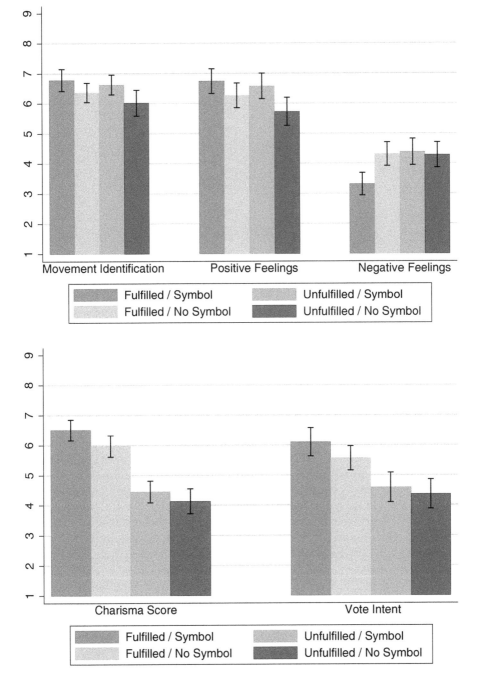

FIGURE 5.1. Mean levels of movement attachment and candidate support by experimental condition in Argentina

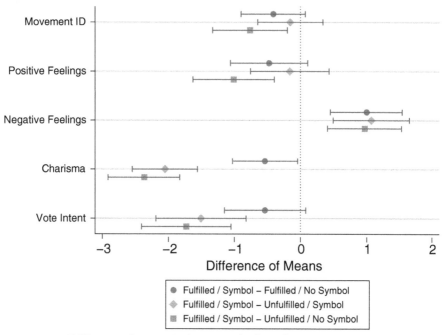

FIGURE 5.2. Difference of means in Argentina for hypothesis I: Pairwise *t*-tests

In Venezuela, the results for HI are mixed. To begin, HI(A) is not supported: In terms of movement attachment, respondents expressed equally strong identification with and feelings toward Chavismo across all four conditions, suggesting that neither bold policies nor symbolic ties had a noticeable effect. Moreover, the Venezuelan respondents expressed much higher and more concentrated levels of attachment than their Argentine counterparts. As shown in Table 5.3, in Argentina, the mean score for identification with Peronism across the four conditions was 6.45 with a standard deviation of 2.44, the mean score for positive feelings was 6.67 with a standard deviation of 2.90, and the mean score for negative feelings was 4.08 with a standard deviation of 2.77. Conversely, in Venezuela, the mean score for identification with Chavismo was 8.54 and a standard deviation of 2.12, the mean for positive feelings was 8.87 with a standard deviation of 1.76, and the mean for negative feelings was 1.57 with a standard deviation of 2.17. In other words, overall, the lower intensity and greater dispersion of attachments in Argentina allowed for differences to reveal themselves across the four conditions, whereas the "ceiling effects" for attachment in Venezuela suppressed any potential differences.

I suspect that these ceiling effects emerged in Venezuela due to the recent nature of Chávez's death, just four years before the survey was conducted. Because Chávez's followers continue to mourn his passing, it is likely that their

TABLE 5.3. *Descriptive statistics for movement attachment and candidate support*

| | Argentina | | Venezuela | |
Variable	Mean	Std. Dev.	Mean	Std. Dev.
Movement ID	6.45	2.44	8.54	2.12
Positive Feelings	6.33	2.90	8.87	1.76
Negative Feelings	4.08	2.77	1.57	2.17
Charisma	5.28	2.66	6.01	3.13
Vote Intent	5.17	3.18	6.46	3.97

attachments to his legacy remain highly activated, resulting in the expression of particularly raw, powerful, and concentrated feelings toward Chavismo – regardless of the behavior of new leaders. Indeed, the survey experiment was administered just four years after Chávez's death, during the rule of Chávez's handpicked successor, Nicolás Maduro – who leaned heavily on symbolic connections to Chávez and likely intensified the emotional salience of the founder's legacy even further. Conversely, Perón died over forty years before the survey was conducted in Argentina. Given the passage of several decades since the founder's death, followers' attachments to Peronism are likely to be more nuanced than their Venezuelan counterparts. Argentines who are *not* exposed to a new leader implementing Peronist cues may therefore be less likely to express their attachments as enthusiastically.

While the Venezuelan respondents' relatively uniform and intense expressions of attachment to Chavismo fail to provide support for HI(A), the results nevertheless attest to the staying power of charismatic attachments in the wake of the founder's death. Indeed, the routinization thesis suggests that citizens' attachments to the movement begin to fade away when the founder disappears, yet in Venezuela, the experimental results suggest that, four years after Chávez's death, many citizens' deeply affective attachments to his movement remain as strong as ever. Still, the comparison of results between Venezuela and Argentina suggests that, over the course of several decades, as the founder's original rule grows more distant, it is possible that the emotional intensity of citizens' attachments to the movement begins to dissipate – albeit much more slowly than routinization scholars indicate. Furthermore, as will be discussed subsequently, it seems likely that the relative importance of the material and symbolic components of the charismatic attachment may shift over time.

Nevertheless, turning to candidate support, the results in Venezuela uphold HI(B): the combined effects of bold policies and symbolic ties caused followers to express the strongest support for the candidate. On average, relative to all other conditions, respondents in the *fulfilled/symbol* condition perceived the candidate as significantly more charismatic ($p \approx 0$ across all pairwise difference-of-means tests) and were more likely to vote for the candidate in future elections ($p \leq .012$ across all pairwise difference-of-means tests).

The significance of these findings is noteworthy: while attachments to Chavismo remain strong among all followers, charismatic attachment to and support for new leaders vary based on the extent to which leaders can (a) demonstrate their own heroic capacities by fulfilling bold policies and (b) convincingly tie that heroism to Chávez's legacy. Thus, to maximize their support, new candidates are incentivized to behave similarly to and associate themselves with the charismatic founder to garner support – actions that perpetuate the founder's legacy. Figures 5.3A and B present graphical illustrations of the results in Venezuela and Figure 5.4 summarizes pairwise *t*-tests between the *fulfilled/symbol* condition and each of the three remaining conditions in Venezuela (full ANOVA results and *p*-values for all pairwise *t*-tests are presented in online Appendix C).

HII: *The marginal effects of bold policies and symbolic ties on followers' (A) expression of attachment to the movement and (B) support for the candidate are stronger than their combined absence.*

The results provide partial support for HII. In terms of movement attachment, respondents in Argentina exposed to *either* bold policies *or* symbolic ties generally expressed stronger attachment than respondents exposed to *neither* of the two cues, supporting HII(A). The results were significant in three of four pairwise *t*-tests ($p \leq .075$), and were in the correct direction in the fourth *t*-test. However, no significant differences were revealed across the three conditions in terms of negative feelings toward the movement, indicating that, unlike the *combined* effect of the two cues, the *marginal* effect of each is insufficient to attenuate respondents' negative sentiments toward the movement.

As for HII(B), the results from Argentina suggest that bold policies by themselves caused respondents to express stronger support for the candidate, whereas symbolic ties had no significant marginal effect. On average, respondents in the *fulfilled/no symbol* condition perceived the candidate as more charismatic ($p \approx 0$) and expressed greater intentions to vote for the candidate ($p = .001$) than in the *unfulfilled/no symbol* condition. In contrast, there was no significant difference between the *unfulfilled/symbol* condition and the *unfulfilled/no symbol* condition. These findings suggest that the impact of symbolic ties on voters' support for the candidate is not as strong as the impact of bold policies. Figure 5.5 displays pairwise *t*-tests pertaining to Hypothesis II in Argentina.

In Venezuela, no significant differences emerged across the four conditions in terms of movement attachment due to the ceiling effects described earlier. However, the results indicate that the marginal effects of bold policies and symbolic ties significantly influenced the respondents' support for the candidate, providing partial support for HII(B). On average, respondents in the *fulfilled/no symbol* and *unfulfilled/symbol* conditions perceived the candidate as more charismatic than respondents in *unfulfilled/no symbol* condition ($p \approx 0$ and $p = .010$, respectively). Furthermore, respondents in the *unfulfilled/*

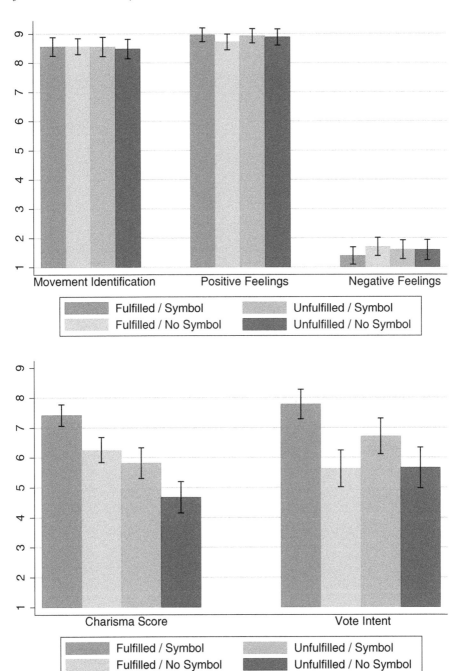

FIGURE 5.3. Mean levels of movement attachment and candidate support by experimental condition in Venezuela

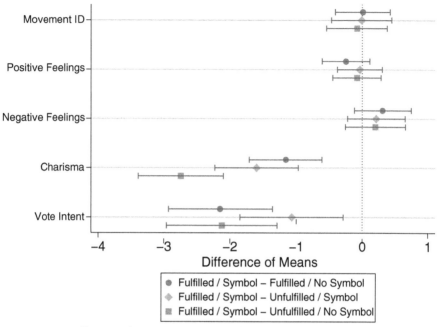

FIGURE 5.4. Difference of means in Venezuela for hypothesis I: Pairwise *t*-tests

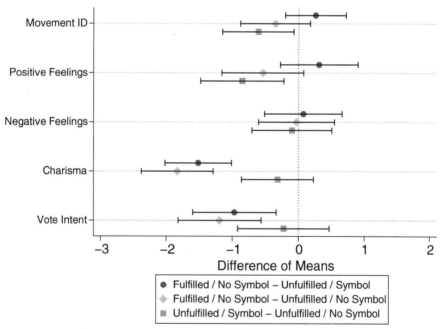

FIGURE 5.5. Difference of means in Argentina for hypothesis II: Pairwise *t*-tests

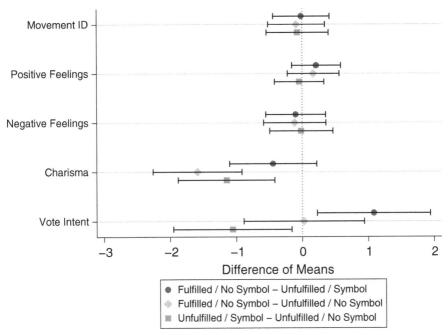

FIGURE 5.6. Difference of means in Venezuela for hypothesis II: Pairwise *t*-tests

symbol condition expressed significantly greater willingness to vote for the candidate than respondents in the *unfulfilled/no symbol* condition ($p = .054$). Figure 5.6 displays pairwise *t*-tests pertaining to these results in Venezuela.

A comparison of the results for HII(B) across Argentina and Venezuela yields further insights regarding the marginal effects of the material and symbolic cues on support for the candidate. As Figures 5.1B and 5.3B illustrate, in Argentina, the marginal effect of the material cue surpassed that of the symbolic cue, whereas in Venezuela, the opposite occurred: the marginal effect of the symbolic cue prevailed over the material cue. In other words, on average, Argentine respondents found the candidate who fulfilled bold policies yet had no symbolic ties to Perón to be more charismatic and worthier of their vote; in contrast, Venezuelan respondents tended to prefer the candidate who *did not* fulfill the policies yet demonstrated his symbolic connection to Chávez!

These findings suggest that the importance of the symbolic and material dimensions of charisma may vary over time, especially as they concern successors' ability to convince the followers they are worthy of the founder's mantle. Specifically, it is possible that, in the aftermath of the founder's disappearance, successors must rely more heavily on the symbolic dimension to portray themselves as rightful heirs. Yet with the passage of time, the material dimension – in particular, the heroic performance of new leaders – may become increasingly consequential for proving their capacity to pick up the founder's baton and revive the movement. Although these findings are speculative, they reveal interesting nuances about the unique effects of the different dimensions of charisma and open up avenues for future research.

To conclude, the findings reveal that the marginal effects of bold policies and symbolic ties influence followers' expressions of emotional attachment to the movement, their perceptions of the new leader's charisma, and their likelihood to vote for the new leader in future elections – though these effects are weaker than the joint effect of the two cues. Interestingly, the marginal effects of each cue vary according to the historical position of the charismatic movement: In Argentina, where the movement's founder died decades ago, the impact of the symbolic cue is relatively weaker than in Venezuela, where the founder died very recently and the movement remains in power. Still, in both countries, the fulfillment of bold policies appears to have a strong marginal effect on support for the *candidate* (with the exception of vote intention in Venezuela, perhaps due to the strength of symbolic ties in the current political climate). In contrast, symbolic ties are potentially more important than bold policies for reviving followers' attachments to the *movement*. These results reinforce my theory that new leaders must fulfill material *and* symbolic cues to fully revive the movement in their own name.

HIII: *Followers' identification with the movement will mediate the effect of the symbolic cue on support for the candidate.*

Finally, to further examine whether symbolic ties increase followers' support for the candidate *by enhancing their identification with the movement*, I turn to the third hypothesis. Following Imai, Keele, and Tingley (2010), I estimate the average causal mediation effect of movement identification on the relationship between symbolic ties and followers' support for the candidate, measured as charismatic perceptions and vote intention (see online Appendix C for equations and full output of the analysis). In Argentina, the results uphold this hypothesis. The direct and total effects of symbolic ties on charismatic perceptions and vote intent are not significant. More importantly, however, movement attachment has a positive, significant effect (see Table 5.4).[19] In other words, the symbolic cue has a significant but *indirect* effect on candidate support: Exposure to symbolic ties increases followers' support for the candidate *by intensifying their identification with the movement*. Thus, although the

---

[19] The mediation analysis includes an assumption that the observed mediator is statistically independent of the observed treatment and pretreatment confounders. In other words, among respondents who share the same treatment status (such as exposure to the symbolic cue) and share the same pretreatment characteristics, "the mediator can be regarded as if it were randomized" (Imai, Keele, and Tingley 2010, 313). To verify the validity of this assumption, I conducted a sensitivity analysis as suggested by Imai et al. (2010), which confirmed for both charisma ($r = .0613$) and vote intent ($r = .0965$) that the assumption was upheld.

TABLE 5.4. *Average causal mediated effect of movement identification on the relationship between the symbolic cue and candidate support (95 percent confidence intervals shown)*

	Argentina		Venezuela	
Average Effect	Charisma	Vote Intent	Charisma	Vote Intent
Mediation	.138	.201	.000	.071
(Indirect)	(.014, .291)	(.016, .413)	(-.046, .048)	(-.122, .275)
Direct	.206	.123	1.16	152
	(-.257, .662)	(-.422, .660)	(.582, 1.72)	(.817, 2.21)
Total	.344	.323	1.16	1.59
	(-.128, .825)	(-.244, .900)	(.592, 1.73)	(.870, 2.33)
Proportion Mediated	.361	.490	.000	.045
	(-2.05, 3.04)	(-6.51, 9.45)	(.000, .000)	(.030, .081)

results from HII(B) suggest that the influence of the symbolic cue on candidate support may have faded in Argentina in the decades since Perón's death, the mediation analysis suggests the lingering influence of the symbolic cue on followers' identification with the movement. In Venezuela, due to the ceiling effects for movement identification across the four experimental conditions, the results were not significant. Nevertheless, the Argentine findings underscore that, in addition to proving their *own* impressive leadership by implementing bold policies, successors who want to maximize their support should link themselves to the founder and his heroic mission to reactivate followers' attachments to the movement.

5.3 CONCLUSION

This chapter has provided important evidence that charismatic movements can persist by sustaining their original, personalistic nature rather than transforming into routinized parties. Specifically, new politicians can tap into followers' latent attachments to the movement to politically reactivate those bonds and garner support as the movement's new savior. Successors do not achieve this by adopting a strategy of routinization, such as developing a strong, consistent programmatic platform or relying on a well-developed party organization. Rather, new leaders restore the movement to power by embracing a personalistic strategy in which they depict themselves as heroic heirs of the founder and claim their devotion to realizing the founder's mission of transcendence. To do so, these leaders must first establish their own charisma by promising and fulfilling bold policies that demonstrate their extraordinary capacities; second, they must symbolically link themselves to the founder and display their commitment to reviving his redemptive mission. These tactics increase the political salience of followers' emotional identification with the movement, which in turn enhance their charismatic perceptions of and electoral support for the successor.

I demonstrate the mechanisms of charismatic attachment reactivation through a survey experiment conducted in Argentina and Venezuela with followers of Peronism and Chavismo, respectively. Similar to the focus groups discussed in Chapter 4, the results illustrate the enduring affective nature of followers' attachments to the movement. These bonds appeared especially strong in Venezuela, but also revealed themselves in Argentina. The survival of charismatic attachments in the latter case is remarkable, given that Juan Perón died over forty years ago and many observers doubt the resilience of the Peronist identity.[20] Moreover, the evidence suggests that new leaders – even ones with whom citizens are unfamiliar, such as a hypothetical presidential candidate – can strategically leverage the founder's legacy to politically reactivate followers' charismatic attachments and increase their own personal allure. Successors who *combine* bold, initially successful policies with symbolic ties to the founder cause followers to express the strongest emotional attachment and elevate the successors' charismatic appeal.

The results also shed light on the marginal effects of material and symbolic cues. The material cue appears to have important, independent effects on support for the candidate, measured in terms of charismatic perceptions and vote intention. This implies that leaning on the symbolic legacy of a charismatic predecessor is, by itself, insufficient to consolidate power: New leaders seeking to inherit the founder's mantle must also independently demonstrate their mighty potential. Yet the results also indicate that symbolic ties have a remarkably strong, marginal effect on citizens' emotional attachments to the movement. Moreover, a causal mediation analysis with the Argentine data indicates the important, *indirect* effect of the symbolic cue on followers' support for the candidate. The strength of this cue and its positive impact on candidate support, which operates by increasing the followers' identification with the movement, underscores the enduring influence of charismatic leaders' symbolic legacies on voters' attitudes and behaviors and suggests that leaders seeking to inherit the founders' power must also tie themselves to those legacies.

Importantly, it is possible that this strategy of charismatic reactivation extends only to the movement's traditional followers – those who come from the popular sectors (i.e., the lower- and lower-middle classes) and claim an affinity, however faint, with the movement. Moreover, the overall impact of the

---

[20] During personal interviews conducted by the author in Buenos Aires between March and July 2016, three public opinion specialists, three political scientists, and four political operatives from across the political spectrum – three Peronists and one non-Peronist – behavior expressed strong doubts that a strong Peronist identity persists among Argentine voters today.

effects can vary: The symbolic cue may be more powerful at the outset, as indicated in Venezuela, whereas the material cue may prove more essential as time goes on, as suggested in Argentina. Implementation of the strategy, therefore, does not guarantee new leaders' rise to power. Nevertheless, the importance of charismatic reactivation should not be underestimated. Indeed, followers need not be active, card-carrying members of the movement; they need only have a latent identification with the movement to be influenced by successors' cues. Popular-sector voters who satisfy this condition constitute a sizeable proportion of the electorate in countries where charismatic movements take root, including Argentina and Venezuela. Thus, politicians have substantial incentives to enact a strategy of charismatic reactivation to enhance their personal appeal. In turn, as demonstrated in the survey experiment, this strategy can increase followers' emotional attachment to the movement, thereby perpetuating its political relevance over time.

Due to the enduring impact of symbolic ties on followers' attachments and the resulting influence on political support, leaders in Argentina and Venezuela have continually linked themselves to their charismatic predecessors. In Argentina, for instance, Carlos Menem justified his audacious free-market reforms in the early 1990s by claiming that Perón would have done the same to resolve the crisis (Comas 1993). Years later, when former president Cristina Fernández de Kirchner sought to regain power as a senator in the 2017 elections, she claimed, "If Perón and Evita were alive, who would they vote for? Evita would vote for Cristina, Perón would vote for Taiana [Cristina's fellow senatorial candidate], and both would vote for Citizen Unity [Cristina's political movement]" ("Evita votaría a Cristina, Perón votaría a Taiana, y los dos juntos a Unidad Ciudadana" 2017). In Venezuela, despite his government's dismal performance, President Nicolás Maduro has also heavily relied on his connection to Chávez to sustain his legitimacy, declaring himself the "son of Chávez" and emphasizing his spiritual connection to the founder (e.g., Scharfenberg 2013; @VTVcanal8 2016). The results of my survey experiment suggest that these leaders' references to the charismatic founders of Peronism and Chavismo are probably strategic attempts to revive popular enthusiasm for the movement and establish a strong foundation for the leaders' support.

In sum, this chapter has clarified the micro-foundational process through which new leaders reactivate citizens' emotional attachments to charismatic movements and increase personal appeal. In Chapter 6, I investigate the macro-level conditions that influence leaders' ability to successfully implement these strategies to win elections and consolidate their own charismatic authority. To do so, I move from the perspective of the movement followers to that of the leaders who seek to revive the movement. By tracing the process through which some leaders succeeded while others failed across three charismatic movements – Peronism, Chavismo, and Fujimorismo in Peru – I indicate the crucial conditions that must be in place for successors to enact the material and symbolic cues described earlier, return the movement to power, and consolidate their own personalistic authority. Given these conditions, Chapter 7 assesses the potential trajectories that charismatic movements can take over the long term and examines the ways in which they threaten liberal democracy and hinder party system development.

PART III

THE SUPPLY SIDE

Charisma from the Leaders' Perspective

6

The Politics of Succession in Charismatic Movements

In previous chapters, I have argued that understanding the striking persistence of charismatic movements requires careful analysis from the perspectives of both the movement's followers and its leadership. In Part II, I focused on the demand side of charisma, identifying from the followers' point of view how their charismatic attachments to leaders form, survive, and become politically reactivated by new politicians. Chapter 3 analyzed public opinion data from Venezuela to demonstrate how followers' powerful, affective bonds to the charismatic founder emerge and overpower alternative (programmatic and organizational) types of linkages. Chapter 4 turned to focus groups conducted in Venezuela and Argentina to illustrate how the followers' ties cultivate a deeply personalistic identity that persists for years after the founder's disappearance. Chapter 5 provided additional evidence from survey experiments in both countries underscoring the resilience of the followers' personalistic identity. Moreover, the chapter showed that new leaders who signal their potential to fill the founder's shoes by enacting bold policies and symbolically associating themselves with the founder cause the followers to express their identity more strongly and have more support for the new leader. In short, my investigation from the demand side of charisma illustrated that citizens' profoundly emotional attachments to the founder and movement form, persist, and become politically reactivated through a *personalistic* mechanism.

Part III places this micro-level analysis in a historical context by turning to the supply side of charisma, incorporating the perspective of leaders who have

This chapter is based on an article by the author that was originally published in 2020 in *Comparative Politics* (Andrews-Lee, Caitlin. 2020. "The Politics of Succession in Charismatic Movements: Routinization Versus Revival in Argentina, Venezuela, and Peru." *Comparative Politics* 52 (2): 289–316, DOI: 10.5129/001041520X15668413926547). Reprinted with permission.

attempted to tap into followers' bonds to revive charismatic movements and consolidate power. To that end, the present chapter analyzes how some leaders succeeded while others failed to reactivate citizens' attachments and become new standard-bearers of the movement. Whereas existing literature argues that such leaders must invest in building an institutionalized party, I argue that they are more successful when they leverage conditions and strategies that conform to the movement's preexisting, personalistic nature.

As indicated in the previous chapter, successors who enact two strategies can reactivate citizens' attachments and garner support: (1) achieving bold performance to "prove" their extraordinary abilities and (2) symbolically tying themselves to the charismatic founder to appear as heroic reincarnations. In reality, however, many leaders have attempted to implement these strategies and have failed. Under what conditions can successors effectively apply these tactics to revive the movement and consolidate their own personalistic authority?

This chapter demonstrates that three conditions shape successors' capacity to reactivate citizen's attachments. The first, crucial condition involves when and how the new leaders emerge. *Anointed successors*, who are often directly handpicked by the founder and immediately take over afterward, encounter formidable obstacles that almost always prevent them from becoming effective leaders of the movement. Conversely, *self-starters*, who rise on their own years after the founder's death, have greater latitude to convince the followers of their heroic powers and assume the founder's mantle. Thus, self-starter status greatly increases the successors' probability of success.

Yet, simply becoming a self-starter is insufficient to ensure successors' victory. In fact, many self-starters attempting to embody the movement founder's legacy have failed. Instead, two additional factors condition whether self-starters can return the movement to power. First, these leaders need a crisis that generates widespread suffering and makes citizens more likely to crave a new savior capable of rescuing them from their problems. Second, self-starters' willingness and ability to adopt a style that plays into the movement's personalistic nature, rather than focusing on party-building and programmatic development, are crucial for their capacity to access the followers' deep, emotional attachments and portray themselves as champions of the people.

To illustrate the importance of these conditions for successors to revive charismatic movements politically and consolidate power, I trace the process through which six successors across three charismatic movements – Peronism, Chavismo, and Peruvian Fujimorismo – attempted to reanimate their predecessors' legacies. Specifically, I rely on interviews with former leaders, analysts, and campaign strategists; focus groups with movement followers; and secondary literature to assess the experiences of two anointed successors (Isabel Perón in Argentina and Nicolás Maduro in Venezuela), two failed self-starters (Keiko Fujimori in Peru and Antonio Cafiero in Argentina), and two successful self-starters (Carlos Menem and the Néstor and Cristina Kirchner couple in

Argentina).[1] In addition to cross-sectional variation provided by the three charismatic movements, this analysis incorporates an overtime component within a single movement by examining at least one successor from Argentina within each paired comparison. In light of this study from the perspective of the leaders, Chapter 7 examines the trajectories of charismatic movements focusing on Argentine Peronism. By investigating the rise and fall of successive charismatic leaders within a single movement over the course of several decades, the chapter reveals how charismatic movements hinder the development of institutionalized party systems over the long term.

6.1 A THEORY OF CHARISMATIC REVIVAL

As stated in Chapter 5, new leaders can politically regenerate a charismatic movement by achieving bold, impressive performance and symbolically associating themselves with the founder. In the following section, I analyze three conditions that impact successors' ability to enact these strategies and reanimate the movement's original, charismatic ethos: their mode of selection, the eruption of a crisis that makes citizens crave a savior, and the successors' adoption of the founder's personalistic style for claiming power.

6.1.1 Mode of Selection

The first condition that shapes successors' capacity to become new standard-bearers of the movement concerns their mode of selection. Some successors depend on the founder's direct anointment. These leaders, who appear to have no choice but to rise up as "chosen ones," typically take power in the immediate aftermath of the founder's disappearance. In contrast, other successors seek a more independent path to power, rising on their own accord when they feel the conditions are conducive to their success – often several years after the founder has gone. Unlike their anointed counterparts, self-starters do not enjoy the founder's explicit blessing. Instead, they must earn the followers' loyalty by using their own tools and strategies to portray themselves as genuine heirs.

On the surface, the founder's direct endorsement would seem to provide anointed successors with a formidable advantage over self-starters. This is because the followers trust the founder's judgment and therefore provide

---

[1] Néstor and Cristina are widely viewed as joint leaders of a single administration, much like Juan and Eva Perón from 1946 to 1952. Long before Néstor's presidential candidacy, both leaders held political offices in their own right and worked together to increase each other's influence. Moreover, Ollier (2015) indicates, "the Kirchner couple planned to alternate power between themselves – as [Cristina] affirmed – but [Néstor's] death [in 2010] made that plan impossible" (author translation). Finally, many Peronist followers compare Cristina to Eva Perón – whose charismatic appeal greatly strengthened and arguably prolonged Juan's position of power – rather than to Isabel, his uncharismatic third wife and anointed successor. For these reasons, I treat the Kirchners' joint presidencies as a single case.

anointed successors with an automatic base of support even before coming to power. In contrast, self-starters must independently gain national recognition and popular approval. Additionally, elites are more likely to back the founder's chosen successor to minimize costly uncertainty and avoid the instability of a power vacuum (Brownlee 2007, 597).[2] Conversely, self-starters usually have to compete against other candidates to earn these elites' support.

However, despite these apparent advantages, I argue that anointed successors rarely succeed. Instead, paradoxically, it is the self-starters – who must rely on their own resources rather than directly inheriting the founder's power – who are better equipped to pick up the founder's baton and rise to greatness.

6.1.1.1 *Anointed Successors*
The struggles of anointed successors stem from the inevitable reluctance of charismatic leaders to select a replacement. As Weber stresses, the charismatic founder considers himself an extraordinary individual with unmatched power (1922/1978, 241–46). For this reason, throughout his rule, the founder insists on his own superiority, concentrates rather than shares power, and demands unwavering loyalty from his staff. Moreover, when forced to face his own mortality, the founder often refuses to groom a successor to take his place. Although a talented successor could safeguard the survival of the founder's movement, training a worthy replacement would threaten the founder's superiority. Therefore, to shield his predominance from potential competitors, the founder prefers to designate a loyal and unintimidating successor rather than a skilled heir.[3] As faithful disciples accustomed to pleasing the founder, anointed successors stand little chance of outshining him. At the same time, however, these handpicked replacements are typically weaklings who lack the independent ambition and authority necessary to lead the movement in the founder's wake. Thus, while the selection of an inadequate successor protects the founder's superior charismatic image, it also places the movement in a precarious position after his rule has ended by leaving it in the hands of a weakling successor who lacks the founder's skill, willpower, and magnetic appeal.

In addition to anointed successors' lack of skill, willpower, and appeal, the situation they inherit from the founder complicates their prospects for success. This is because, by the end of the founder's rule, his audacious policies are likely to be nearing exhaustion. Since these haphazard and personalistic programs are designed to prove the founder's heroic capacities, they tend to lack the infrastructure to endure. While the performance of the policies may begin to decline during the founder's tenure, he can stave off the negative consequences by

---

[2] Specifically, Brownlee argues that "elites will accede to the ruler's choice of heir apparent" in the context of authoritarian regimes where the leader predates the party – as is the case for charismatic founders, who predate their own movements.

[3] Self-starters rarely compete for power under these circumstances, as they must face the candidate personally anointed by the beloved founder and are therefore unlikely to win.

draining available resources and using his charisma as a shield (Merolla and Zechmeister 2011, 30). Yet, neither of these tools is available to anointed successors. By the time the disciples take power, the country's resources are likely to be depleted; furthermore, anointed successors have no charisma of their own to protect their reputation. Consequently, these new leaders – rather than the adored founder – are likely to be blamed by followers for the policy failures.

Given the collapse of the founder's policies, anointed successors would do well to initiate drastic reforms. However, the extraordinary initial success of these policies, which remains fresh in the followers' minds, pressures the new leaders to become excessively risk averse. Indeed, the fearful prospect of disappointing the followers and sacrificing fragile legitimacy, which rests entirely on their connection to the founder, prompts handpicked successors to cling to the status quo rather than implementing drastic reforms. To make matters worse, these successors struggle to convincingly blame other actors for the policy failures and resultant crisis. To avoid blaming the beloved founder, even though the fault for these problems lies predominantly with him, they may attempt to place blame on classic enemies of the movement. However, this is unlikely to win much sympathy from the followers. From the followers' perspective, the founder successfully warded off threats from these malevolent opponents; anointed successors' inability to do so only further substantiates their weakness. In short, while the founder's endorsement may initially boost anointed successors' support, multiple obstacles related to skill, timing, and resources prevent these individuals from becoming successful new leaders of the movement.

Existing studies of charisma support the notion that anointed successors struggle to uphold their predecessors' movements. Yet in contrast to my theory, scholars tend to interpret this as evidence that the movements *must* routinize to survive. For example, Kostadinova and Levitt state, "When [the founder] withdraws from politics or dies, the organization faces an enormous challenge: it either replaces the leader with a functionary who is not remotely comparable with the predecessor, or else it splinters or simply dissolves. In either case, electoral loss is a more likely outcome than revival" (Kostadinova and Levitt 2014, 500–1). Similarly, Madsen and Snow claim, "the ability of any [anointed successor] to maintain a direct tie with his/her following is very much diminished." Thus, "charismatic movements, if they are to survive for an extended period, will *inevitably* develop structure and with that structure will come some decentralization of influence" (Madsen and Snow 1991, 25–28, emphasis added).

I argue that this logic of routinization underestimates the resilience of followers' affective attachments to the founder, which – as demonstrated in Chapter 4 – cultivate a remarkably stable identity (Huddy 2001, 127–56; Meléndez and Rovira Kaltwasser 2019, 3). Even in the absence of the founder, cultural symbols – such as images of the founder and stories of his/her heroism – can help sustain the identity among the followers (Huddy 2001, 143–4). In fact, these symbols may trigger especially intense feelings of sadness and yearning when the founder dies, making it very difficult for proponents of routinization to replace the followers' identity with depersonalized partisanship. As I will illustrate in subsequent sections, successors who adopt a strategy of routinization – including Antonio Cafiero in Argentina – overlook the intensity of the followers' enduring, charismatic attachments and therefore fail to tap into this reservoir of deep emotional support.

In sum, anointed successors face overwhelming obstacles that almost always preclude success. But, the resilience of citizens' affective attachments to the founder and movement signals the potential for self-starters to reactivate those bonds, revive the founder's transformative mission, and consolidate independent authority when conditions are more apt. Even so, success is anything but guaranteed. In fact, most self-starters who attempt to revive the movement in their own name fall short of establishing themselves as powerful heirs. The next section assesses the conditions under which self-starters can achieve this objective and carry the movement forward.

6.1.1.2 *Self-Starters*

Self-starters circumvent two obstacles faced by anointed successors and therefore have greater possibilities for successfully reviving charismatic movements and consolidating power. First, because they have greater freedom to seek power on their own timeline, self-starters can bypass the "status-quo bias" that encumbers handpicked successors; they can also avoid inheriting the crisis caused by the founder's collapsed programs. Thus, not only can self-starters seek power unencumbered by the burdens shouldered by anointed successors, but they can also convincingly blame the crisis on someone else – such as the unfortunate leader who immediately replaced the founder. Second, because these leaders choose when they seek power, they often rise years after the founder's rule, and can sidestep the founder's desire to appoint an underwhelming replacement. While this fact alone does not ensure self-starters' success, it encourages the emergence of more talented and promising candidates capable of exercising greater individual agency and appearing as strong leaders reminiscent of, rather than beholden to, the founder.

Scholars of routinization would claim that these two factors could not revive charismatic movements. Indeed, Weber, who perceives charisma to be fundamentally unstable, would argue that the movement could not live on without transforming into a more stable – traditional or bureaucratic – form of authority during the founder's rule or shortly after his death (1922/1978, 249–51). Shils, who contends that charisma can survive only through inanimate objects, would likewise doubt the possibility that an individual leader could reactivate the movement in personalistic fashion years after the founder's disappearance (1965, 205). Finally, Jowitt, who claims that the charisma of *programs* – but not of *leaders* – can persist, would find it unlikely that a self-starter could claim the founder's mantle. In short, these scholars would contend that charismatic movements' lack of organizational structure would cause disintegration before self-starters could bring them back to life.

By contrast, I argue that charismatic movements can tolerate much more leadership volatility than institutionalized parties precisely *because* of their weak structure and their firm emotional foundation. As shown in Chapter 4, unlike conventional partisanship, the profoundly affective and personalistic nature of citizens' identification with the movement, which is rooted in the founder's legacy, can endure even if the movement suffers an organizational decline. While the intensity of charismatic attachments may fade during such periods, ambitious leaders who "embody the prototype" of the movement – that is, leaders who signal their likeness to the founder – can politically reactivate citizens' ties and earn their loyalty as new standard-bearers (Haslam, Reicher, and Platow 2011, 137; Hogg and Reid 2006, 19; Huddy 2001; Meléndez and Rovira Kaltwasser 2019). Indeed, while it is difficult to change the personalistic nature of citizens' identity, the evidence in Chapter 5 suggests that, in some contexts, talented successors can strategically "shift the intensity" of the followers' identity to increase its political significance (Huddy 2001, 148).

6.1.2 Conditions for Self-Starters' Success

Many self-starters emerge, but few succeed in reviving the movement and becoming its preeminent leader. One reason for this failure is that success requires the emergence of a severe crisis, which is an exogenous condition over which self-starters have little control. Similar to the founder's initial rise to power, a crisis is important because it makes citizens hungry for a savior to rescue them. Not only does a crisis intensify *existing* followers' longing for such a leader, but it also makes citizens who were not previously followers of the movement – such as newly marginalized groups and younger generations who may not have directly experienced the founder's rule – look for an exceptional leader to provide them with relief (Madsen and Snow 1991; Merolla and Zechmeister 2009a; Weyland 2003). Just as with the initial rise of the charismatic founder, the eruption of a crisis provides a crucial opportunity for self-starters to prove their independent capacity to establish a heroic image and an impressive base of support.

However, the existence of a crisis does not guarantee the success of self-starters. To connect with and earn the devotion of the followers, these leaders must also adopt the founder's personalistic style. To do so, self-starters must *use* the crisis – they must "perform" and "mediate" it – to prove their heroic power and write themselves into the founder's symbolic narrative as true heirs who are destined to pick up the founder's baton (Moffitt 2015, 189). To achieve this, self-starters must exercise individual agency by relying on their own leadership skills and charisma. Rather than investing time and energy into party-building, as the routinization thesis would suggest, self-starters must use superb communication skills and magnetic appeal to reignite followers' emotional attachments and claim those bonds for themselves.

Moreover, self-starters must use symbolic tactics to play up the crisis and increase the political relevance of the founder's narrative under new circumstances. Specifically, in addition to portraying themselves as heirs of the founder, self-starters must revive the personalistic cleavage and intensify the polarizing dynamic of the movement by blaming their opponents for the crisis and framing them as menacing enemies of the people. This enhances cohesion among the followers while alienating the self-starters' critics as evil adversaries. Additionally, self-starters must use speech, dress, gestures, and other symbols to restore the relevance of the founder's mission of salvation and frame their actions as necessary for fulfilling this noble promise.

To recapitulate, I claim that the revival of charismatic movements requires a combination of structural conditions and new leaders' agency. Structurally, successors must arise as self-starters to emerge from the founder's overbearing shadow. These leaders must also seek power after the eruption of an acute crisis in order to convincingly portray themselves as saviors capable of meeting the people's needs. Once these two structural conditions have been met, self-starters must then rely on their own skills and charisma to embody the founder's personalistic style. By fulfilling all three of these conditions, successors are much more likely to return the movement to power and declare themselves true heirs and heroes in their own right.

6.2 TESTING THE THEORY: CHARISMATIC SUCCESSORS IN LATIN AMERICA

To test my theory of charismatic revival against the routinization thesis, I focus on Peronism, Chavismo, and Fujimorismo, the three most prominent charismatic movements in recent Latin American history. Specifically, I examine three sets of successors from across these movements: two anointed successors, two failed self-starters, and two successful self-starters.[4] To begin, I analyze Isabel Perón and Nicolás Maduro, the only two anointed successors from these movements. Subsequently, I explore the paths of two failed self-starters: Keiko Fujimori and Antonio Cafiero. While many self-starters have attempted and failed to revive charismatic movements, I analyze Fujimori and Cafiero because their candidacies were widely considered as viable and competitive. Finally, I analyze the complete set of successful self-starters from these cases: Carlos Menem and the Kirchners in Argentina.

Using interviews with former leaders and campaign experts, original campaign materials, newspaper articles, and secondary sources, I trace the process

---

[4] By definition, successors who seek to revive the movement must openly identify with its label.

through which each set of leaders failed or succeeded to return the movement to power and assess the relevance of the three conditions outlined in my theory. Next, I return to the focus groups discussed in Chapter 4 to highlight followers' personal impressions of the founder and subsequent leaders.[5] While the focus group participants do not constitute a representative sample of followers, their discussions provide multiple accounts that corroborate my leader-focused research regarding the strengths and weaknesses of different types of successors (Cyr 2016, 247).

As outlined in Chapter 2, I use three criteria to distinguish "success" from "failure." First, to embody the founder's legacy, I argue that successors must publicly associate themselves with the founder; otherwise, they may be perceived as independent leaders keen to start a new movement that threatens to overshadow the beloved founder. Second, like the founder, successors must rise to the chief executive office. Crucially, declaring themselves as heirs of the founder and becoming the nation's leader is insufficient; after all, most anointed successors achieve this without any real accomplishment of their own. To become true heirs of the founder, successors must also establish a strong popular mandate by drawing mass support in a sustained way once they are in office. To indicate the establishment of mass support, I turn to executive approval ratings.[6] In particular, I argue that successful leaders must secure the approval of a majority of the population (at least 50 percent) for at least one year in executive office. Table 6.1 displays the six successors analyzed here with their scores for each of the three criteria.

6.2.1 Anointed Successors: Isabel Perón and Nicolás Maduro

I begin by assessing the trajectories of two anointed successors: Isabel Perón, who inherited the Argentine presidency in 1974 from her husband, Juan Perón; and Nicolás Maduro, whom moribund Hugo Chávez handpicked as president of Venezuela in 2013. While both Isabel and Maduro became chief executives of their respective countries, their support rapidly diminished shortly after they took office. After two disastrous years, Isabel was ousted by a military coup in 1976, while Maduro became an authoritarian leader who managed to cling to power using repression rather than charisma. While both leaders assumed the top office, they projected an uninspiring symbolic image and failed to reform their predecessors' collapsing policies. The weak leadership of these anointed successors led to the temporary deflation of the movement; however, citizens' charismatic attachments survived, setting up

---

[5] Because focus groups were not conducted in Peru, this type of evidence is not used for the case of Keiko Fujimori.
[6] Approval ratings are drawn from the Executive Approval Database, Carlin et al. 2016, available for download at www.executiveapproval.org.

TABLE 6.1. *Scoring of successors under analysis: Anointed successors, failed self-starters, and successful self-starters*

Successor Type	Leader Name (Country)	Public Tie to Founder	Chief Executive	Highest Annual Exec Approval
Anointed Successor	Isabel Perón (Argentina)*	Yes	Yes (1974–76)	–
	Nicolás Maduro (Venezuela)	Yes	Yes (2013–present)	37.91 (5/2013–4/2014)
Failed Self-Starter	Antonio Cafiero (Argentina)	Yes	No (1989 campaign)	–
	Keiko Fujimori (Peru)	Yes	No (2011, 2016 campaigns)	–
Successful Self-Starter	Carlos Menem (Argentina)	Yes	Yes (1989–99)	60.13 (8/1989–7/1990)
	Néstor Kirchner (Argentina)**	Yes	Yes (2003–7)	69.00 (6/2003–5/2004)
	Cristina Kirchner (Argentina)***	Yes	Yes (2007–15)	58.84 (1/2011–12/2011)

* As her husband's vice president, Isabel Perón became president upon his death rather than being elected. Her approval numbers are not listed due to the scarcity of public opinion data from this tumultuous period in Argentine history. Nevertheless, her broad unpopularity as president is widely documented (e.g., Madsen and Snow 1991, 134; McGuire 1997, 165–70), suggesting that her approval numbers would have fallen below the 50-percent threshold.

** Néstor Kirchner and Carlos Menem advanced to a second round of presidential elections in 2003. Due to Kirchner's overwhelmingly superior numbers, Menem dropped out of the race before elections were held.

*** Though Cristina immediately succeeded Néstor as president, I consider her as a self-starter rather than an anointed successor because, from their initial rise to national executive power in 2003, the two ambitious leaders planned a *joint project* to become Argentina's new saviors.

the future possibility of movement revival by self-starters – an outcome that routinization would not predict.

6.2.1.1 Isabel Perón

As will be described in further detail in Chapter 7, Juan Perón rose to the presidency in 1946 and consolidated a powerful charismatic movement alongside his second wife, Eva, by granting unprecedented benefits to millions of socioeconomically and politically excluded citizens. Though Eva died of cancer in 1952 and a military coup exiled Juan to Spain in 1955, outlawing Peronism for nearly two decades, Perón remained Argentina's most prominent political figure throughout his lifetime. Indeed, during his exile (1955–73), he influenced politics through proxy leaders and his unmatched support base.[7]

Perón frequently spoke of creating an "organized community" of followers, suggesting that his movement might one day routinize (Perón 1974). In practice, however, he undermined the organizational dimension of his movement by allowing the proliferation of ideological rifts within it and maintaining unchallenged personalistic control over it (McGuire 1997, 50; Page 1983, 161). These tactics deepened the "chameleonic" nature of his political brand and prevented the rise of powerful protégés while reinforcing his position as supreme leader (Ciria 1974, 30). Indeed, personal loyalty to Perón constituted the only thread uniting his otherwise bitterly divided followers. Upon returning to Argentina to serve a third presidential term in 1973, he displayed reluctance to share his power. Despite old age and a delicate political and economic context, he appointed his most faithful servant, Isabel, as his vice president and eventual successor (McGuire 1997, 164). By nominating a complete political novice rather than a more experienced leader, he showed his desire to dominate the movement.

As her husband's reluctant successor, Isabel lacked the political familiarity and skill to maneuver her government out of the crisis and claim her place as the new leader of Peronism. Instead of reaching out to console the devastated masses, she failed to take ownership of the deep bonds her husband had cultivated. Thus, while followers expressed euphoria upon Juan's return to Argentina in 1973, they viewed Isabel as weak and out of touch. In fact, her presidency was widely perceived as a "leaderless situation," and voters "assumed that she would not be able to remain, even as a figurehead" for the movement (Di Tella 1983, 69).

Isabel's failure to inspire the followers was compounded by her inability to reform her husband's dysfunctional policies of economic nationalism. While these policies had once created impressive growth and delivered prosperity to millions of Argentine workers, they were already approaching exhaustion when

---

[7] During this period, presidents owed their victories to Perón's endorsement or the abstention of his followers; military dictators seized power in response to elected presidents' inability to sustain a popular mandate and stable government in Perón's absence (Kirkpatrick 1971, 49–78).

Perón was exiled in 1955. Because Perón had prioritized the short-term impact of the policies over their sustainability, the policies were inherently "self-limiting" (Waisman 1987, 256). Thus, as the economy began to stagnate in the early 1950s, the policies generated a distributional conflict between the productive agricultural sector and the unproductive industrial sector; this, in turn, created a crisis of "illegitimacy and political instability" (ibid.). Because subsequent regimes struggled to implement adequate reforms, they were held responsible for the declining trade, expanding debt, increasing inflation, low growth, and political volatility that resulted.

This inability of non-Peronist regimes to address the crisis in the 1955–73 period provided Perón with a second opportunity to prove his heroic power upon returning to Argentina in 1973. At the time, he proposed the "Social Pact," a series of bold programs – enhancing Argentina's economic independence from the United States, freezing inflationary prices, and increasing workers' wages – to return the country to the prosperity of his prior rule (Pion-Berlin 1983, 59). As before, these policies *initially* delivered favorable results and sustained Perón's superhuman reputation for the rest of his life, which lasted just nine months, until July 1, 1974. Shortly thereafter, the policies quickly imploded, causing a grave crisis that Isabel was forced to shoulder (ibid., 59–60).

Despite the urgent need for reform, Isabel feared that altering her husband's policies would impose a painful cost on the followers and demonstrated little desire to undertake this challenge. Instead, in a half-hearted effort to maintain the support of her husband's increasingly fractious rank and file, she promised to continue rather than reform his deeply problematic platform of economic nationalism through wage hikes and industrial expansion (Waisman 1987, 280). This strategy soon shattered the economy, forcing Isabel and her closest advisor, José López Rega, to enact a series of stabilization plans that substantially decreased workers' real incomes (McGuire 1997, 167). Consequently, Lorenzo Miguel, the leader of the General Confederation of Labor (*Confederación General del Trabajo* – CGT), launched a crippling, two-day general strike against Isabel's government. Unable to recover from this political and economic disaster, Isabel was ousted by a military coup on March 24, 1976 (ibid., 170).

Isabel's weak image and utter lack of leadership led Peronist followers to view her as a tremendous disappointment rather than her husband's genuine heir. Thus, while their loyalty to Perón and Eva survived, their attachments never transferred to Isabel. In fact, "Isabel is not Perón" and "there is only one Evita" became common refrains among the Peronist left during Isabel's administration (Gillespie 1982, 164). Decades later, in 2016, followers in focus groups with the author emphasized their distaste for Isabel. They stated, "I am Peronist of [Juan] Perón"; "I am an *original* Peronist"; "I follow Eva and her masses, but Isabel was a disaster"; and "Isabel was chaos." Crucially, while her rule gave way to a military dictatorship in March 1976, these statements suggest that followers disassociated Isabel from Perón, thereby preserving their attachments to his heroic legacy.

6.2.1.2 *Nicolás Maduro*

As described in Chapter 3, Hugo Chávez took Venezuela by storm upon rising to the presidency in 1999. During his fourteen-year rule, he took drastic measures to destroy the unpopular, corrupt, and dysfunctional regime he replaced and establish his image as a true champion of the poor. Although the dramatic impact of his reforms depended on unsustainably high oil prices and drastic overspending, they provided unmatched benefits to millions of citizens and solidified Chávez's status as their everlasting savior. Correspondingly, when he revealed that he had cancer on July 1, 2011, he assured his followers that he would combat the illness; in the meantime, while undergoing treatment in Cuba, he promised he would continue to personally govern the country rather than appoint a successor, emphasizing his irreplaceability (Primera 2011). Thus, when he announced his cancer was terminal in December 2012, he appeared as surprised and devastated as his followers that he would not live on to serve as their immortal protector. As though resigned to the fact that any successor would be inadequate, Chávez anointed Nicolás Maduro, an obsequious follower with scant ambition or domestic political experience, as his heir. The choice surprised many within and outside of Chavismo. However, the anointed successor's lack of skill made Chávez appear even more impressive; furthermore, Maduro had devoted years of service to Chávez – a characteristic of paramount importance to the founder (Corrales and Penfold 2015, 160).

Since becoming president in 2013, Maduro has utterly failed to claim true leadership of Chavismo. His attempts to legitimate his authority have hinged exclusively on his appointment by Chávez rather than the establishment of an independent charismatic image. For instance, he has declared himself the "son of Chávez," referenced the founder constantly in speeches, and covered public spaces with images of his predecessor. Perhaps as a result, support for Maduro remains at about 28 percent – a surprisingly high figure, considering his catastrophic mismanagement of the economy and society in general (GBAO Strategies 2019). Nevertheless, whereas Chávez relied on his captivating charisma to consolidate support, Maduro has used despotic tactics to remain in power, including jailing opposition politicians, outlawing (or holding fraudulent) elections, and repressing civilians (Freedom House 2018). Furthermore, his claims to have assumed the founder's mantle appear absurd to many followers, who have been forced to endure hyperinflation, extreme shortages of basic goods, and even starvation (Corrales and Penfold 2015, 171; Gill 2017).

Like Isabel Perón in Argentina, Nicolás Maduro has also proven unwilling and unable to transform his predecessor's foundering policies. To sustain the flow of benefits to his followers during his rule, Chávez squandered the state's oil profits and recklessly interfered with the economy. Maduro therefore inherited an administration that severely undermined economic production and embraced drastic overspending, triggering inflation, shortages, corruption, and crime. Despite these problems, the successor's only political asset – Chávez's personal endorsement – made him unwilling and unable to introduce desperately needed reforms, which has caused a devastating crisis. Furthermore, Maduro's attempts to blame the domestic opposition politicians and foreign "imperial" powers, such as the United States and Europe, have appeared thoroughly unconvincing – even to followers, who have long distrusted these "enemy" groups. Consequently, many Chavistas view the new leader as responsible for their suffering. As several followers expressed in focus groups conducted in 2016, "Maduro is a bad Chavista"; "we are more Chavista than Maduro is"; and "what a shame that Maduro is the one representing Chavismo today." Because of Maduro's refusal to reverse policy failures, about half of Chávez's followers opposed Maduro in 2015, two years into the anointed successor's rule (Briceño 2015a).

Several scholars have taken Maduro's failure as evidence that Chavismo has died – a testament to the fleeting nature of charismatic movements (e.g., López Maya 2014, 68–87; Rondón 2017). Conversely, I argue that the stark contrast between Chávez and Maduro has caused many followers to *reinforce* their attachments to the former while distancing themselves from the latter. Indeed, half of Chávez's most devoted followers – about 16 percent of the electorate – identify as "Chavistas *no Maduristas*" (Briceño 2015a). Moreover, a 2020 poll by Venezuelan firm Datanálisis indicates that while Maduro's approval rating stands at a dismal 13 percent, fully 62 percent of voters maintain favorable views of Chávez (Datanálisis: Encuesta Nacional Ómnibus 2020). And in focus groups conducted with Chavista followers in 2016, participants expressed disdain for Maduro while declaring their love for Chávez and expressing faith that a more competent successor will appear someday: "I am with the future, and we are going to get it with Chavismo"; "one looks to the future and one sees Chávez." Others declared that their future leader should be "charismatic," "honorable," "capable of restoring order," and "100 percent Chavista." Contrary to the logic of routinization, wherein citizens' bonds must transform into depersonalized organizational linkages, the survival of citizens' affective ties to Chávez suggests the potential for his movement to one day reemerge in its original charismatic form under a more appealing successor.

6.2.2 Failed Self-Starters: Keiko Fujimori and Antonio Cafiero

Self-starters are more likely to restore charismatic movements to power because they control their own timeline and can therefore steer clear of the founder's desire to marginalize skilled leaders who might steal the limelight and escape blame for the collapse of his policies. But, being a self-starter alone does not guarantee success. These leaders must also rise during a crisis to appear as new saviors and portray themselves symbolically as new standard-bearers devoted to reviving the founder's mission to transform society. I analyze two self-starters who failed to fulfill one of these two conditions: Keiko Fujimori in Peru, who tried to rise in the absence of crisis conditions, and Antonio Cafiero in Argentina, who chose a strategy of routinization rather than adopting a personalistic approach.

6.2.2.1 *Keiko Fujimori*

In June 1990, political outsider Alberto Fujimori was elected president of Peru during a period of hyperinflation and insurrection. He immediately implemented drastic policies of economic stabilization, bringing hyperinflation to a screeching halt, and soon launched a campaign to combat the insurgent groups (Weyland 2002, 150–58). Combined with his personal allure and his inspiring mission to "reengineer Peru," these bold initiatives helped him consolidate impressive popular support (Carrión 2006, 126–49). Devotion to Fujimori proved especially strong among the poor, who had suffered the most from the economic crisis and political violence prior to his rule. Indeed, his popularity remained well above 50 percent in 2000, ten years after his rise to power, when he won a third (unconstitutional) term (Arce and Carrión 2010, 37–38).

While he retained a large and devoted following, Congress threatened to depose Fujimori following his electoral victory in 2000, citing accusations of corruption and misconduct. Reluctantly, he resigned that November while in Japan and remained in self-imposed exile until 2007, when he was imprisoned for human rights abuses committed during his rule (ibid.; Levitsky and Zavaleta 2016, 433). When he was forced to step down in 2000, Fujimori's personalistic legacy left the country in a leadership vacuum. In fact, in subsequent years, Peru endured a series of disliked presidents characterized by "broken promises" (Dargent and Muñoz 2016, 147).

Over time, however, Keiko Fujimori, Alberto's daughter, demonstrated her potential to return Fujimorismo to power and become its new champion.[8] When she competed in presidential elections in 2011 and 2016, she built a larger and more consistent support base than any other political party. In fact, in 2016, she claimed 39.9 percent of the vote in the first round – nearly twice as much as the runner-up candidate (Dargent and Muñoz 2016, 145–47).

To build this support, Keiko first established herself as a self-starter. As the daughter of the exiled founder, in some ways she appeared to be her father's handpicked heir. Indeed, she made her political debut as First Lady of Peru during her father's presidency, after her parents had separated. Years later in 2011 when she first sought the presidency, many speculated that Alberto had helped orchestrate her campaign from prison (Romero 2011). In turn, Keiko leaned heavily on her flesh-and-blood connection to Alberto throughout the

---

[8] I am grateful to Carlos Meléndez for sharing his insights on the case of Keiko Fujimori.

2011 campaign to enhance her popularity among his followers, calling him "the best president in Peruvian history" (Loxton and Levitsky 2016, 127).

Despite her close relationship with her father, however, Keiko's experience in the 2011 and 2016 presidential campaigns indicates that she earned her status as a self-starter. First, while she took advantage of her familial connection to boost her popularity, her father never explicitly designated her as his successor. Rather than leaning on his overt endorsement, she sought the presidency on her own, a full decade after his resignation. Moreover, Keiko ran under a party label of her own creation, Popular Force (*Fuerza Popular* – FP) (Levitsky 2011).[9] In doing so, she injected fresh energy into the movement and added her own "personal stamp" to expand its political influence (Meléndez 2019; Vergara 2018, 67).

In contrast to anointed successors, Keiko also navigated an increasingly tense personal relationship with her father during her quest for power (Meléndez 2019). Indeed, unlike political advisers who had faithfully served Alberto and continued to display sycophantic tendencies throughout the 2000s – such as Martha Chávez, his handpicked candidate for the 2006 presidential election – Keiko exercised independent ambition that sometimes conflicted with and threatened to overshadow her father. For instance, whereas Chávez unabashedly praised even the most unsavory aspects of Alberto's legacy, Keiko carefully tied herself to his most popular accomplishments – namely, stabilizing the economy, restoring law and order, and lifting up the poor – while distancing herself from his more violent and authoritarian tendencies ("Martha Chávez Aplaude Ataque a Monumento 'Ojo que Llora'" 2007; Meléndez 2019).

In the most overt demonstration of her independence, during her 2016 campaign, Keiko publicly vowed *not* to pardon her father for his past crimes and release him from prison if elected (Vergara 2018, 83). In contrast, Keiko's brother, Kenji, remained faithful to his father, fiercely advocating for his release from prison – which finally occurred in December 2017 (ibid.).[10] While this family drama added to the growing rift between Keiko and Alberto, it helped the former secure her hard-won position as the movement's new leader. Indeed, the number of "Keikistas" within the movement – who support both her father's legacy and her new leadership – continued to grow even as she distanced herself from him (Levitsky and Zavaleta 2016, 436–37).

While positioning herself as a self-starter, Keiko also fulfilled the second condition for successful movement revival by adopting key elements of her father's personalistic style to win over traditional Fujimoristas. For example, rather than campaigning on a specific platform, she made sweeping promises to reverse economic stagnation and meet the needs of citizens "tired of waiting for

---

[9] During her 2011 campaign, her party label took the name of *Fuerza 2011*, which was subsequently altered to become *Fuerza Popular*.

[10] In January 2019, a Supreme Court judge overturned Fujimori's pardon, returning the leader to prison ("Peru's Fujimori, Pardon Annulled, Forced Back to Prison" 2019).

solutions to their pressing problems" (Dargent and Muñoz 2016, 152). She also donned her father's approachable, "down-to-earth" style and traveled the country to forge direct ties with voters as Alberto had years earlier.

Importantly, even as she consolidated personalistic appeal, Keiko also tried to establish a party organization more than any other presidential candidate. Her new party, FP, organized local-level committees throughout Peru, and nominated candidates for subnational elections under its label (Meléndez 2019). Perhaps as a result, FP achieved some electoral successes, including an absolute majority in Congress in 2016 with 36 percent of the legislative vote (Birnbaum 2017; Tegel 2017).

Despite these efforts, Keiko prioritized her charismatic allure over her party-building efforts at crucial moments. During her presidential campaigns, she created a "personalistic vehicle" that overshadowed her nascent party (Dargent and Muñoz 2016, 152). Her supporters also came to call themselves "Keikistas" rather than FP partisans, indicating their loyalty to the individual over the party. In short, Keiko's "success at party-building [was] far from guaranteed," whereas her image as a fresh leader capable of delivering prosperity to the suffering masses – as her father did two decades earlier – played to the personalistic foundations of Fujimorismo (ibid., 155).

Though Keiko achieved self-starter status and adopted an engaging personalistic style, she narrowly lost the elections in both 2011 and 2016, failing to secure the presidency. Contrary to the successful self-starters discussed subsequently, she did not manage to win an impressive, landslide victory over her opponents. Thus, she was unable to restore her father's movement and exercise power as the people's new savior.

I argue that Keiko failed due to the absence of a crisis – another crucial condition for self-starters' success. An economic boom in the mid-2000s, driven by international demand for Peru's copper, gold, and natural gas, generated substantial growth and acted as a "buffer against social malaise" (ibid., 147). Indeed, this boom, combined with solid macroeconomic policies and structural stability, enabled the country to achieve high growth, low inflation, and substantial poverty reduction in the post-Fujimori period. Peru's average GDP grew at an annual rate of 6.1 percent between 2002 and 2013, while poverty fell from 52.2 percent to 26.1 percent between 2005 and 2013, and extreme poverty fell from 30.9 percent to 11.4 percent during the same period (*The World Bank in Peru: Overview*, April 2019). Consequently, while Peruvians expressed disappointment in their political leaders, they did not desperately crave a hero as they did prior to Alberto's rise in 1990. Keiko's promises to once again "reengineer Peru" and restore prosperity did not resonate enough with the public to catapult her into power.

6.2.2.2 *Antonio Cafiero*
In Argentina, Antonio Cafiero, a talented and experienced leader, had the potential to become a successful self-starter when he competed in the presidential

primaries for the Peronist Justicialist Party (PJ) in July 1988. By then, memories of Isabel's failures had been overshadowed by the even-worse performance of the military during the 1976–83 dictatorship. Moreover, seeking power fifteen years after Perón's death, Cafiero rose as an independent leader and not as a submissive protégé of the founder. Without the inherent weaknesses of anointed successors, Cafiero's path to power seemed more promising than that of his Peronist predecessor.

Additionally, Cafiero sought power amidst a terrible economic crisis, further enhancing his prospects for becoming the new leader of Peronism. The outgoing president from the (non-Peronist) Radical Civic Union (UCR) party, Raúl Alfonsín, had failed to stimulate growth, reduce inflation, or ameliorate the country's ballooning debt. Despite Alfonsín's attempts to stabilize the economy, unemployment worsened, wages stagnated, and prices soared, increasing social conflict while destroying his popularity (McGuire 1997, 185–86). This provided a unique opportunity for Peronist self-starters such as Cafiero to seek power: with Alfonsín delegitimized and the crisis worsening every day, citizens grew eager for a new leader to rise up and relieve their misery (Weyland 2002, 138). As Cafiero's grandson, Francisco Cafiero, stated, Argentines were desperate for "a leader to put an end to the economic cancer...to take action to confront the crisis."[11]

Despite these advantages, Cafiero failed to reactivate followers' attachments and secure the Peronist presidential nomination. I argue that this is because he did not play to the movement's charismatic foundations. Rather than promising to save his people through whatever means necessary, as Perón had done, Cafiero committed himself to the "Peronist Renovation," an effort to transform Peronism into a strong, institutionalized party (Cafiero 2011).[12] He adopted this approach because, in line with scholars of routinization, he believed that "Peronism could only survive ... to the extent that it clearly assumed the form of a *party*, detached itself from authoritarian traditions, and stopped trying to center itself around a plebiscitarian leadership that had not existed since Perón's death" (McGuire 1997, 167–68, emphasis added).

While Cafiero's attempt to transform the movement into an institutionalized party appealed to middle-class intellectuals, it distanced him from traditional, popular-sector (lower- and lower-middle-class) Peronists, who simply wanted a strong leader to resolve their pressing problems.[13] Furthermore, Cafiero's lack of affinity with Perón's personalistic legacy caused the followers to perceive the

---

[11] Author interview with Francisco Cafiero, Secretary of International Affairs for Defense and grandson of Antonio Cafiero, April 5, 2016.

[12] Although the PJ was already technically a political party, it suffered tremendous institutional weakness and was historically subordinated to the power of the overarching movement and of Perón himself (see McGuire 1997, 1–3).

[13] Author interview with Alberto Kohan, Menem's political adviser, former Cabinet Chief, and Minister of Health, November 4, 2016.

successor and his team as "a bunch of urbane intellectuals mesmerized by an exotic leftist ideology perhaps appropriate for Sweden or Germany but alien to Argentina's nationalist tradition" (McGuire 1997, 211). Cafiero's dry communication style also projected "formality, wordiness, and lukewarm progressivism," further alienating him from traditional Peronist followers (ibid.). In fact, compared to his alluring competitor, Carlos Menem, Cafiero was so unpopular with the masses that, a week before the July 1988 primaries, pundits predicted that his victory over Menem would depend on *low* turnout among Peronist voters ("Evita votaría a Cristina, Perón votaría a Taiana, y los dos juntos a Unidad Ciudadana" 2017). In the end, Cafiero suffered a humiliating defeat: to the chagrin of PJ elites, he lost in 19 of 24 electoral districts, by a total margin of more than 100,000 votes ("Menem, Candidato Presidencial Del PJ" 1988).[14] As the incumbent Governor of the Province of Buenos Aires – a traditional Peronist stronghold – Cafiero even lost his own province to Menem by over 23,000 votes! ("Replanteo en el Justicialismo tras el triunfo de Carlos Menem" 1988).

In brief, Cafiero's failure to win the Peronist nomination for president demonstrates the unviability of routinization for reviving charismatic movements. His commitment to party institutionalization over the cultivation of an inspiring, charismatic image prevented him from appearing as Perón's heroic descendant. Though he was a self-starter in a time of crisis, he attempted to create a programmatic organization rather than simply playing to Perón's personalistic legacy. This strategy of routinization alienated followers and marked Cafiero as an elite politician rather than a hero capable of reviving Perón's ambitious mission to transform society.

As the experiences of Keiko Fujimori and Antonio Cafiero illustrate, self-starters fall short of reanimating charismatic movements when they fail to meet both of the essential conditions. First, as Keiko's unsuccessful quest for power shows, leaders who emerge in the absence of crisis cannot leverage citizens' desperation for a new savior and thus struggle to establish a charismatic image reminiscent of the founder. Second, Cafiero demonstrates that self-starters who attempt to routinize the movement into a structured party rather than filling the absent founder's shoes fail to tap into supporters' profound, affective bonds and thus struggle to cultivate their own charismatic allure.

6.2.3 Successful Self-Starters: Carlos Menem and the Kirchners

I now turn to two sets of Argentine self-starters who successfully revived Peronism: Carlos Menem, who governed from 1989 to 1999, and Néstor and Cristina Kirchner, who ruled from 2003 to 2015. Both Menem and the

---

[14] The electoral districts include the country's twenty-three provinces plus the Federal Capital of Buenos Aires.

Kirchners dominated the movement, kept its organization weak, and demonstrated through stark policy reversals that they had little interest in programmatic routinization. Instead, these self-starters focused on embodying the movement's preexisting, personalistic nature and linked themselves symbolically to the founder. Consequently, both sets of leaders convincingly portrayed themselves as genuine heirs of the founder, reinvigorated citizens' attachments, and restored the movement to power under their own charismatic authority.

6.2.3.1 Carlos Menem

Carlos Menem defied the expectations of party elites by securing the PJ presidential nomination in July 1988 against Cafiero, the favored candidate, and becoming president the following year. Subsequently, Menem established a new chapter of Peronism, giving the movement new life and becoming the most beloved leader of Argentina since Perón. Indeed, Menem swept the May 1989 elections by more than ten points; enjoyed approval ratings as high as 70 percent within two years of assuming office; successfully revised the constitution to allow for reelection; and won a second term in 1995 by a margin of more than twenty points (Carlin et al. 2016).

In addition to consolidating impressive popularity, Menem's charismatic leadership revitalized Peronism as the country's predominant political force. In fact, while deliberately undermining the efforts of Cafiero and the "Peronist Renovation" to institutionalize the movement – a process I will discuss in greater detail in Chapter 7 – he inspired followers to express their attachments with renewed strength. This is reflected by the dramatic increase in the proportion of citizens who expressed their identification with the movement after his rise to power. According to public opinion surveys from local firms, whereas about 16 percent of citizens openly identified with Peronism in 1985, more than 40 percent identified themselves with the movement in 1992, just three years into Menem's presidency. In contrast, over the same period of time, the proportion of citizens who identified with the UCR – the main opposition party and the party of Menem's predecessor, Alfonsín – declined precipitously, from about 32 percent in 1985 to 20 percent in 1992 (Consultoria Interdisciplinaria En Desarrollo 1985; Romer & Associates 1992).[15]

Like Cafiero, Menem's presidential candidacy was aided by his self-starter status and his rise during a severe crisis. The difference in the two leaders' fates, I contend, lies in their contrasting leadership styles. As described in the previous section, Cafiero's efforts to routinize the movement led to his downfall. He believed that working through the party's nascent institutional channels,

---

[15] Both of these polls were accessed through the Roper Center for Public Opinion Research. The 1985 poll, conducted by Consultoria Interdisciplinaria en Desarrollo S.A. (CID), was a nationally representative, face-to-face survey of 1,504 young and mature adults (aged 16 and older). The 1992 poll, conducted by Romer y Asociados, was a sample of 1,229 adult residents from eight of Argentina's twenty-three provinces.

establishing a platform for effective programmatic governance, and accumulating the support of party elites would lead to victory. In reality, however, this approach alienated Cafiero from the Peronist rank and file, effectively cutting him off from the movement's most powerful asset.

In contrast, Menem's deliberate effort to revive Perón's personalistic approach and apply his own charisma resonated deeply with the followers. By portraying himself as a hero in times of dire crisis, he explicitly recognized and promised to address the hopes and fears of the people. As summarized by the major national newspaper, *La Nación*, in the aftermath of the 1988 primary election, "The Cafiero … ticket represented rationality. It had a structure behind it and a more homogenous project. Menem worked principally on folklore and the emotional content of Peronism" ("Replanteo en el justicialismo tras el triunfo de Carlos Menem" 1988). For this reason, Menem was able to politically mobilize Peronist voters, vanquish his opponent, and restore the movement to power in his own name for a full decade.

Consistent with my theory laid out in Chapter 5, I argue that Menem's successful adoption of a personalistic approach depended on a combination of symbolic and material strategies. To begin, the leader established direct, affectionate communication with Peronist supporters, reinforcing his symbolic image as the founder's authentic and charismatic heir. In contrast to the elitist appearance of his opponents – including Cafiero in the 1988 primary election and the UCR's Eduardo Angeloz in the 1989 general election – Menem embraced a "swashbuckling personal style," donned casual clothing and sideburns that rivaled those of historic caudillo Facundo Quiroga, and traveled tirelessly to personally connect with ordinary people (McGuire 1997, 208). Alberto Kohan, a close advisor who would become Menem's chief of staff, recalled how massive crowds would greet Menem as his campaign bus pulled into each town. After years of suffering under disappointing leaders, Kohan stated, citizens felt inspired by Menem's charisma.[16] Carlos Corach, who became Minister of the Interior, explained that, like Perón, Menem could "interpret the sentiments, both good and bad, of the people," and used this understanding to "tell the people what they wanted to hear."[17]

Additionally, during his 1989 presidential campaign, Menem promised citizens relief from the crisis and a return to the prosperity of Perón's rule, rather than articulating the programmatic details of his proposals. On the surface, the candidate's platform seemed consistent with Perón's policies of economic nationalism. For instance, he proclaimed he would increase workers' wages through his "*Salariazo*" and would reignite Perón's state-sponsored "productive revolution" (Arias 1995). Despite these vague programmatic references, however, Menem focused primarily on his promise to save the people

---

[16] Author interview with Kohan, July 20, 2016.
[17] Author interview with Carlos Corach, Menem's political adviser and former Minister of the Interior, July 14, 2016.

from their suffering – a duty he claimed that the outgoing radical administration had failed to uphold. For example, two weeks before the May 1989
elections, he stated, "The current government has been unable to resolve [the
country's] problems, and has made them even worse. There is even more
hunger, and [the government] has failed to guarantee the right to health, to a
dignified home, to social protection, and the rights of the elderly" ("Menem:
'No ofrezco falsas promesas, sino trabajo y más trabajo,'" 1989).

Moreover, rather than focusing on the details of his own policies, Menem
pledged to do whatever was necessary to reverse the failures of the outgoing
regime and "pulverize the crisis" ("Hay que enfrentar la crisis y pulverizarla,
dijo Menem" 1989). In doing so, he became the first leader to bring Perón's
mission of salvation back to life. As he stated on the campaign trail:

> [I have no commitments] to unions or business people. The only [commitment] I have is
> to the people, and with your support, we are going to pick up the productive revolution.
> We are going to create the conditions and the infrastructure for development and
> growth. I'm not here to promise anything, I only pledge to work hard, which is the only
> thing that can lift Argentina out of stagnation and weakness. ("Menem: 'No ofrezco
> falsas promesas, sino trabajo y más trabajo'" 1989)

In addition to assuring the people that he would resolve the crisis and deliver
prosperity through whatever means necessary, Menem implored Peronists to
have faith in his leadership, as demonstrated by his campaign slogan, "Follow
me! I will not let you down."[18] Through these tactics, he shifted the public's
attention away from programmatic substance and successfully embodied the
charismatic spirit of Perón.

Shortly after coming to power in July 1989, Menem performed a programmatic about-face by implementing stark free-market policies. The new president
fearlessly launched unconventional alliances with private companies and business elites long demonized by Peronism, namely the multinational corporation
Bunge y Born; enacted structural adjustment measures that were even more
extreme than the recommendations of international financial institutions; and
committed Argentina to a fundamentally liberal economic model. Then, in
1991, Menem followed these adjustment programs up with the Convertibility
Plan, a "highly risky" policy that pegged the Argentine peso to the US dollar
(Weyland 2002, 112–15).

Predictably, most PJ elites criticized Menem's bold gestures as brazenly anti-
Peronist (Cafiero 2011, 464–65; Levitsky 2003, 148–49). Yet, while the substance of these policies contradicted those of Perón, they provided tangible
evidence of Menem's charismatic power by putting a swift and seemingly
miraculous end to the hyperinflationary crisis that the new president had
inherited from his predecessor, Alfonsín. Indeed, by straying from the substance
of Perón's original programs, Menem embodied the founder's daring spirit and,

---

[18] In Spanish, Menem's campaign slogan read: "Síganme! no los voy a defraudar."

in the short term, rescued the followers from their misery. For example, the Convertibility Plan reduced inflation from 1,344 percent in early 1990 to 17.5 percent in 1992 and to 3.9 percent in 1994 (Weyland 2002, 158). The plan also increased the purchasing power of poor Argentines – many of them Peronist followers – in an extraordinary fashion (Gantman 2012, 338). Menem's audacious structural adjustment policies also paved the way for impressive economic growth, achieving an annual rate of 7.5 percent between 1991 and 1994, as well as a substantial decline in poverty, from 21.6 percent in October 1991 to 16.1 percent in May 1994 (Weyland 2002, 158).

The impressive, stabilizing impact of his policies on inflation and prices granted Menem overwhelming popular support, even if the policies ultimately hurt poor Peronists by generating high unemployment, social spending cuts, and a devastating economic crash in 2001. Crucially, both Menem and his supporters interpreted the remarkable, though short-lived, success of his programs as evidence of his genuine Peronist roots. In fact, throughout his presidency, Menem skillfully invoked Perón to justify his actions in the name of protecting the people from harm. As he declared in 1993, "This country, this president, is doing exactly what Perón would have done if he had to govern Argentina today" (Comas 1993). Ten years later, during his third (and ultimately failed) campaign in 2003, he declared, "Carlos Menem is the best and most authentic disciple of Juan Perón and of Eva Perón" (Sued 2003). Even today, long after his fall from power, many Peronists personally attribute their 1990s prosperity to him. As followers reported in the focus groups, "thanks to Menem, I bought my first house, there was credit available, and there wasn't inflation"; "Menem was good to my dad"; "with Menem, we could eat well." While some leaders strongly opposed Menem, followers praised him for quickly resolving their problems and fulfilling Perón's mission to deliver prosperity.

By communicating in a direct and emotive fashion, tying himself to Perón, and rescuing citizens from hyperinflation-induced suffering, Menem embodied Perón's most alluring traits. His policies eventually collapsed and unleashed an even deeper crisis. Indeed, beginning with Menem's second presidential term in 1995, unemployment, inequality, and crime steadily increased (Gantman 2012, 338–44). Moreover, in the aftermath of his presidency, from 1999 to 2002, the economy sharply contracted, hitting rock bottom in December 2001. The dollar-to-peso convertibility came to a halt with a devaluation of the peso in January 2002, which led to an economic contraction of 11.74 percent that year (ibid., 332, 339–44). In spite of this implosion, the impressive short-term effects of Menem's policies, combined with the leader's captivating appeal, had successfully reactivated citizens' charismatic attachments to Peronism for several years and had expanded his base to include the business-oriented middle class. Consequently, Menem achieved tremendous personalistic authority that endured for a decade. More importantly, by embodying the charismatic legacy of Perón, he successfully returned the Peronist movement to power and demonstrated its capacity to reemerge as a predominant political force without shedding its deeply personalistic nature.

6.2.3.2 *Néstor and Cristina Kirchner*

As described earlier, Menem's unsustainable policies, especially the problematic Convertibility Plan, unleashed a terrible economic crisis in December 2001. In turn, this disaster delegitimized the political system: the government cycled through five presidents in eleven days, beginning with Fernando De La Rúa, Menem's non-Peronist successor who resigned on December 21, and ending with Eduardo Duhalde, a Peronist who served as interim president from January 2, 2002, to May 25, 2003 (Gantman 2012, 345). During this transition, Peronism fragmented and did not nominate an official presidential candidate for the 2003 elections. Instead, three Peronist politicians – Carlos Menem, Adolfo Rodríguez Saá, and Néstor Kirchner – ran on independent tickets. Menem won the first round of elections with just over 24 percent of the vote but dropped out of the race, fearing he could not win in a run-off against Néstor, who was overwhelmingly the favored candidate. Thus, Néstor, a governor from the far-flung, southern province of Santa Cruz, became president (Mora y Araujo 2011).

While the new leader owed his presidential victory in 2003 in large part to the weak profiles of the other candidates, he and his wife, Cristina, leveraged favorable conditions to redefine Peronism on their own terms and dominate politics for the next twelve years. First, like Menem in 1989, Néstor became president in 2003 as a self-starter rather than an anointed successor. He achieved this by waiting four years after Menem's fall to seek power and avoiding any association with his defamed Peronist predecessor. Moreover, he distanced himself by turning against Menem. This allowed the former president's economic policies to break down under De La Rúa, a non-Peronist; softened his once-powerful grip on Peronism; permitted Néstor to frame Menem as a neoliberal traitor; and created the opportunity to reconfigure the movement by promising a return to Perón's economic nationalism.

Second, Néstor's rise after the 2001 economic collapse was essential to his reactivation of Peronism. To address the crisis and alleviate citizens' extreme suffering, Duhalde, Néstor's immediate predecessor, implemented painful economic stabilization policies in 2002, including a massive devaluation of the peso. This, combined with rapid growth in global commodity prices, produced much-needed relief during Néstor's presidency. Indeed, between 2003 and 2007, Argentina's gross domestic product grew at an annual rate of about 9 percent, the value of the peso stabilized, unemployment declined from 21.7 to 8.5 percent, and wages increased by over 50 percent (Damill and Frenkel 2015, Table 1).

Crucially, the self-starter capitalized on this remarkable recovery to frame himself as the people's savior. To begin, he aggressively attacked others for causing the crisis, including Menem, the International Monetary Fund, and other foreign creditors (Gantman 2012, 345). For instance, during his 2003 campaign, Néstor blamed Menem for intentionally undermining the well-being of the people and weakening Argentina's democracy, stating that the former president "robbed Argentines of their right to work, then their right to eat, to study, and to hope; then, he came after the last right they had, to vote" ("Kirchner acusó a Menem de dar un 'golpe a la democracia'" 2003). Subsequently, in December 2005, Néstor canceled Argentina's debt payments to the International Monetary Fund, blaming the international financial institution for inflicting "pain and injustice" on Argentina during the 2001 crisis through pressuring the country to enact "policies that undermined economic growth" ("Argentina cancela su deuda de 9.810 millones de dólares con el Fondo Monetario Internacional" 2006). This confrontational approach suited Néstor's "fighting" personality and accentuated his appeal as a strong, charismatic leader.[19] Moreover, his aggressive style connected him to a key dimension of the Peronist legacy: the deep cleavage between the humble people and the selfish elites. Consequently, this strategy established emotional connections between Néstor and the movement's followers without explicitly tying the new president to the Peronist label, which would have risked associating him with Menem's disastrous failures.

In addition to deepening the cleavage between "elites" and "the people," Néstor took personal credit for the economic recovery, even though it resulted largely from the stabilization measures imposed by Duhalde in 2002, prior to his rise to power (Damill and Frenkel 2015). Establishing this impression proved relatively easy for him, as his presidency coincided with notable improvements in employment, wages, salaries, and economic growth (Mora y Araujo 2011). In fact, thanks in large part to the concrete results of this recovery, Néstor's approval soared to 74 percent by July 2003, just two months into his presidency (Carlin et al. 2016), and Peronists seemed convinced that he would become a heroic reincarnation of the founder. Indeed, as evidenced in the focus groups conducted by the author in 2016, many followers went beyond positive evaluations of Néstor's performance to worship him as a savior. "The world was sunken, and he saved us," one participant declared; "the people began to believe in their president once again"; another stated, "Néstor brought love back to the people, he brought the return of Peronism," a third said, "I had purpose in my life again when Néstor came to power"; a fourth confessed; "Perón's legacy [was] alive in Néstor," fifth expressed. Yet another participant claimed, "My father said that, since Perón, nobody had been capable of filling his eyes with tears until Néstor. When I saw [Néstor] on television, I felt butterflies in my stomach, I wanted to hug him and thank him [for touching my father]." In short, because the new president depicted himself as responsible for the seemingly miraculous economic recovery, he consolidated

---

[19] Mora y Araujo (2011); Author interviews with Kohan, Corach, and two anonymous advisers from the Kirchner administration (on April 6, 2016, and April 13, 2016, respectively).

impressive, personalistic power and revived Peronism on his own terms, as a separate chapter from that of Menem (ibid.; Ollier 2015).

Once Néstor proved himself worthy of the people's adoration, he and Cristina set about consolidating their symbolic image as charismatic heirs of Juan and Eva Perón. To do so, the leading couple behaved in a deeply personalistic fashion and resurrected components of the Peronist narrative that played to their strengths while further separating them from their Peronist predecessor. For example, as mentioned earlier, the Kirchners adopted a polarizing, openly confrontational attitude toward their opponents, including Menem, agro-industrial elites, figures associated with the 1976–83 military dictatorship, international financial institutions, and supporters of the neoliberal development model in general (Wortman 2015). This strategy recharged followers' enthusiasm for the movement by reminding them of Eva's defiant attitude toward anti-Peronist "oligarchs" and it differentiated the Kirchners from Menem, who had a much more conciliatory leadership style.[20]

The Kirchner couple also portrayed themselves as unparalleled champions of human rights. This appealed to young, middle-class, and leftist Peronists whose relatives and friends had suffered persecution and repression during the 1976–83 military dictatorship (Wortman 2015). Interestingly, while President Alfonsín had courageously defended human rights and democracy in the immediate aftermath of the dictatorship, the Kirchners downplayed the contributions of this non-Peronist leader and instead "considered themselves to be the authors of human rights in Argentina."[21] By consolidating an image as passionate defenders of victimized people, Néstor and Cristina boosted their charismatic appeal, especially among middle-class and leftist Peronists.

Finally, upon becoming president in 2007 in what was intended to be a strategy of alternation in power with Néstor, Cristina focused on rekindling direct, emotional ties with Peronists from the popular sectors. This strategy solidified the Kirchners' symbolic position as true Peronists and, in combination with the extraordinary economic recovery under Néstor, curried favor with the movement's traditional rank and file. Indeed, several Kirchner-affiliated political strategists stressed that, especially once the initial euphoria brought by the economic recovery began to fade, forging affective linkages with Peronist followers in this fashion was essential for the leading couple to "return Peronism to power," "interpret and refresh the identity," and consolidate their position as the undisputed heirs of Juan and Eva.[22]

As president, Cristina reconnected with Peronist followers by portraying herself as "Evita reloaded," mirroring the founder's wife in speech, dress, and

---

[20] Mora y Araujo (2011); author interviews with Kohan, Corach, and two anonymous advisers from the Kirchner administration (April 6, 2016, and April 13, 2016, respectively).

[21] Author interview with Kohan, July 20, 2016.

[22] Author interviews with two anonymous political advisers from the Kirchner administration (April 6, 2016, and May 10, 2016, respectively).

interactions with voters (Wortman 2015). This activated followers' passionate, visceral connections to the movement and associated Cristina with Eva's saint-like image – "a combination of Christ, Che, and Robin Hood."[23] After Néstor's unexpected death from a heart attack in 2010, Cristina also portrayed him as a martyr alongside Juan and Eva, drawing explicit comparisons between the two leading couples. Consequently, Cristina won reelection in 2011 with an overwhelming 54 percent of the vote. Reflecting on this period, followers declared in the focus groups, "Perón is embodied by Néstor, and Eva by Cristina"; "for me, Cristina is a reflection of Eva"; "Perón and Eva, Néstor and Cristina, they are the most important leaders in Argentina."

During Cristina's second term, the Kirchners' policies of economic nationalism began to deteriorate, resulting in rising inflation, poverty, and crime (Salvia 2015). Correspondingly, similar to Menem at the end of his presidency, some followers came to view Cristina as a failed Peronist leader. As non-Kirchner Peronists in the focus groups stated in 2016, one year after her fall from power, "I didn't like Cristina at all, I hope she never returns, she makes me so mad because of the things she did"; "Cristina spoke about being 'national and popular,' but the government was a cash register for her"; "the era of Cristina was terrible, she disgusts me." Other followers expressed frustration with Cristina's attempts to portray herself as the contemporary Eva. For example, one participant stated, "Cristina wanted to be like Eva, but she didn't have a single hair in common." Another declared that Cristina's attempt to imitate Eva "was a costume she used to keep robbing the people." A third stated, "she tried [to be like Eva] but she didn't succeed by a long shot." A fourth said, "She tried to dress and speak like [Eva], but she didn't actually imitate her." A fifth stated, "she wanted to be like Eva but she didn't ever succeed." A sixth explained, "Evita was a common woman. Cristina wanted to be like that, but she fell victim to her own selfishness and ego." As reflected by these statements, Cristina's declining performance led Peronist followers to view her as a fraudulent Peronist, and symbolically excommunicated her from the movement while reaffirming their own attachments to its founders.

The Kirchner administration receded from power in 2015 with the presidential election of Mauricio Macri, a non-Peronist. Yet, while the leaders' government ultimately fell, I argue that Néstor's rise as a self-starter; his policies, which became associated with dramatic growth and economic prosperity; and both Néstor and Cristina's symbolic strategies to reignite the followers' emotional attachments to the movement enabled them to establish a formidable new episode of Peronism. In doing so, the Kirchners – like Menem before them – deepened the widespread perception in Argentina that Peronism is the only force capable of governing the country.

---

[23] Author interview with an anonymous communications strategist from the Kirchner administration, April 6, 2016.

6.3 CONCLUSION

This chapter has argued that charismatic movements persist to dominate politics long after their founders disappear. Contrary to existing studies, which suggest that survival depends on routinization, I claim that many such movements endure by retaining their personalistic core and welcoming new leaders who recharge their charismatic nature. Thus, rather than establishing stable development trajectories like more conventional parties, these movements unfold in a "spasmodic" pattern. After their founders disappear, charismatic movements become latent and the whole country seems adrift. Yet new crises enable subsequent leaders to emerge, reactivate citizens' emotional attachments, and restore these movements to power. This process does not rely primarily on party organizations, as scholars of routinization would argue. Rather, it depends on successors' ability to convincingly portray themselves to the followers as charismatic saviors who have come to revive the founder's mission to rescue society.

As illustrated in this chapter, successors must fulfill three conditions to revive the movement in new contexts: achieve self-starter status; rise up amid a crisis; and play to the movement's personalistic nature. While many politicians have attempted to restore charismatic movements to power in Latin America and beyond, it is the leaders who have leveraged these conditions, such as Carlos Menem and Néstor and Cristina Kirchner, who have been able to consolidate independent authority as heirs of the founder.

Importantly, the power of successful self-starters is temporary. Like charismatic founders, their bold performance eventually collapses. Unless they leave power before this implosion, it dampens their heroic image and dilutes their connection to the founder. But these failures do not destroy the movement because citizens' attachments remain rooted in charismatic founders, not in successors. Indeed, followers label disappointing successors as "traitors" to the founder. The movement then enters a period of leaderless fragmentation until conditions ripen once more for a new self-starter to rise and pick up the founder's baton.

Based on the findings discussed in this chapter, the next chapter investigates the long-term trajectories of charismatic movements and assesses their negative impact on democracy. The analysis focuses on the rise and fall of charismatic successors in the context of a single movement: Argentine Peronism. In contrast to the conventional wisdom, which suggests that surviving charismatic movements routinize and therefore have a stabilizing impact on democracy, the chapter demonstrates that enduring charismatic movements make for political systems characterized by pernicious personalism, perpetually weak institutions, and frequent crises.

7

The Spasmodic Trajectories of Charismatic Movements

The preceding two chapters demonstrated that leaders who seek to revive charismatic movements in their own name must leverage specific strategies and conditions to reactivate the followers' fervent attachments and consolidate independent authority. Chapter 5 indicated that new leaders must combine material and symbolic cues – impressive performance to demonstrate heroic capacities and symbolic ties to the founder and his mission of transcendence – to reinvigorate the followers' identification with the movement and enhance the new leaders' charismatic appeal. In turn, Chapter 6 demonstrated that, to effectively implement these strategies, successors must fulfill three conditions. First, they must achieve self-starter status by rising to power years after the founder's disappearance; second, they must emerge following the eruption of a crisis that makes people once again feel the need to be saved; third, the new leaders must adopt a personalistic style reminiscent of the founder in order to establish unmediated, affective connections with the followers.

Given the strategies and conditions required to revive charismatic movements, the present chapter investigates the pattern in which these movements unfold over time and indicates the negative consequences for democracy. To do so, I examine the trajectory of a single charismatic movement – Argentine Peronism – over the course of seven decades. This historical analysis reveals how the personalistic mechanism identified in the previous chapters generates a spasmodic and self-perpetuating cycle of politics in which periods of predominant charismatic leadership alternate with periods of leaderless fragmentation. I demonstrate how this mechanism of movement revival weakens democracy by diluting the quality of citizens' representation, repeatedly subjugating democratic political institutions to the hegemonic authority of charismatic leaders, and undermining the development of a robust programmatic party system.

This chapter challenges the conclusions drawn by scholars of routinization regarding the pattern in which charismatic movements unfold and influence democracy. Existing literature states that the survival of charismatic movements requires institutionalization – a process in which the movement loses its personalistic nature, intermediaries within the movement establish a programmatic brand, and they develop an organizational network to sustain the support of loyal partisans (Jowitt 1992, 107; Madsen and Snow 1991, 29; Shils 1965, 202–5; Weber 1922/1978, 246). Because these components of routinization are positively associated with democracy (Campbell et al. 1960; Converse 1969; Lupu 2014; Samuels and Zucco 2014), this argument implies that, by setting in motion a process of routinization, charismatic movements can actually lead to the development of stable, democratic party systems.

In contrast, I claim that the personalistic core of charismatic movements remains intact over time and continues to shape key characteristics of the political system. Successors adopt the founder's charismatic style of leadership in order to claim the followers' preexisting attachments and consolidate power. To prove extraordinary capacities and appear as the symbolic reincarnations of the founder, self-starters enact bold initiatives that overtake party politics and disregard institutional constraints. During this process of approbation, these new leaders mimic the founder by engaging in top-down, authoritarian behaviors, overriding mechanisms of vertical and horizontal accountability, and marginalizing those who question their authority. This personalistic approach makes the successors appear triumphant, but only temporarily. Indeed, the nearsighted nature of their audacious policies, combined with the weakness of institutional safeguards, also set the leaders up for eventual failure. Through this erratic, up-and-down process, charismatic movements perpetually inhibit programmatic and institutional development.

The following section presents a theoretical discussion that integrates the perspectives of movement followers and leaders to explain the spasmodic trajectories of charismatic movements. I argue that, while generating tremendous political and economic volatility, the spasmodic pattern in which these movements develop reinforces rather than dilutes the personalistic nature of the movement. I then discuss the consequences of this process for democracy at the individual and system levels. Next, I illustrate this self-reinforcing cycle using the case of Peronism, which has experienced four distinct waves of charismatic leadership over its eighty-year history. The first wave rose with Juan Perón's ascension in the 1940s and receded with his forced exile in 1955; the second culminated in Perón's return to power in 1973 and faded with his death in the following year; the third arrived with Carlos Menem's rise in 1989 and retreated with the end of his second administration in 1999; the fourth transpired with Néstor Kirchner's presidency in 2003 and declined with Cristina Kirchner's exit in 2015. I conclude by briefly discussing the fifth wave of Peronism, which recently emerged with the election of Alberto Fernández to the presidency (and Cristina to the vice presidency) in 2019.[1] While a comprehensive account of this period lies beyond the scope of this chapter, for each wave I highlight key events and processes that have contributed to the charismatic revival of the movement.

Through this investigation, I illustrate how each wave of Peronism reinvigorated citizens' charismatic identity and temporarily strengthened each leader's personalistic control while simultaneously sowing the seeds for the leader's demise. The results underscore the endogenous nature of charismatic movement revival and stress its deleterious impact on democracy. The findings also illustrate how, paradoxically, such movements generate periods of political strength and coherence as well as periods of recession and political fragmentation, the latter of which, in turn, helps ready the soil for the movement's re-emergence.

7.1 THE FITS AND STARTS OF CHARISMATIC MOVEMENTS

The survival of charismatic movements hinges primarily on the resilient nature of citizens' emotional attachments to the founder and his eternal promise of transcendence. While the political salience of these attachments waxes and wanes depending on the circumstances, the personalistic nature of the bonds persists, even during times in which there is no leader to guide the way (Huddy 2001, 49). Thus, when favorable conditions return, self-starters who convincingly portray themselves as heirs of the founder can inject the followers' latent attachments with renewed energy. The capacity to mobilize these followers into political action grants self-starters a formidable advantage over other candidates and paves the way for the movement's revival.[2]

In contrast to the stable nature of the followers' charismatic bonds, the influence of new leaders is contingent and time-bound. One reason for this is that these self-starters – like the founder – must seek power under conditions of crisis. Without a crisis, citizens would not feel the need to be saved and would therefore be less likely to view even compelling self-starters in a heroic light. Additionally, to substantiate their extraordinary abilities, new leaders must enact policies that trade sustainability for an impressive, short-term impact. Accomplishing this requires successors to exercise their own skill and appeal, but it also depends on factors that lie beyond the leaders' control, such as an amenable geopolitical environment, a favorable socioeconomic context, or natural resource windfalls available for exploitation. Because these conditions occur intermittently, the revival of charismatic movements

---

[1] For clarity, I refer to Cristina Fernández de Kirchner as "Cristina" throughout this chapter while referring to Alberto Fernández as "Fernández."

[2] As indicated in previous chapters, the rank-and-file followers of Peronism and Chavismo constitute approximately one-third of the voting population in Argentina and Venezuela, respectively. In both cases, this core group of supporters has remained fairly stable over time.

unfolds in an episodic manner that contrasts with the stable, linear development of institutionalized parties.

Ambitious self-starters who successfully leverage the abovementioned conditions, achieve heroic performance, and tie themselves to the founder's mission of salvation to consolidate remarkable authority. Yet their personalistic victory also plants the seeds for their eventual demise, deepening the erratic nature of charismatic movements. First, the bold policies of self-starters are inherently unsustainable. To achieve an impressive impact, these policies weaken institutional checks designed to safeguard the policies' sustainability (Bersch 2016, 207; Levitsky and Murillo 2013, 100). Additionally, because the early success of the policies temporarily alleviates popular suffering, citizens' intense need for a charismatic savior also fades away. Self-starters' symbolic association with the founder therefore becomes increasingly strained, especially as their extraordinary performance begins to wane.

Self-starters further limit their own power by surrounding themselves with faithful confidants rather than experienced bureaucrats and party leaders. Upon rising to the presidency, these successors tend to establish these personalistic ruling coalitions – which consist of loyal friends, family members, and other sycophants – to overcome party constraints and limit institutional checks on their authority. Initially, such yes-men help pave the way for self-starters to dominate politics. But as conditions grow more challenging and performance begins to decline, these advisers' lack of experience and inability to challenge the opinions of the self-starters, no matter how imprudent, further jeopardize the leaders' prospects for continued popularity and success. Moreover, because underlings often enjoy kickbacks in exchange for their loyalty, accusations of corruption can further erode the legitimacy of the once-popular self-starters.

In short, the combination of followers' resilient personalistic attachments and successors' dramatic but short-lived power causes charismatic movements to develop oscillating trajectories that contrast with the steady path of routinization. At the outset, the charismatic founder establishes a heroic legacy as an everlasting savior by providing the suffering masses with unprecedented recognition and tangible, seemingly miraculous benefits. Crucially, the founder disappears before his policies fully collapse, exonerating him and protecting his legacy. Soon after, the combination of his disappearance and the exhaustion of his policies unleash a crisis and power vacuum. This causes the movement to recede from power and ushers in a period of leaderless fragmentation. However, the disintegration of parties, the weakness of democratic institutions, and the followers' ongoing devotion to the movement make it difficult for unaffiliated leaders and parties to rise up, coalesce around a meaningful identity that reaches beyond mere opposition to the movement, and stabilize the country on their own terms. Consequently, the country can languish for years under conditions of crisis, uncertainty, uninspiring leadership, and institutional weakness.

Under these circumstances, scholars of routinization contend that it is virtually impossible for charismatic movements to regenerate themselves (Kostadinova and Levitt 2014, 500–1; Madsen and Snow 1991, 25–28). Conversely, I argue that citizens' suffering and frustration with weak leadership during such periods make them yearn for a new hero to rise up and resolve the situation in a manner reminiscent of the founder. Thus, paradoxically, the "leaderless" period following the founder's disappearance eventually creates the opportunity for self-starters to revive the movement by playing to its personalistic roots. In particular, when the context shifts to favor self-starters – when the crisis has erupted and conditions realign to enable these new leaders to avoid blame and rise independently – the followers are likely to find the self-starter's personalistic style, as well as her promise to provide them with much-needed relief, reminiscent of the founder. Thus, leveraging the combination of crisis conditions and personalistic tactics, self-starters can catapult the movement back into power.

Even so, because the legitimacy of self-starters rests on the movement's charismatic foundation, these leaders can only restore the movement to power temporarily. When the performance of their audacious policies inevitably crests, their loyal advisers are unable to provide guidance; political institutions, which have been starved of power, cannot easily correct these policy failures; and the successors' symbolic influence erodes. Yet because the followers' loyalty remains grounded in the founder's heroic legacy, the fall of self-starters – while disappointing – does not compromise these citizens' underlying faith in the movement. Rather, many supporters come to view failed self-starters as fraudulent representatives of the movement. As these citizens suffer from the resultant crisis, they begin to look for another, more convincing savior to pick up the founder's baton. Eventually, this search for a new hero positions the movement to surge back to power on another wave of charismatic leadership, led by a different self-starter who can don the founder's mantle.

In sum, charismatic movements unfold in fitful waves. After the founder has gone, self-starters rise to power and consolidate authority using favorable conditions and personalistic tactics, which ultimately lead to their downfall. In turn, the failures of these leaders generate crises that cause suffering citizens to long for a new savior who seems capable of resolving the situation. Therefore, the movement swings back into power under new and momentarily compelling self-starters. The rise of the new personalistic leader causes the cycle to repeat, generating a self-reinforcing pattern of political and economic volatility.

7.2 THE CONSEQUENCES OF CHARISMATIC MOVEMENT REVIVAL FOR DEMOCRACY

7.2.1 Individual-Level Consequences

The spasmodic trajectories of charismatic movements undermine democracy in several ways. At the individual level, the personalistic nature of followers' attachments dilutes the quality of their programmatic and organizational representation. First, the followers expect new leaders to achieve seemingly miraculous performance to prove themselves worthy of the founder's mantle. In the short term, the followers receive benefits such as food, medical care, jobs, homes, and even toys, all of which tangibly improve their lives. However, this expectation motivates self-starters to achieve early success at great expense, compromising the programmatic integrity and sustainability of their policies (Bersch 2016; Levitsky and Murillo 2013). To take personal credit for these policies, charismatic leaders carry them out in a direct and impromptu fashion rather than working through institutional channels, which further undermines the policies' effectiveness and durability (Bersch 2016, 207). In short, by incentivizing new leaders to implement daring, irresponsible reforms without regard for substantive content or sustainability, charismatic movements weaken vertical accountability and compromise citizens' programmatic representation.

In addition to programmatic concerns, the intimate nature of followers' unmediated bonds to the movement's leaders hinders the development of strong organizational linkages. On the surface, charismatic leaders frequently tout their movements as driven by a strong grassroots spirit. Indeed, both Perón and Chávez publicly declared their movements to be propelled by an "organized community" of followers. In reality, however, charismatic founders and their successors exercise direct authority and cultivate paternalistic, top-down attachments with their supporters (Kampwirth 2010, 12). Moreover, as I will illustrate in the following section, followers tend to *openly embrace* the top-down nature of their attachments with these leaders: while perceiving themselves as lowly and humble, these citizens view their leaders as superior. Thus, the rank-and-file profess ongoing loyalty to the movement not because they feel empowered to become politically active, but because they wish to maintain close ties to their beloved leaders. This intensely hierarchical relationship between charismatic leaders and their followers suppresses the development of organizational ties that inspire followers to become empowered, politically engaged citizens.

7.2.2 System-Level Consequences

At the system level, charismatic movements undermine democracy by encouraging authoritarian behaviors in their leaders and weakening political institutions crucial to sustaining democratic accountability. Charismatic leaders seek to personally dominate the party (or parties) affiliated with the movement in order to ward off internal threats to their power and demonstrate that they answer directly to the people rather than to self-seeking party operatives. To achieve this, they often appoint themselves or their close confidants to serve as head of the party once they have risen to power; they also take measures to keep the party bureaucracy weak and drown out potential voices of contention from within. Additionally, charismatic leaders often create new parties and party labels that are more directly associated with their personal image – while maintaining control over the original, movement-affiliated party – to enhance their individual power. As a result of these efforts to increase personal influence, parties tied to the movement tend to remain weak, fragmented, and dependent on the individual leader. This outcome contrasts with the routinization thesis, which holds that charismatic movements that survive the death of their founders lead to the emergence of depersonalized parties that accumulate institutional strength over time.

In addition to weakening parties aligned with the leader, charismatic movements make it difficult for opposing actors to coalesce and develop a coherent, well-institutionalized alternative. The symbolic narrative crafted by the charismatic founder and reinforced by subsequent leaders accentuates the personalistic cleavage defined by citizens' allegiance or aversion to the movement while suppressing the relevance of more traditional political divides (Ostiguy and Roberts 2016, 26). Furthermore, the leaders' intolerance of dissent – expressed through acerbic rhetoric, discriminatory legalism, and even occasional repression – marginalizes opposing voices and curtails the resources of potential rivals (Weyland 2013). Consequently, the opposition to charismatic movements tends to be comprised of programmatically heterogeneous actors that struggle to unite and rally voters based on principles beyond their shared aversion to the movement. Thus, over time, interactions between movement leaders and their adversaries reinforces the personalistic division of society into followers and opponents of the movement while continually undermining the development of coherent principles and programs crucial to programmatic parties.

Finally, the emergence and revival of charismatic movements undermine the development of other political institutions, including the legislature, courts, and government agencies. To tighten their grip on power and take personal credit for impressive performance, movement leaders often override the legislature and rule by emergency decree. They also attack institutions that threaten to check their power, such as Congress, the courts, the Census Bureau, and the Central Bank. For example, charismatic leaders often stack these institutions with loyalists; distort information to discredit institutions that threaten their authority; revise existing laws to limit the power of those institutions; and create new institutions to tighten their personal grip on power. Because each self-starter that revives the movement adopts these destructive behaviors, charismatic movements repeatedly erode the transparency, effectiveness, and stability of institutions from across the political system that are vital to the development of a healthy democracy.

The recurrent damage that charismatic movements inflict on political parties, opposition actors, and institutions establishes a vicious cycle of political and economic volatility. Each successive leader must demonstrate superhuman capacities by implementing bold, irresponsible, and short-lived policies with little infrastructure. To ensure the success of these policies, the leader suppresses dissent and bulldozes institutional constraints from within the party and across the political system. Thus, when the self-starter's policies collapse and crisis erupts, the country's weak institutional foundation does little to mitigate the consequences. Thus, the burden of the leader's failure falls on the citizenry.

Remarkably, however, while citizens may blame particular successors for each collapse, their faith in the charismatic founder and his mission of salvation endures. Moreover, the widespread suffering caused by the crisis, combined with the powerless state of institutions, cause citizens to seek out yet another savior capable of rescuing them from their desperate situation. This desire creates the opportunity for a new self-starter to ascend to and consolidate power based on the promise to embody the founder's mission to provide the people with a more prosperous future. Thus, the volatile cycle of charismatic leadership repeats, intensifying problems of executive aggrandizement, institutional decay, and recurrent crises.

The remainder of this chapter demonstrates the spasmodic nature of charismatic movements by examining the historical trajectory of Argentine Peronism. As shown in Figure 7.1, I analyze four waves that Peronism has completed in which leaders surged to power, dominated the political system, and subsequently receded, leaving economic and political crises in their wake. I also briefly discuss the beginning of the movement's fifth wave, which emerged with the election of Alberto Fernández in October 2019.

As I illustrate subsequently, during each wave of the movement, the leader used charisma to establish a magnetic cult of personality, concentrated executive power, exerted hegemonic control over the movement, marginalized opposition parties, and successfully overpowered political institutions. Between each of these waves, society suffered a serious crisis, opposition administrations failed to govern effectively, and the movement endured extensive fragmentation. By stringing these waves together, I demonstrate how charismatic movements can perpetually harm democracy and generate an endogenous cycle of economic and political booms and busts.

7.3 THE REVIVAL OF CHARISMA AND THE TUMULTUOUS HISTORY OF THE PERONIST MOVEMENT

7.3.1 The First Wave Rises: Juan Perón and the Foundation of the Movement

Juan Perón made his political debut in Argentina in the wake of the *Década Infame*, a ten-year period following the Great Depression of 1930 in which a repressive authoritarian government called the *Concordancia* ruled. During this time, the country's agricultural economy collapsed, leading millions of poor citizens to flee from the countryside to overcrowded cities in search of jobs in the growing industrial sector (Madsen and Snow 1991, 44; Page 1983, 41–43).

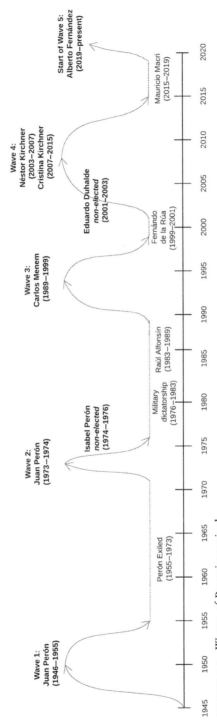

FIGURE 7.1. Waves of Peronist revival

While many found employment in the Federal Capital and surrounding Province of Buenos Aires, rapid urbanization and the absence of workers' rights caused these newly urban laborers – who constituted a majority of the population – terrible suffering in the form of low wages, long hours, job insecurity, and deplorable living conditions (James 1988, 8; Kirkpatrick 1971, 30–34; Madsen and Snow 1991, 47; McGuire 1997, 47–48).

The suffering endured by the masses, combined with their right to vote, provided the impetus for Perón to found a powerful charismatic movement.[3] Whereas the military and conservative politicians discounted and even repressed these citizens, Perón perceived them as "a ready reservoir of support" (Page 1983, 66). To win their favor, he became Secretary of Labor after participating in the 1943 military coup that toppled the *Concordancia*. His fellow officers ridiculed him for assuming this modest position, which oversaw the decrepit National Labor Department that workers referred to as the "elephants' graveyard" (Corach, author interview, 2016; Page 1983, 63). But Perón used his new post to forge profound, unmediated connections with the neglected masses, who had been searching for a savior to improve their desperate circumstances (Madsen and Snow 1991, 46–48).

7.3.1.1 Establishing Charismatic Attachments

Perón fulfilled the first condition for the establishment of charismatic attachments by using his position as Minister of Labor to reach out to the neglected masses and grant them a role in politics for the first time in the country's history. Thanks to his leadership, poor and working-class Argentines underwent a transformation from voiceless outsiders to dignified citizens who occupied a meaningful role in society (James 1988, 17). In addition, Perón satisfied the second condition by implementing bold and extensive reforms on behalf of his *descamisados* (shirtless ones). Due to his reforms, millions of Argentinians enjoyed unprecedented material benefits, including newfound job security in urban factories, a 40-percent wage increase, paid vacation, and new homes (Ascher 1984, 51; Madsen and Snow 1991, 52). Grateful for their elevated status and material prosperity, these people came to worship Perón as their savior (ibid., 46–48).

Over the next two years, some factions of the military came to resent Perón's rapidly increasing power (Page 1983, 112–19). On October 12, 1945, in an attempt to curb his power, they came together to arrest the Colonel with the naïve hope that removing him from politics would diminish his influence. However, the military vastly underestimated the political capital Perón had gained through his working-class supporters. Days later, on October 17, millions of poor Argentines flooded the plaza in front of the presidential palace to

---

[3] Unlike previous generations, who were immigrants to Argentina, many of these individuals were born in Argentina and thus had the right to vote (James 1988, 17).

demand his release from prison – a day that would henceforth be commemorated annually as "Loyalty Day" (ibid., 127). A few months later, in February 1946, Perón went on to win the presidential election (James 1988, 9).

During two presidential terms (1946–55), Perón deepened the direct, emotional bonds he had cultivated with his followers by recognizing the suffering and exclusion they endured prior to his rise to power and vowing to resolve their misery. Perón's second wife, Eva, accentuated her husband's appeal by portraying herself as his humble servant and quickly establishing her position as the poor's most passionate advocate (Madsen and Snow 1991, 52; Page 1983, 79). Together, the leading couple continued to deliver new rights and material gains to the popular sectors through labor reforms, economic growth stimulated by import substitution industrialization (ISI), and social assistance channeled through the Eva Perón Foundation (Madsen and Snow 1991, 52). Perón also fulfilled the third condition of charismatic attachment and solidified his bonds with the people by crafting a powerful symbolic narrative that glorified him as a hero and "Evita" as a saint, attacked his opponents as selfish oligarchs and "defenders of class privilege," and instilled a profound hope in Peronist followers for a more dignified and prosperous future (James 1988, 18–21; Page 1983, 144). As a result of these actions, millions of Argentines developed steadfast affective connections to Perón and pledged quasi-religious devotion to him.[4]

7.3.1.2 Concentrating Hegemonic Authority

During his first two presidencies, Perón used the charismatic bonds he established with his followers to launch his paradigm-shifting movement concentrate power. Indeed, though he gave workers some political voice, he never relinquished significant control to union leaders. Thus, while some have suggested that Perón intended to establish a corporatist political system (e.g., Waisman

---

[4] Some scholars question the extent to which the charismatic linkages that Perón cultivated with his followers were foundational to his political movement. Most notably, while acknowledging Perón's personal appeal, James contends that the core identity of Peronism rested on the empowerment of organized labor rather than on the unmediated, emotional bonds that the leader formed with his rank and file (1988, 12–18). According to this interpretation, citizens' enduring support for Perón and his movement grew primarily out of their connection to Peronist unions and organizations – actors that worked alongside Perón to achieve socioeconomic and political inclusion. In contrast, I argue that Perón's deep, unmediated, and emotional attachments to his followers were – and remain – central to the movement's ethos. In claiming this, I do not wish to discount the importance of political recognition, feelings of dignity, and material gains that followers experienced under Perón. Rather, I argue that the intensely personalistic, top-down nature in which these rights and benefits were granted by Perón fundamentally shaped the nature of citizens' identification with the movement and its leaders. I base this claim in part on several previous studies that identify the crucial role of Perón's charisma for the formation of the movement (Levitsky 2003, 36; Madsen and Snow 1991, 46–51; McGuire 1997, 50). However, as illustrated throughout this book, I also move beyond existing studies by drawing on original research to demonstrate how charisma has helped perpetuate the Peronist movement over time.

1987, 117; Wiarda 1973, 2009), which structures society into a rigid hierarchy under the State, in reality he maintained a direct relationship with his constituents in labor and industry. As Wynia states, "Perón was a very impatient and ambitious leader ... who jealously guarded his authority from business and industrial leaders who sought to limit it" (Wynia 1978, 54, 60). Rather than ceding authority to unions, as a corporatist model would have required, the founder empowered the state (and, thus, himself) through an aggressive program of economic nationalism and ISI. With his bold policies, he gained personal control over commodity trading and lucrative industries, which enabled him to construct state institutions through which to distribute impressive benefits directly to his rank and file (ibid., 47).

Between 1946 and 1949, Perón's daring reforms produced a "golden age" in Argentina. The GNP grew by 25 percent and the working and popular sectors experienced unprecedented upward mobility (Wynia 1978, 52). This period of growth resulted in immeasurable gains for poor citizens, including a newfound sense of respect, dignity, and material prosperity (James 1988, 18). Yet by deepening citizens' adoration of Perón, these victories also accelerated his executive aggrandizement. In fact, the apparently miraculous impact of his policies caused his followers to perceive him as "the ultimate guarantor" of their well-being and thus reinforced the emotional depth and political asymmetry of their relationship with him (ibid., 99).

Emboldened by the fervent loyalty of his supporters, Perón dominated the political system for several years, undermining the development of parties and overpowering political institutions that threatened his superior status. Within his own "Peronist party," a loose conglomeration of conflicting factions, he "cultivated contention and disarray," such that unwavering allegiance to him constituted the only thread uniting his fractious constituents (Page 1983, 161). He also filled his administration with personal confidants who pledged unwavering devotion to him. Most prominently, he relied on Eva, his most trusted servant, to run many important affairs – including the Ministry of Labor, arguably the most important branch of his administration (Madsen and Snow 1991, 51–52). From her position next to Perón, Eva played a crucial role in sustaining and deepening his emotional connections to his followers, while always openly subordinating herself to his authority (Page 1983, 198–99).

In addition to consolidating his influence over his own supporters, Perón stifled leaders and parties who opposed him. For example, he quickly smothered attempts by the Labor Party, namely the powerful union leader Cipriano Reyes, to maintain independence from his movement (McGuire 1997, 161). He also fragmented the main opposition party, the Radical Civic Union (UCR), by enticing some of its prominent leaders to join him while repressing others (ibid., 108, 208–9). To Perón's delight, the UCR facilitated his efforts by adopting a strategy of obstruction that accelerated its own disintegration. Radical leaders used obscure legal tactics to attack Perón and publicly question his political legitimacy. Rather than tarring Perón as a criminal, this strategy accentuated the UCR's reputation for "intellectual snobbery" and demonstrated how out of touch the party had become with the general public, who adored the new president (ibid., 162–63).

Beyond opposition parties, Perón limited the influence of other political institutions that threatened his power. For example, in 1945, even before he was elected president, he began issuing executive decrees such as the *Aguinaldo* – which increased nearly all workers' wages, provided an annual bonus equal to a full month's pay, and protected workers from being fired for unjust cause (Page 1983, 143). After becoming president, Perón treated Congress as an extension of his personal will, relying on the "unquestioning obedience" of inexperienced and faithful legislators, who constituted 69 percent of the Chamber of Deputies and 93 percent of the Senate (ibid., 162–64). He also frequently bypassed actors and institutions that questioned his bold actions, ranging from economic advisors to the Central Bank to the Supreme Court (Wynia 1978, 68–70). In fact, he "Peronized" the entire judicial system by stacking courts with loyalists and impeaching those critical of him on grounds of "malfeasance" (Page 1983, 165–67).

In sum, the combination of Perón's charismatic appeal and his efforts to silence competing voices within his own ranks and across the political system granted him "virtually limitless power" (Page 1983, 228). The steadfast devotion of his support base was crucial to this concentration of his hegemonic authority. In turn, his profoundly personalistic influence helped reinforce his glorification. His single-handed initiation of bold economic programs to "rescue" the people made him seem even worthier of his followers' adoration. The shortsighted and self-serving character of these policies would eventually cause them to implode, destabilizing the system and harming Perón's own supporters (McGuire 1997, 59–60). Nevertheless, driven by their thirst for recognition and their charismatic perceptions of the leader, Peronist citizens would remember the initial, extraordinary success of the policies as part of a "golden age" and would blame others for the policies' eventual failures. As I will illustrate subsequently, the founder's legacy – combined with the military's violent intervention, which attempted to destroy that legacy – would help the movement survive during Perón's exile and eventually establish the conditions for his return nearly two decades later.

7.3.2 The First Wave Recedes: Coup, Exile, and Chaos

7.3.2.1 *Policy Exhaustion*
During Perón's second presidential term (1952–55), the immediate payoffs of his shortsighted economic policies began to fade as structural weaknesses surfaced. By this time, his aggressive ISI program had drained the state's reserves of gold and foreign currency, while industrial growth had slowed and agricultural exports had plummeted (Wynia 1978, 66–68). The economic

slump that followed affected the popular sectors – his rank and file – in the form of stagnant wages, inflation, and shortages of basic goods such as meat and grain (Page 1983, 269). To protect his magnetic appeal, Perón responded to the downturn by firing his economic advisors and blaming them for problems of corruption and mismanagement. The fact that many of these individuals, including Central Bank President Miguel Miranda, had been personally appointed by Perón and had simply been following his orders did not implicate him in their guilt (Wynia 1978, 69). To the contrary, their dismissal actually vindicated Perón in the eyes of his followers and reinvigorated their support for him (Page 1983, 271–72).

Having preserved his heroic image, Perón reluctantly addressed the crisis through his Economic Plan of 1952 (Wynia 1978, 70). Composed in secret, the Plan reversed many of his prior pro-labor policies by opening Argentina to foreign capital, inviting private investors, and initiating an anti-inflationary monetary policy to stabilize the economy. Perón justified these ideological reversals using the same promise of political, economic, and social justice that he declared during his initial presidential campaign, underscoring the persona-listic – rather than programmatic – nature of his leadership (Page 1983, 287). He also blamed selfish rural interests and "foreign imperialists" for attempting to thwart his righteous effort to transform Argentina, even though his excessive state intervention had generated many of the problems in the first place (Wynia 1978, 70–71). Thus, as circumstances began to improve, Perón did not suffer for reneging on his earlier policies. Instead, from the followers' perspective, his about-face reinforced his reputation as the ultimate problem-solver and corrob-orated his "genius" (ibid., 288).

Nevertheless, while Perón successfully redirected blame for the downturn and temporarily salvaged the economy, he failed to address the fundamental weaknesses of his state-centered policies, resulting in a saturated market, slug-gish growth, a weakened agricultural sector, and low entrepreneurial confi-dence (Waisman 1987, 121; Wynia 1978, 73). Furthermore, his brazen refusal to cooperate with entrenched elites – including opposition politicians, agricul-tural exporters, industrial and financial leaders, elements of the military, and the Catholic Church – placed his regime on increasingly precarious ground, even though his charismatic appeal and popular support remained strong. Consequently, an elite-backed military coup ousted Perón in September 1955, forcing him to flee the country and remain in exile for eighteen years (McGuire 1997, 72–75).

7.3.2.2 Resistance to Routinization
Based on the routinization theory, Perón's sudden disappearance should have caused his movement to fade away or transform into an institutionalized party. Yet his abrupt and violent ouster by the military only enraged his followers and deepened their affective attachments to him. Moreover, the timing of the coup – after Perón had achieved a modest economic recovery, before the complete

deterioration of his policies – helped protect his legacy and generated in his followers an intense nostalgia for the prosperity they had experienced in prior years thanks to his leadership. Throughout Perón's exile, his supporters expressed "elements of a regressive fantasy for 'the good old days' of a 'golden era' – a plaintive reflection on a glorified, utopian past" (James 1988, 98).

As I will describe subsequently, similar to routinization scholars, both the backers of the 1955 coup and subsequent democratically elected presidents underestimated the resilience of citizens' devotion to Perón. This miscalculation, combined with the intractable challenges of governing an economically dysfunctional and politically fragmented society, undermined non-Peronist actors' efforts to achieve political legitimacy. The failure of the opposition to achieve independent legitimacy, in turn, facilitated Perón's efforts to maintain his personal grip over the movement and established the conditions for his eventual resurgence in 1973.

To maintain control over his movement during his exile, Perón began by reinforcing the loyalty of his followers. His eventual successor in Argentina's presidency, General Pedro Aramburu, facilitated this task by proscribing the Peronist party, banning Perón's inner circle from participating in politics, and outlawing the use of proper names for parties (McGuire 1997, 80). Aramburu assumed that these measures would diminish Perón's influence and re-route followers' support to more traditional parties who offered "bread-and-butter unionism" (ibid., 81–82). Had Peronism routinized by this juncture, Aramburu's strategy would likely have been effective. However, the new leader's efforts only emphasized the enduring charismatic appeal of Perón – whom poor citizens viewed as single-handedly responsible for their newfound prosperity (Ciria 1974, 25). Perón took advantage of Aramburu's oversight by rallying his followers to resist the military government and fight for his return to power. Perón's supporters from across the country responded by mobilizing in a wave of "ill-defined ... insurrection" to demand his homecoming (James 1988, 83). Thus, the proscription of Peronism actually *reinforced* the followers' identification with the movement and deepened their resistance to the new regime.

To further tighten his grip on his movement while legally barred from power, Perón undermined attempts by politicians within his own ranks to reestablish his movement without him. His followers, who had never been organized into a "well-institutionalized Peronist party," facilitated this effort by refusing to support leftists and "neo-Peronist" leaders who proposed anything "less than the complete return of Perón" (James 1988, 83; McGuire 1997, 79). Capitalizing on this unmediated support, Perón also invoked a tactic that had served him well during his presidency: he encouraged divisions between the different factions of his movement, including hard-liners who promoted an aggressive strategy of resistance against the military regime, soft-liners who sought to negotiate with the new government, and a third group who preferred a middle path (McGuire 1997, 87).

Beyond Peronism, the opposition struggled to establish independent legitimacy and thereby contributed to Perón's position of strength. In 1957, the UCR divided into two factions: Arturo Frondizi's Intransigent UCR (UCRI), which proposed allying with Peronists to defeat Aramburu, and Ricardo Balbín's UCR of the People (UCRP), which refused to partner with Peronists and sought power independently (McGuire 1997, 84). Perón deepened this fissure by backing Frondizi's candidacy in the 1958 presidential election and calling on his supporters to vote for the UCRI candidate. Not only did this strategy further divide the UCR, but also thwarted efforts to institutionalize Peronism, as it drew a significant proportion of Peronist votes toward Frondizi and away from neo-Peronist leaders (Corach 2011).

As president, Frondizi inherited an ungovernable situation. The Peronist voters to whom he owed his victory expected him to continue the founder's bold and beloved redistributive policies. Instead, the saturated domestic market, combined with pressure from the military, led him to enact a program of strict stabilization (Wynia 1978, 87–92). This "astounding about-face" caused an uproar among workers, resulting in a series of debilitating union strikes over the course of the new leader's presidency (Ascher 1984, 187–89). Furthermore, because Frondizi failed to inspire the cooperation of industrial and agricultural leaders, his painful structural adjustment program attracted little foreign investment and fell short of providing a satisfactory economic recovery (ibid.; Wynia 1978, 96–98). The president's massive unpopularity and lackluster performance strengthened the campaign for Perón's return. The military capitalized on Frondizi's failure as justification to oust him in March 1962 and call for new general elections to be held in July of the following year (Ascher 1984, 193).

With Peronists banned from the ballot and the UCRI delegitimized by Frondizi's disastrous performance, the UCRP candidate, Arturo Illia, won the 1963 election with a meager 26 percent of the popular vote (Wynia 1978, 112). Because he rose under more favorable economic conditions than Frondizi, Illia managed to enact more popular expansionary policies. In stark contrast to Perón, however, the new president enacted these policies in a cautious and gradual manner, "reinforcing the ... impression that Argentines had elected a man with no program at all" (ibid., 116). Moreover, because Peronists viewed his election as illegitimate, Illia failed to earn the support of the movement's rank and file, even though his redistributive policies produced modest, short-term improvements in their wages. To make matters worse for the president, his policies alienated the country's other major actors, including agricultural and industrial elites. Thus, when labor protests erupted in 1964 and 1965, the military intervened again, removing yet another unpopular president with a coup in 1966 (ibid., 122–27).

The failures of Frondizi and Illia strengthened Perón's reputation as the only leader capable of effectively governing Argentina. To sustain his favorable position, however, Perón also had to minimize threats from within his

movement, which had gathered strength during Illia's presidency. Most importantly, Augusto Vandor, an experienced union leader, sought to build a routinized Peronist party during this period that would sustain the movement's
traditional, pro-labor policies while leaving the founder behind (James 1988,
162). A passionate defender of Argentine workers and a pragmatic leader,
Vandor would likely have protected Peronist followers' interests more effectively than Perón himself (McGuire 1997, 133). Yet the founder deliberately
sabotaged Vandor's attempts to carry Peronism forward without him. To do
so, Perón empowered the radical left wing of his movement – the Revolutionary
Peronist Movement – a faction with which he had very little in common
ideologically (Gillespie 1982, 42; McGuire 1997, 91). While emboldening this
radical branch, Perón constantly shifted his support between it and the labor
branch, the latter of which was sympathetic to Vandor, throughout the 1960s
and early 1970s. This "deliberate strategic ambiguity" incited chaos and violence between the factions, compromising the well-being of Perón's own followers (Gillespie 1982, 45). Crucially, however, it also safeguarded his personal
control over his movement, further demonstrating his preference for charismatic power over programmatic substance.

In short, chaos, fragmentation, and instability defined the interregnum
between Perón's ouster in 1955 and his return to power in 1973. Both opposition and neo-Peronist parties failed to grow roots and attract sufficient political
support to establish a stable, democratic party system. Instead, the military,
obsessed with erasing Peronism while unconfident in other parties' capacity to
govern, regularly interfered. In fact, Frondizi and Illia, the only democratically
elected presidents who served during the period, were ousted by military coups;
the third, Héctor Cámpora, served only as a stand-in candidate for Perón and
was replaced by the founder just months after his election in 1973 (Wynia
1978, 14).

I argue that citizens' charismatic attachments to Perón, combined with the
exiled leader's ongoing interference, helped sustain his image as the only person
capable of rescuing the country from crisis and turmoil – even though he played
a direct role in generating the upheaval. With his charisma intact, the triumphant Perón therefore returned to Argentina in 1973 to begin his third presidential
term amid throngs of fervently loyal followers.

7.3.3 The Second Wave Rises: Perón's Brief Return to Power

7.3.3.1 *Recharging Charismatic Attachments*
Like his first rise in the mid-1940s, Perón relied on his enduring personalistic
appeal to return to power in 1973. In a conciliatory gesture, the military regime
permitted the Peronist party – though not Perón himself – to participate in
elections scheduled for that March. The regime invited the participation of the
Peronist party in the hopes that "the 'Perón myth' would have eventually
vanished during his long exile" (Ciria 1974, 30). As in 1955, however, the

military once again underestimated the depth of citizens' affective ties to their leader. By 1973, the charismatic founder had not just sustained the devotion of his original followers, but he had also grown his base by incorporating middle-class and leftist activists (Page 1983, 453). While the interests and values of these new supporters starkly contrasted with those of his working-class rank and file, he appealed to all of them: to his traditional followers, he symbolized a return to the "golden age" of his prior rule; to his new constituents, he appeared as an inspirational and revolutionary figure, "almost a local version of Mao or Fidel" (Ciria 1974, 29–30). Regardless of their interpretations, however, all of Perón's supporters became convinced that their vision of the future required his *personal* resumption of power.

7.3.3.2 Reasserting Hegemonic Authority

Harnessing the faith of his followers, Perón revived his movement in typical charismatic fashion. His handpicked proxy, Héctor Cámpora, ran in the March 1973 presidential election. A "staunch supporter and personal representative of Perón," Cámpora posed little threat to the founder and vowed to immediately step down upon winning the election to restore Perón to power (Ciria 1974, 32). With Perón's blessing and the campaign slogan, "Cámpora to the presidency, Perón to power," the proxy candidate won in a landslide ("Triumph for Perón" 1973). True to his word, Cámpora welcomed Perón back to Argentina and stepped down from power in July, just four months after being elected. Perón won a newly scheduled election that September with 62 percent of the vote and, on October 12, greeted masses of jubilant – if internally divided – followers from the presidential palace (Page 1983, 477).

7.3.4 The Second Wave Recedes: Death, Dictatorship, and the Return to Democracy

7.3.4.1 Policy Exhaustion

As discussed earlier, Perón resumed the presidency after nearly two decades of exile by leaning on his charismatic authority and fighting attempts to destroy or institutionalize his movement. These efforts facilitated his comeback, but they also presented him with intractable challenges, including an unstable political situation, a disjointed movement, and a fragile economy. Perón temporarily sidestepped these issues by condemning the failures of the prior military regime and making vague promises to restore independence, prosperity, and social justice to Argentina through projects such as the "Social Pact" and the "Reconstruction and Liberation Project" (Ciria 1974, 34; Wynia 1978, 252). Given the perilous state of the economy and explosive divisions – not only within his movement, but also across other sectors of society including opposition parties, the revolutionary left, and the military – his grand gestures would not last long. Fortunately for his legacy, he died before disaster ensued, just nine months after assuming office (Pion-Berlin 1983, 54). Rather than blaming him for the dark period that followed, his devotees sustained their glorified perceptions of their beloved *Conductor*.

As described in Chapter 6, during Isabel Perón's short-lived and disastrous presidency from July 1974 to March 1976, she reinforced her husband and predecessor's dysfunctional economic policies while using repression to quell popular dissent. Subsequently, the military ousted her and instilled a brutal dictatorship under General Jorge Videla. Over the next six years, the military dictatorship increased state-sponsored repression to horrific levels in its quest to "annihilate" the revolutionary left – and anyone even remotely associated with the left – in the name of reestablishing order (McGuire 1997, 170–71). The regime "disappeared" tens of thousands of civilians, killed thousands more outright, and pushed more than two million others to flee the country (Haberman 2015).[5] Economically, Videla sought to stabilize the country by demobilizing the working class and aggressively reenacting a free-market model to curb inflation and stimulate growth. Although these extreme measures led to a modest economic recovery during the first three years of the dictatorship, the regime – despite claiming to be a beacon of economic discipline and efficiency – indulged in "gargantuan borrowing" and destroyed industrial productivity, leading to widespread implosion of financial institutions (McGuire 1997, 171–73). The resulting economic collapse, combined with a last-ditch effort to shore up political legitimacy through a failed invasion of the British Falkland Islands, forced the regime to usher in a caretaker government and restore democratic elections in 1983 (ibid., 178–79).

7.3.4.2 *Resistance to Routinization*

During the military dictatorship, Peronism fragmented even more than during the founder's eighteen-year exile. While the regime's unspeakable acts of torture suppressed the Peronist left, rifts grew in the movement's more traditional, union-centered base due to disagreements regarding how to confront the dictatorship. Some union leaders, such as Saúl Ubaldini of the beer workers' union and Roberto García of the taxi workers' union, adopted a combative approach in which they led general strikes and openly expressed their opposition. Others, including Lorenzo Miguel of the steelworkers' union and Jorge Triaca of the plastic workers' union, chose a more conciliatory path that involved negotiation with the regime in hopes of securing a role in the eventual transition to democracy (ibid., 173–74). Like the Peronists, opposition parties also suffered repression and fragmentation, albeit to a lesser extent. Similar to union leaders, Radical politicians disagreed about how to deal with the military regime. For example, UCRP leader Ricardo Balbín endeavored to cooperate with the military in order to gain a more prominent

---

[5] The "Disappeared" refers to the citizens whom the military captured, clandestinely tortured, and often murdered.

role in a transitional regime, whereas Raúl Alfonsín openly opposed the regime throughout its six-year tenure (ibid., 177).

Despite these divisions, the military dictatorship's unabashed brutality and failed economic policies ultimately caused the regime to collapse, motivating Peronist and UCR leaders to form a united front to facilitate a transition to democracy. This coalition, dubbed the *multipartidaria*, played an active role in scheduling elections for October 1983 (Corach 2011). Due to the deep fissures within Peronism, which had intensified due to the absence of its charismatic founder and the unrelenting repression of the dictatorship, the movement failed to present a compelling candidate for the election. Instead, its fractious leaders nominated Ítalo Luder – an unintimidating and perfunctory lawyer with no connection to the movement's rank and file (Madsen and Snow 1991, 139).

In contrast to the behind-the-scenes politicking of Peronist leaders who all coveted the presidency, the UCR held a transparent, democratic primary election in which candidates had the opportunity to appeal directly to voters. Thus, unlike their Peronist counterparts, UCR leaders overcame internal divisions and coalesced behind Raúl Alfonsín (McGuire 1997, 183). An inspiring leader who promised to restore light, hope, and democracy to the country after years of repression and darkness, Alfonsín swept Luder in the elections and became Argentina's first post-transition president.[6]

As the first post-transition president, Alfonsín attempted to launch a new political movement, which he dubbed the "Third Historical Movement," that would rise above the existing parties and movements including the UCR and Peronism (Zelaznik 2013, 424). At the time, many of Alfonsín's supporters thought he would succeed: endowed with his own charismatic appeal, he seemed to personally embody the light, hope, and democracy that Argentines so desperately craved after several years of darkness, turmoil, and repression.[7] However, as I will illustrate susbequently, Alfonsín, like many leaders before him, underestimated the resilience of Peronism. Ultimately, this oversight foiled his ambitions to start a new movement and led to his premature departure from the presidency.

Specifically, although problems of leaderless fragmentation prevented Peronism from returning to power during this period, the Peronists capitalized on their enduring influence over the working class to obstruct Alfonsín's capacity to govern. While unable to return society to the "glory days" under Perón, these politicians could mobilize Peronist workers to undermine the new administration by highlighting how Alfonsín's proposals to stabilize the economy – which included scaling back benefits Perón had granted decades earlier – betrayed the founder's legacy. Using this logic, Peronism's otherwise divided union leaders, including Ubaldini and Triaca, joined forces to oppose the new

---

[6] Author interview with María Patricia Vischi, October 7, 2016.
[7] Author interview with Vischi.

president's reforms. In fact, over the course of Alfonsín's term, these leaders coordinated thirteen general, nationwide strikes (McGuire 1997, 200). These tactics greatly hindered Alfonsín's success and played a crucial role in the leader's premature exit from power in July 1989, several months before the official completion of his term.

In short, while no leader emerged as Perón's clear heir in 1983, the movement's capacity to mobilize followers and obstruct opposing forces sustained its political relevance throughout Alfonsín's presidency. Perhaps more importantly, by inhibiting the leadership capacities of Alfonsín, the rebellious behavior of union leaders throughout the 1980s created a deep crisis of governability and demonstrated to Peronist followers the inability of non-Peronists to meet their needs. In turn, the desperate economic and political circumstances that had worsened during Alfonsín's presidency established a ripe opportunity for a new charismatic savior to arise, pick up Perón's baton, and save the people from their distress.

7.3.5 The Third Wave Rises: Carlos Menem

7.3.5.1 *Recharging Charismatic Attachments*

As described in Chapter 6, Carlos Menem rose toward the end of Alfonsín's chaotic presidency to restore Peronism to power and – temporarily – become Argentina's preeminent leader. A self-starter seeking power in the midst of a terrible crisis, Menem embraced a personalistic style of leadership that "echoed Perón's," revitalizing citizens' emotional attachments to the movement and restoring their faith in its promise to bring them peace and prosperity.[8] As I will describe subsequently, Menem's charisma played a crucial role in reviving Peronism and establishing his authority. But, just as with the first two waves of the movement under Perón, Menem's personalistic tactics ultimately led to his downfall and yet another period of tumultuous crisis.

In contrast to his failed predecessor, Menem secured the loyalty of Peronist citizens in part because he portrayed himself as a genuine successor of Perón. He boasted a lifelong record as a devout Peronist: he had participated in the party as a young activist during Perón's second presidential term, endured five years of imprisonment under the military dictatorship, and served three terms as the Peronist governor of the rural Western province of La Rioja (McGuire 1997, 207–8). Leveraging these strong connections to the movement, he rose above political infighting and portrayed himself as uniquely capable of picking up the founder's baton and restoring the people's faith in the movement's promise of redemption.[9] Thus, Menem distanced himself from Alfonsín's failed administration; triumphed over Cafiero in the 1988 Peronist primary; handily

---

[8] McGuire (1997, 212); author interview with Kohan, November 14, 2016.
[9] Author interview with Kohan, November 14, 2016.

defeated the UCR candidate, Eduardo Angeloz, in the 1989 general election; and began his presidency backed by a powerful, emotionally charged base of supporters.

As president, Menem solidified his image as a charismatic savior by implementing daring reforms. Most prominently, his Convertibility Plan, which artificially fixed the Argentine peso to the US dollar, attacked and eventually ended hyperinflation, dramatically increasing the purchasing power of ordinary Argentines (see Chapter 6). Menem enacted the Plan in April 1991 after a cascade of neoliberal reforms that directly contradicted Perón's original, state-centered policies and far outpaced Alfonsín's proposed structural adjustment plans (Weyland 2002, 20–21).

While Menem's policies appeared to contradict those of Perón, I contend that his behavior was quintessentially Peronist, as he ended the crisis and provided the suffering masses with much-needed relief. Between 1990 and 1994, inflation dropped from 1,832 percent to 4 percent. Additionally, newly privatized public services – which had been hopelessly dysfunctional before Menem's rise – became efficient and affordable (McGuire 1997, 219–20). Thanks to Menem's neoliberal policies, the country achieved sustained economic growth and Argentines enjoyed a higher quality of life than they had experienced in decades. In short, while his audacious programs horrified the principled leaders of the center-left Peronist Renovation – the coalition dedicated to institutionalizing the movement – Menem's emotional appeal and extraordinary performance during his first presidential term enabled him to revive the movement in all its personalistic glory.

7.3.5.2 Concentrating Hegemonic Authority

Capitalizing on his success, Menem followed Perón's model by deepening his control over politics. First, the self-starter conquered the Peronist party by marginalizing prominent leaders of the Renovation and replacing Cafiero as president of the PJ. He also filled his cabinet with trusted friends rather than experienced party officials. For example, he appointed three individuals to important posts based on personal rather than party connections: Roberto Dromi (Minister of Public Works), Alberto Kohan (Chief of Staff), and Eduardo Bauzá (Minister of the Interior). He also selected several previously anti-Peronist leaders as prominent advisers, including Alvaro Alsogaray and Octavio Frigerio, further demonstrating that he was not beholden to party officials (ibid., 242).[10] To deepen his control over the PJ, Menem personally endorsed political outsiders ranging from celebrities to speedboat racers to corporate CEOs for legislative and gubernatorial positions rather than supporting party leaders (ibid., 242–43). In doing so, he stifled the efforts of many to

---

[10] Prior to being appointed by Menem, Alsogaray was a longtime member of the conservative party, Union of the Democratic Center (UCeDé), while Frigerio belonged to the Movement for Development and Integration (MID), an offshoot of Frondizi's UCRI (McGuire 1997, 242).

routinize the PJ, coopted important opposition leaders, and strengthened Peronism's personalistic nature.

In addition to overpowering parties within and beyond the Peronist movement, Menem undermined political institutions that constrained his authority. For example, he bypassed the legislature to enact hundreds of emergency decrees that ensured the swift implementation of his free-market reforms, which many politicians found worrisome and irresponsible. By the end of 1993, he enacted over three hundred such decrees – about ten times more than the country had experienced over the previous 140 years combined (ibid, 256).[11] Similar to Perón, he also sidestepped legal challenges to his executive power by increasing the number of Supreme Court justices from five to nine and handpicking loyalists to fill the new vacancies. To reinforce his image of indomitable popularity, he meddled in electoral rules to benefit his administration, adding twenty-three new seats to the Chamber of Deputies representing sympathetic districts and, most prominently, pushing through a new constitution to permit his reelection in 1995 (ibid., 255–57). Through these tactics, Menem successfully overcame constraints imposed by the other branches of government and solidified his charismatic power in a manner reminiscent of the founder.

Lastly, to ensure his personal control over the state, Menem allowed corruption to proliferate throughout his administration and often orchestrated illicit activities. When scandals erupted involving his personal advisors and other loyal politicians, he responded by demonizing the press for unjustly accusing these individuals (ibid., 259). Crucially, thanks in large part to his charismatic image and close attachments with Peronist followers, the accusations of corruption failed to reach Menem personally during his presidency. As Kohan, Menem's Chief of Staff, stated in an interview with the author, opposition leaders "accused Menem of everything ... and even then, we continued to win elections. They still haven't been able to prove anything."[12] Thus, the president remained popular and exercised largely unchecked power throughout his first and much of his second presidential term.

To recapitulate, like Perón, Menem harnessed the fervent loyalty of Peronist followers and the early success of his economic reforms to achieve hegemonic control over the political system. As with the charismatic founder, his direct appeals to the popular sectors helped catapult him into power. Then, as president, Menem used his personalistic authority to reinforce his heroic image and temporarily provide his supporters with determined reprieve from economic crisis. Ultimately, Menem's actions undermined his followers' long-term programmatic interests, destroyed the efforts of the Renovation leaders to routinize Peronism, and weakened political institutions vital to the consolidation of democracy. Nevertheless, Menem's charismatic leadership strengthened

---

[11] By the end of his two presidencies, Menem had enacted a total of 545 emergency decrees (Capriata 2008).

[12] Author interview with Kohan, July 20, 2016.

Peronism by reenergizing the followers' enthusiasm for the movement and causing them to worship him as its new chief. Thus, while his impressive reign would not last, I argue that it played a crucial role in perpetuating the personalistic nature and spasmodic trajectory of the movement.

7.3.6 The Third Wave Recedes: Menem's Fall and The Convertibility Crisis

7.3.6.1 *Policy Exhaustion*

During Menem's second presidential term (1995–99), the structural deficiencies of his audacious policies began to emerge. In particular, it became increasingly difficult to ignore the unsustainable nature of the Convertibility Plan, as the official value of the peso far exceeded its real worth. While Menem refused to publicly acknowledge this disturbing reality, anxiety rose among ordinary Argentines, whose livelihood had become dependent on the artificial exchange rate (Weyland 2002, 187). Adding to this fear were the social consequences of Menem's neoliberal reforms, which included growing inequality and unemployment (Gantman 2012, 338–41). Although the Peronist rank and file continued to view Menem favorably, these problems directly impacted their lives and began to erode his reputation as a heroic problem-solver.

Unable to run for a third presidential term in 1999, Menem was forced to yield the Peronist candidacy to Eduardo Duhalde. A programmatically principled leader and longtime rival of Menem's, Duhalde enjoyed the backing of Peronist Renovation leaders who had grown frustrated by the president's hegemonic behavior and his waning performance (Weyland 2002, 194). Yet, Menem's influence over the movement remained significant. Furthermore, many of the outgoing president's conservative supporters backed his former Economy Minister, Domingo Cavallo. This fragmentation deprived Duhalde of valuable votes and ultimately cost him the election. Thus, Fernando de la Rúa, a dreadfully uninspiring candidate aptly nicknamed "baby pacifier" (*el chupete*), came to power backed by a loose alliance of anti-Peronist parties (ibid.).[13]

As with the recession of the first two Peronist waves in 1955 and 1974, Menem's delicate economic and political balance collapsed upon his departure from power in 1999. Throughout his presidency, he had enforced political cohesion and economic stability from the top-down using his unmediated charismatic authority. His sudden absence, combined with the exhaustion of his shortsighted policies, ushered in a chaotic period without a leader to guide the way. Indeed, the virtually powerless de la Rúa failed to take charge of the situation upon rising to office and thus resigned in December 2001

---

[13] The Alliance supporting de la Rúa's candidacy consisted of the UCR, a center-left coalition called Frepaso, and several smaller parties (Weyland 2002, 194–95).

(Weyland 2002, 195). The combination of economic collapse and feeble leadership de-legitimized the political system and led citizens to riot in the streets (Krauss 2001).

In the eleven days between de la Rúa's resignation and Duhalde's appointment as interim president, Argentina endured a profound leadership crisis in which five presidents rose and fell. Remarkably, the military did not intervene during this tumultuous period – a testament to the country's commitment to a minimal level of democracy as well as its strong aversion toward violence. Nevertheless, the crisis revealed the disintegrated state of the party system and demonstrated how little the country's political institutions had progressed over the previous decade.

In terms of political parties, the UCR grew even weaker during the 1999–2003 period than it had been when Alfonsín stepped down from the presidency prematurely in 1989 (Zelaznik 2013, 425). The party's inability to compete in the 1999 elections without crafting an alliance with several other parties was an illustration of its frailty; De La Rúa's feeble presidency and resignation in 2001 only exacerbated the party's failure to thrive. Consequently, in the wake of the crisis, the UCR would play only a minor role in stabilizing the country and would never again present a stand-alone candidate for presidential elections (Roberts 2007, 12).

7.3.6.2 Resistance to Routinization

Peronism remained divided in the aftermath of Menem's presidency. For his part, Duhalde led a large group of party stalwarts against Menem and his neoliberal policies. The rival's faction had begun to accumulate strength in 1997, as Menem's performance had begun to wane. Yet Duhalde's group encountered several obstacles that prevented it from assuming control over the party. One obstacle is that, as previously mentioned, Cavallo also ran for president under a separate ticket in a blatant attempt to split the PJ (Cassese 1999). In addition, Menem retained control over important factions of the PJ, hindering the efforts of his Peronist opponents to dethrone him. Thus, while constitutionally barred from running for a third presidential term in 1999, Menem managed to get himself reelected as president of the PJ until 2003 (Ventura 1999).[14]

When Duhalde scheduled presidential elections for 2003, the PJ refrained from endorsing an official candidate, reflecting the lack of cohesion within the party. As a result, three leaders with Peronist affiliations ran on separate tickets: Menem; Néstor Kirchner, the Governor of Santa Cruz and Duhalde's preferred candidate; and Adolfo Rodríguez Saá, the Governor of San Luis. Notably, despite running independently, the three candidates did not attempt to break

---

[14] Duhalde challenged the legality of the PJ internal elections, but the Menem-backed Supreme Court upheld the results, securing Menem's place as the party president (Ventura 1999).

away from Peronism and start new parties. Instead, each depicted himself as a true successor of Perón while targeting the others as frauds threatening to denigrate the founder's legacy. Most explicitly, Menem claimed throughout his campaign to be Perón's most faithful successor. He even declared during his campaign finale in the iconic River Plate Stadium in the Federal Capital, "Carlos Menem is the authentic and best disciple of the Lieutenant General Juan Domingo Perón and of Eva Perón" (Sued 2003).

Although Kirchner downplayed his ties to the PJ in order to distance himself from Menem, he also implicitly connected himself to the charismatic founder. For example, just as Menem claimed to reinvigorate Perón's "productive revolution" during his 1989 campaign, Kirchner promised an economic "model of production and work" – a clear association with the founder's original platform (Ybarra 2003). Similarly, while less popular than Menem or Kirchner, Adolfo Rodríguez Saá titled his electoral coalition after the founders' movement, "National and Popular Movement," and referenced Perón's promise of salvation by titling his caravan "The March of Dreams" (Colonna 2003). In short, while the infighting between Peronist leaders kept the PJ fragmented and weak during the 1999–2003 period, each candidate's efforts to associate himself with the founder underscore the ongoing influence of Perón's charismatic legacy.

In addition to weak parties, political institutions during this period remained frail. The judicial branch remained deeply politicized and the legislature was virtually powerless, as evidenced by its failure to implement much-needed economic reforms and prevent the 2001 collapse (Ventura 1999). With weakling De La Rúa at the helm, the executive office also lost its decisive authority. Given the utter disempowerment of the three major branches of government, the State had little capacity to address the crisis, causing citizens throughout the country to become thoroughly disillusioned with the government and detached from politics in the ensuing years (Quiroga 2005, 322–23).

Despite the discredited status of political parties and institutions, however, Peronism sustained its reputation as the only force capable of governing the country during the transitional period from Menem to Kirchner (Mora y Araujo 2011; Ollier 2015). In fact, I contend that Argentina recovered from the 2001 collapse primarily due to the ongoing legitimacy of Peronism and the strength of the chief executive office relative to other political institutions. Paradoxically, while undermining democratic institutions, the movement's popular legitimacy and its monopoly over executive power saved Argentina from worse fates. Moreover, while the 2001 crisis made citizens feel utterly fed up with politics, it also reinforced their perception of Peronism as the only force capable of rescuing the country from desperate circumstances. Thus, even while rejecting contemporary politicians, Peronist followers sustained their attachments to the movement and their faith in the founder's promise to deliver salvation. As I will discuss in the next section, it is for this reason that the followers would come to worship another set of charismatic saviors soon after the crisis, restoring Peronism to its position of power.

7.3.7 The Fourth Wave Rises: Néstor and Cristina Kirchner

7.3.7.1 *Recharging Charismatic Attachments*
As discussed in the previous chapter, Néstor Kirchner won the 2003 presidential election thanks in large part to Menem's departure from the race, combined with the wave of economic recovery that Duhalde had initiated in the previous year. Taking personal credit for the reestablishment of prosperity, Néstor – and subsequently, his wife, Cristina – consolidated tremendous popularity and reinvigorated followers' emotional attachments, thereby ushering in the fourth wave of Peronism.

Initially, the Kirchners tried to establish a unique movement that superseded (but still incorporated) Peronism. For example, Néstor responded to the PJ's refusal to endorse any candidate for the 2003 election by creating a new party label, Front for Victory (*Frente para la Victoria* – FPV), which he claimed would be a "transversal" coalition that would incorporate Peronist and non-Peronist actors alike. Julio Cobos, the Radical governor of Mendoza, also served as Cristina's vice president during her first presidential term (2007–11). Mora y Araujo (2011) indicates that the Kirchners initially pursued this strategy because, when Néstor rose to power, his control over Peronism was anything but guaranteed. Indeed, Néstor won the presidency with less than 23 percent of the vote; Menem, who had gained over 24 percent of the vote in the first round of the election, still enjoyed the loyalty of many Peronist followers. The Kirchners sought to strengthen their position by building a broader coalition that reached beyond Peronism and drew support from opposition groups, such as ideologically moderate and left-leaning Radicals like Cobos.

However, similar to Alfonsín's attempts to create a "Third Historical Movement" in the 1980s, the Kirchners' attempts to establish a new movement failed, causing them to double down on their Peronist identity. The leading couple's renewed embrace of Peronism occurred in large part because they resisted making concessions to the diverse members of the transversal coalition; in turn, the coalition members felt increasingly irritated and alienated by the Kirchners' domineering style (Mora y Araujo 2011). Thus, as the Kirchners' joint administration progressed, their non-Peronist alliances fell apart, especially during Cristina's presidency (Calvo and Victoria Murillo 2012, 151; Mora y Araujo 2011).

At the same time, Néstor and Cristina's popularity among Peronist followers increased substantially over the course of their joint rule due to Argentina's impressive economic recovery as well as Menem's fading prominence (Mora y Araujo 2011). In an especially notable illustration of the Kirchners' newfound control over the movement, Cristina defeated Duhalde's wife, "Chiche," in the

2005 senate race for the Province of Buenos Aires, arguably the most important Peronist stronghold in the country (Calvo and Victoria Murillo 2012, 161). As a result of their increasing dominance over Peronism and the defections of their Radical allies, the Kirchner era became widely perceived as a formidable new chapter of Peronism rather than an independent movement (Ollier 2015).

Interestingly, some scholars and Peronist activists insisted in interviews with the author that the Kirchners brought Peronism back to life using a programmatic approach: namely, by constructing a state-centered, nationalist economy similar to Perón's original platform.[15] For instance, Santiago Cafiero, a grandson of Antonio Cafiero who would become President Alberto Fernández's cabinet chief in 2019, stated that, whereas Menem claimed the Peronist label through superficial "iconography," the Kirchners resurrected the programmatic substance of Peronism through reinstating "concrete policies of state-centered economics and social redistribution."[16] Based on this reasoning, one might conclude that, in contrast to Menem, the Kirchners successfully transformed Peronism into the routinized, center-left party envisioned by Antonio Cafiero and other leaders of the Peronist Renovation a decade earlier.

Yet, as I argue subsequently, the Kirchners intentionally undermined others' attempts to routinize Peronism and strengthened the charismatic heart of the movement. They achieved this by adopting the same strategies that Perón and Menem utilized in the past to consolidate decisively personalistic authority. However, to distance themselves from Menem's tainted administration, they employed the strategies of charismatic leadership in reverse order: they began by enacting daring and initially successful programs, then embraced their roles as the heirs of Juan and Eva Perón.

Whereas Menem stressed his symbolic role as a Peronist before implementing bold reforms, Néstor kicked off his presidency by enacting audacious policies that produced extraordinary, though unsustainable, benefits. The outcomes of his daring reforms reenergized Peronist followers and secured the loyalty of new supporters from the lower and middle classes. His decision to repay Argentina's massive debt with the International Monetary Fund in one fell swoop in December 2005 exemplifies this approach. This astonishing initiative created a "climate of euphoria" across Argentina by instantaneously liberating the country from the "tutelage" of one of its most detested and powerful overlords ("Histórico: el país saldará en un solo pago la deuda con

---

[15] Author interview with Santiago Cafiero, Chief of the Cabinet of Ministers of Argentina under Alberto Fernández and grandson of Antonio Cafiero, July 5, 2016; author interview with Delfina Rossi, Peronist activist, former Director of the National Bank of Argentina, and daughter of Agustín Rossi, May 15, 2015; author interview with Macarena Kunkel, Peronist activist and daughter of Carlos Kunkel, April 19, 2016; and author interview with Juan Ernesto Gullo, son of Juan Carlos "Dante" Gullo, July 11, 2016. Cafiero, Rossi, Kunkel, and Gullo expressed similar views that the Kirchners managed to revive the (leftist) programmatic substance of Peronism and thus advanced efforts to routinize the movement.

[16] Author interview with Santiago Cafiero.

el FMI" 2005; Ollier 2015). Moreover, it cast Néstor in a heroic light and distinguished him from Menem, whom the public widely perceived as selling out to the IMF in the first place. The loan repayment accelerated the economic recovery, bringing about substantial increases in employment and wages, thereby causing Néstor's popularity to skyrocket to 74 percent by July 2003 (Mora y Araujo 2011).

As president in subsequent years, Cristina implemented similar state-centered programs to display her own determination and capacity to transform Argentina. For example, in a bold move in 2008, she renationalized the pension system that Menem had privatized in 1993. She presented the decision as a radical effort to "protect our pensioners and our workers," from the evils of Menem's neoliberalism as well as the greedy interests of developed countries, "economic conglomerates," and "large banks" (Arza 2012, 48–49; Datz 2012, 116). In reality, the policy revealed Cristina's "political short-termism and executive strength," and undermined "long-term concerns about the stability of the social security system" (Datz 2012, 101). However, the renationalization deepened the enthusiasm of her followers, greatly enhanced her control over the country's fiscal resources, and enabled her to restructure and temporarily alleviate the country's large and growing public debt. By the end of her presidency, 1.28 million Argentines received noncontributory pensions thanks to the reform (Nogueira 2015). In short, while complicating the country's economic stability, this daring fiscal policy strengthened Cristina's image as the common people's central protagonist and proved her willingness to stand up on the world stage to defend her supporters against powerful enemies.[17]

Once they achieved impressive performance and distanced themselves from Menem, the Kirchners proceeded to portray themselves as symbolic reincarnations of Perón and Eva, thereby reviving the movement's quasi-religious mystique. Néstor did this implicitly by portraying himself as the champion of Argentine workers (Wortman 2015). He also reanimated the cleavage Perón had emphasized between the privileged and the poor – a dimension of the Peronist narrative that Menem had downplayed. For example, he verbally attacked Menem, human rights abusers from the military dictatorship, and international financial institutions as selfish elites.[18] Conversely, he praised Argentine workers, the progressive middle class, youths, and the poor masses as model citizens (Wortman 2015).

When Cristina rose to power in 2007, she reinforced this cleavage between the "haves" and "have-nots" and explicitly embodied Evita's persona as the mother of the impoverished masses.[19] Throughout her presidency, she mingled

---

[17] Author interview with anonymous communications strategist from the Kirchner administration, April 6, 2016.
[18] Author interview with Corach.
[19] Wortman 2015; author interview with anonymous communications strategist from the Kirchner administration, April 6, 2016.

FIGURE 7.2. Cristina Kirchner announces a new bill in the "Evita Room" of the presidential palace, 2012

with poor Argentines during public acts, used passionate rhetoric to defend the "people" against the malevolent upper class, and depicted herself as personally responsible for redistributing wealth to more virtuous Argentines via her social programs. She introduced many such programs in the "Evita Room" of the presidential palace, with an image of the founder's wife projected prominently behind her, as exemplified in Figure 7.2.

However, it was Néstor's sudden death from a heart attack in October 2010 that would catalyze the Kirchners' most powerful symbolic connection to the Peróns' charismatic legacy. Following this tragedy, Cristina doubled down on her efforts to create an "idealized image" of her husband that explicitly associated both of them with the founders (Cherny 2014, 156). For example, following Néstor's death, images proliferated of Cristina and her late husband mimicking the founders' passionate embrace during massive campaign rallies (see Figures 7.3 and 7.4). Cristina also publicly mourned Néstor's death for an extensive period of time and continually referred to "Him" as Christ-like during the final years of her presidency, intensifying her allure as a brave and tenacious widow. And just as Perón immortalized Eva's saintly image upon her tragic death, Cristina solidified Néstor's charismatic legacy by incorporating his image into propaganda spread throughout the country; renaming streets, public buildings, and neighborhoods after him; and constantly referencing his extraordinary contributions to society (Cherny 2014, 156; Wortman 2015).

FIGURE 7.3. Cristina and Néstor Kirchner embrace

FIGURE 7.4. Juan and Eva Perón embrace

7.3.7.2 *Concentrating Hegemonic Authority*

Contrary to the hopes of some party activists and intellectuals, the Kirchners did not use their charismatic authority to oversee the construction of a leftist, institutionalized party. Rather, the leading couple seized control of the PJ and leveraged their powerful appeal to vanquish threats from the party's mid-level agents. Initially, Néstor adopted a conciliatory tone to win the support of diverse leaders within and beyond the PJ (Cherny 2014, 150; Mora y Araujo 2011). Yet, as he became more popular, these actors – especially Duhalde – quickly went from critical sources of support to obstacles threatening to hinder the Kirchners' consolidation of power. As these fragile political alliances grew more strained, the leading couple abandoned their transversal movement and established a new chapter of Peronism that they could define on their own terms (Dagatti 2013; Ollier 2015).

To establish a formidable and distinctly *Kirchnerista* chapter of Peronism, Néstor used his overwhelming popular support to demand loyalty from Peronist governors and legislators throughout the country. He also punished PJ leaders who questioned him by nominating parallel lists with his own candidates during the 2005 mid-term elections, and his nominees easily won thanks to their association with him. Furthermore, he weakened dissident Peronist governors by placing loyal mayors (*intendentes*) with new executive powers in the governors' districts. When some Peronist officials attempted to create a united front to oppose the president's aggressive behavior, he responded by pressuring influential members of the PJ to resign, effectively deactivating the party (Cherny 2014, 151–54). Finally, as previously mentioned, Cristina competed against Duhalde's wife, "Chiche," in the 2005 elections for senator of the Province of Buenos Aires. Unfortunately for Duhalde, his experience as a two-term governor of the province was no match for the Kirchners' popularity. Cristina emerged as the victorious senator, delivering a decisive blow to dissident Peronists, extinguishing Duhalde's influence, and paving the way for the Kirchners' undisputed control over the movement (ibid.; Mora y Araujo 2011; Ollier 2015).

Throughout the remainder of their combined presidencies, the Kirchners controlled the PJ in a hegemonic manner reminiscent of Menem and Perón. In fact, Néstor became president of the PJ in 2008, less than one year after handing the presidency of the nation to his wife. Time and again, the leading couple overcame internal threats to their power by deepening their direct connections with their adoring followers. Cristina continued to dominate the party on her own in the aftermath of her husband's death in October 2010, as evidenced by her landslide reelection in the following year. Before Néstor's death, a group of important Peronists had been plotting to wrest the party from the Kirchners' grasp (Cherny 2014, 155). Yet his death reinvigorated the followers' attachments to Cristina and glorified her husband as a martyr. Capitalizing on this emotional support, Cristina won reelection with an overwhelming 54 percent of the vote, smothering threats to her power from PJ challengers and enjoying supreme control over the movement and the country for several more years.

As the Kirchners established hegemonic authority over the nation and consolidated their influence over the Peronist movement, they also helped accelerate the fragmentation of opposition parties. Early on in his presidency, Néstor lured Radical leaders into his transversal coalition, thereby preventing the country's most influential opposition party from reestablishing a coherent bloc. This, combined with the UCR's implication in De La Rúa's humiliating (mis) management of the 2001 crisis, produced a precipitous decline in the UCR's representation in Congress (Zelaznik 2013). In fact, from 1999 to 2007, the party went from occupying eighty-five seats in the Chamber of Deputies and twenty seats in the Senate to forty seats in the Chamber and thirteen seats in the Senate (Ollier 2015).

When Cristina became president in 2007, her polemic style and actions fomented greater division between the government and the opposition. Most prominently, in 2008, she issued an emergency decree to increase export taxes on agricultural products, namely soybeans – an aggressive challenge to the country's powerful agricultural sector. This bold gesture deepened the divide between her followers and opponents. For the former group, it strengthened her symbolic image as a true savior of the poor, as she promised to use the resulting funds to finance massive social programs. For the latter group, which included much of the middle class, the action was interpreted as a transparent ploy to enhance the power and influence of the Kirchners themselves (Calvo and Victoria Murillo 2012, 154).[20] The increased polarization that resulted from this debacle presented an important opportunity for opposition groups to form a united front against Cristina. However, even in the face of Cristina's divisive leadership style, the opposition struggled to establish a cohesive force.

Finally, similar to their charismatic predecessors, the Kirchners weakened political institutions in the quest to sustain their personalistic authority. Like Menem, Néstor made ample use of emergency decrees to rapidly and single-handedly enact his policies – a total of 270 over the course of his presidency, an average of one every six days (Capriata 2008). While Cristina passed fewer than 50 decrees during her two presidential terms combined, she also used this tool strategically to enhance her charismatic image.[21] Like Perón, the Kirchners also interfered with the National Institute for Statistics and Census of the Republic (INDEC) to falsify statistics and mask the rising inflation that had resulted from their unsustainable state-centered economic policies. By 2012, the disparity between real and "official" inflation rates reached nearly 15 percentage points (Streb 2015). To strengthen their appearance as heroes defending the people against nefarious enemies, the Kirchners attacked media outlets critical of their administration and dominated public spaces with propaganda. Most prominently, in 2008 Cristina launched an all-out attack against the media giant *Clarín* for criticizing her efforts to increase taxes on the agricultural export sector to fund her social spending (Becerra 2015).

In sum, Peronism surged back to power under the Kirchners just as it had under Menem. Had the movement become institutionalized, this impressive comeback would have been unlikely. Yet its persistent charismatic nature enabled ambitious new leaders to restore its position as the country's

---

[20] As protests erupted across the nation in opposition to Cristina's decree, she attempted to have Congress enact a law to increase the export tax. However, in July 2008, the bill ultimately failed due to the tie-breaking vote of Cristina's own vice president, Cobos (Calvo and Victoria Murillo 2012, 154).

[21] For example, Cristina's attempt to increase agro-export-taxes in 2008 occurred through an emergency decree. Though she ultimately failed to enforce the new policy, the decree deepened the divide between her followers and opponents while increasing her symbolic image as a true savior among the poor.

predominant political force following the 2001 crisis. Specifically, citizens' enduring attachments to Peronism and their faith in the founder's mission of salvation caused them to crave a new hero capable of resolving their misery. The Kirchners capitalized on this opportunity to rise up and demonstrate their charismatic power. They oversaw an impressive economic recovery and boldly reversed Menem's neoliberal program through reinstating the economic nationalism and state interventionism of the past, reinvigorating citizens' intense nostalgia for Perón's golden age. Over time, the leaders also strategically reconstructed the movement's symbolic narrative by writing Menem out and depicting themselves as the contemporary manifestations of Perón and Eva. In doing so, Néstor and Cristina politically reactivated the followers' affective bonds, dominated the PJ, and weakened institutions that threatened their executive power.

As with Menem, this charismatic style of leadership allowed the Kirchners to consolidate hegemonic power – but only for a limited period of time. As I will illustrate in the next section, their shortsighted programs eventually imploded, compromising their heroic image. The Kirchners' collapse would once again usher in a period of leaderless fragmentation. Rather than destroying the movement, this recession, which would occur under non-Peronist president Mauricio Macri, would simply provide the opportunity for Cristina to stage an impressive comeback four years later, this time as vice president under Néstor's close confidant and Cabinet Chief, Alberto Fernández.

7.3.8 The Fourth Wave Recedes: Another Temporary Fall

7.3.8.1 Policy Exhaustion
Over the course of Cristina's two presidential terms, unchecked social spending and protectionist economic policies resulted in increasing inflation, rising prices, and shortages of basic material goods (Damill and Frenkel 2015). Rather than addressing these problems, Cristina upheld the policies and used personalistic tactics to try to preserve her power. Speculation blossomed regarding her potential plans to legalize "re-reelection," which would enable her to serve a third presidential term (Rebossio 2012). Meanwhile, she blamed the economic struggles on "evil" opponents including speculators, international financial institutions, and private corporations (Wortman 2015). She also denied the severity of the looming crisis, distorted inflation statistics, further increased social spending, and relentlessly spread propaganda in praise of her administration's progress, which she came to label "The Victorious Decade" (*La Década Ganada*).

As Cristina's second presidency unfolded, it became increasingly difficult to sustain the illusion of prosperity with these stopgap measures. Moreover, in large part due to her declining performance, her plans for "re-reelection" failed, forcing her to step down in 2015 (Gilbert 2015). As with Menem in 1999, the combination of growing economic woes and the charismatic leader's inability to remain in executive power caused the Peronist movement to recede from power once again.

Due to economic deterioration and Cristina's looming departure, Peronism once again suffered a crisis of fragmentation. The 2015 elections revealed these internal divisions. Cristina reluctantly endorsed Daniel Scioli, the lackluster Governor of the Province of Buenos Aires and Menem's original protégé, as the PJ candidate (Raszewski 2015). As in 2003, two additional Peronist candidates ran on independent tickets: Sergio Massa, a prominent national deputy from the Province of Buenos Aires and Cristina's former cabinet chief, and Adolfo Rodríguez Saá, the governor of San Luis and perennial presidential hopeful.

Similar to 1999, the fragmentation of Peronism greatly facilitated the opposition. Despite their ongoing struggle to unite, opposition groups managed to coalesce around a single candidate: Mauricio Macri, the center-right, wealthy businessman and Governor of the Federal Capital. Macri won and stepped into the presidency, backed by an ideologically variegated, seven-party coalition called "*Cambiemos*" (Let's Change), whose sole unifying foundation was its opposition to Cristina. Notably, Macri won in the second round of the election.[22] In the first round, he won a mere 30 percent of the vote; in contrast, the Peronists won a combined 61 percent (about 38.5 percent for Scioli, 20.5 percent for Massa, and 2 percent for Rodríguez Saá). While Peronism clearly remained the country's most popular political force, its internal divisions permitted Macri to participate in a runoff against Scioli, in which the non-Peronist won by two percentage points. In short, Macri owed his narrow victory to Peronists disillusioned with the Kirchner regime who refused to support her weakling successor.

7.3.8.2 *Resistance to Routinization*
Macri broke with historical precedent by becoming the first non-Peronist president to complete a full term in office (2015–19) since Perón's first electoral victory in 1946. Nonetheless, his presidency was marked by struggle and controversy, in large part because the crisis he inherited from his predecessor worsened substantially under his watch. By the end of his term, inflation had soared to 50 percent, GDP had shrunk by over three percent, and his approval dropped from a high of 62 percent after the 2017 mid-term election to a low of 28 percent in 2019 (Gillespie and Do Rosario 2019; Murillo and Rodrigo Zarazaga 2020). Therefore, Macri lost his October 2019 bid for reelection by a full eight points to the Peronist presidential candidate, Alberto Fernández, whom Cristina chose as her running mate (with Cristina as vice president) just

---

[22] The 1994 Constitution of Argentina requires that, in presidential elections, the first-place candidate win either 45 percent of the popular vote or 40–44 percent of the popular vote *and* defeat the runner-up candidate by at least 10 percentage points. Otherwise, the top two candidates must compete in a second round.

three months prior to the election. In short, while Macri temporarily overcame enormous challenges to assemble a successful non-Peronist coalition and complete his presidential term, his weak leadership – marked by his glaring inability to address the worsening economic crisis – ultimately paved the way for Peronism's fifth resurgence.

As with the presidencies of Alfonsín and De La Rúa, I argue that the persistent, charismatic nature of Peronism severely impacted Macri's leadership potential and contributed substantially to his political demise. Even while out of power during Macri's presidency, Peronism continued to shape citizen's expectations for a strong leader to provide a heroic resolution to the growing crisis. Yet Macri's non-Peronist background, coupled with his unwillingness and inability to adopt the personalistic style typical of Peronist leaders, prevented him from filling this role. Instead of working to establish a charismatic image, the new president endeavored to project a principled, business-like style. Indeed, while he held influential political roles in the past – most importantly, as the Chief of Government (equivalent to Governor) of the City of Buenos Aires – he leaned on his credentials as a civil engineer and businessman rather than portraying himself as a talented and inspirational leader in his own right. Throughout his campaign and presidency, he also openly criticized the "hyperpresidentialism and ... polarizing style" of Peronist leaders, namely Cristina, and depicted himself as the humble manager of a "team" of bureaucrats (Lupu 2016, 47–48). Members of Macri's political administration insisted that this technocratic approach, which intentionally downplayed any emotional connection between the president and the citizenry, would help the president differentiate himself from his melodramatic predecessor and enhance his capacity to govern.[23]

However, instead of strengthening his image, Macri's strategy of depersonalization demonstrated his grave underestimation of the affective power of the Peronist identity, which hinges on citizens' deeply emotional bonds to charismatic leaders. Thus, although the president believed his so-called de-dramatization of power would inspire Argentines to invest in a more "horizontal" and egalitarian concept of leadership, his approach appeared to many as a brazen attempt to erase the legacies of Argentina's most beloved heroes – Perón above all (Rodríguez and Touzon 2020, 55, 70). In other words, by belittling the charismatic style of past leaders, especially Perón and the Kirchners, Macri and his team of technocrats (perhaps unknowingly) insulted the hopes and dreams that many citizens felt those leaders had fiercely defended (Rodríguez 2019). Consequently, Macri failed to connect on an emotional level with ordinary Argentines and fell short of their expectations of strong leadership.

---

[23] Author interview with Soledad Planes, polling adviser to Cabinet Chief Marcos Peña, June 21, 2016.

In addition to denying the symbolic power of Peronism, Macri enacted lukewarm policies rather than providing bold and decisive action to confront the economic crisis he inherited from his predecessor. Ironically, during his campaign, he vowed to end poverty, inflation, and corruption while jumpstarting Argentina's economy – audacious promises not unlike those of Peronist heroes. Yet, as president, he lacked the confidence and support to enact bold structural adjustments and provide the swift relief that many Argentines expected (Kovalski 2019). His cautious approach unfolded into a "meandering road to stability and growth" rather than bringing about miraculous recovery (Sturzenegger 2019). Then, in 2018, the Turkish debt crisis and a terrible drought exacerbated the recession (Kovalski 2019). Desperate to resolve the situation, the president turned to the International Monetary Fund – the most detested institution in Argentina – for help, securing the largest loan in history, at US$5.7 billion; in exchange, he promised to enact much stricter structural adjustment measures (Murillo and Rodrigo Zarazaga 2020, 129). By this time, Argentines had lost faith in his capacity to rescue them from crisis. They also felt betrayed by his decision to sell the country out to the IMF and suffered from the painful adjustment measures.

Similar to his non-Peronist predecessors, Macri's weak leadership reinforced the maxim that only Peronist leaders are capable of governing the country. His presidency strengthened the cleavage between Peronists and anti-Peronists, injecting Peronism with a much-needed boost of legitimacy. As the "Macrisis" worsened during the final two years of his presidency, the fragile unity of his non-Peronist coalition eroded substantially (Rapoza 2019). Meanwhile, the ideologically heterogeneous array of Peronist leaders grew increasingly motivated to "put aside their differences and coalesce" (Murillo and Rodrigo Zarazaga 2020, 126).

In short, as with Alfonsín and De La Rúa decades earlier, the fall of Peronism in 2015 enabled Macri, a non-Peronist, to rise to power. At the same time, the charismatic ethos of the movement once again largely precluded the non-Peronist from becoming a successful leader. Indeed, Macri's inability and unwillingness to emotionally connect with Peronist-identifying citizens or miraculously resolve the economic crisis through bold, unilateral action set him up for failure and paved the way for Peronism's impressive comeback.

7.3.9 The Fifth Wave Rises: Fernández and Fernández

Energized by Macri's disastrous presidency, the fragmented Peronists managed to reunite and take back the presidency in 2019. To achieve this, Cristina positioned herself as vice presidential candidate with Alberto Fernández, her husband's ideologically moderate cabinet chief who had defected from her in 2008, at the head of the ticket. This cunning political maneuver enabled the movement's two major factions – one led by Cristina and the other by her defectors – to unify under a new coalition, "Front for All" (*Frente de Todos*).

In contrast to Macri's narrow, second-round win over Scioli in 2015, Fernández enjoyed an overwhelming victory in the first round of the 2019 election, with 48 percent of the vote to Macri's 40 percent. The Peronists also swept the gubernatorial and senate elections, gaining the support of twenty of twenty-four governors and forty-three of seventy-two senators (Murillo and Rodrigo Zarazaga 2020, 132).

At the time of writing in September 2020, Alberto Fernández faces several challenges, including the ongoing economic recession, yawning fiscal deficit, novel coronavirus pandemic, and ideological divisions within its own ranks. However, as with previous Peronist leaders, his position at the head of both the charismatic movement and the country has enabled him to use these conditions of crisis as a launchpad to exert strong, personalistic leadership. Already, he has demonstrated his potential to achieve this. Most importantly, he has confronted the pandemic with decisive policies, including a strict, months-long quarantine. While the economic consequences of the pandemic could be catastrophic, some analysts speculate that the health crisis grants the new president greater leeway to work with (or stop paying) the country's creditors (Mander 2020). Moreover, Fernández's policies have slowed the spread of the virus far more than in neighboring countries, earning him international praise and elevating his approval by more than twenty points, from 56.8 percent in December 2019 to 78 percent in April 2020, according to national polling firm Trespuntozero (Horwitz 2020).

In addition to increasing his popularity, Fernández's courageous response to the pandemic has enabled him to exert greater control over the Peronist movement. In particular, while some wondered during the presidential campaign whether Cristina would use him as a puppet to exert her own power (Jourdan and Raszewski 2019), it has become clear that his political capital far exceeds her own (Di Giorgio 2020). Indeed, like Menem in 2003, Cristina continues to command the fervent support of certain groups – but her disapproval ratings consistently outweigh her approval ratings, the latter of which stood at a mere 27.5 percent as of August 2020 (Mander 2020). In contrast, Alberto's approval has soared since he became president. While his numbers have receded somewhat since the peak of the pandemic in April, at well over 60 percent they remain higher than that of any other politician in the country (Guadalupe 2020). And whereas Cristina remains a divisive figure tainted by corruption scandals, a majority of Argentines view Fernández as the politician most likely to achieve dialogue and consensus to move the country forward (Di Giorgio 2020). Citizens also generally view Fernández as the leader most capable of rescuing the country from the pandemic and striking a favorable deal with foreign creditors to address the country's formidable economic crisis (Horwitz 2020).

In sum, the mechanisms through which Peronism recently returned to power under the leadership of Alberto Fernández suggest that the movement's personalistic core remains intact. He has consolidated impressive popularity by taking bold actions in the face of a global pandemic and a serious economic recession, and has connected on an emotional level with Argentines to a far greater extent than Macri, his technocratic and non-Peronist predecessor. Additionally, Fernández has drawn on his resounding popular approval to begin to impose greater coherence on the Peronist movement, using informal channels to maintain the unity of diverse officials within his *Frente de Todos* coalition. Fernández's leadership mirrors that of Néstor Kirchner, who established impressive political capital shortly after assuming the presidency in 2003 and used it to dominate the Peronist movement two years later by overtaking Duhalde. To be sure, Fernández continues to face enormous economic and political challenges, and the future of Peronism remains uncertain. But if he continues to exercise charisma in the face of hardship, it is not unlikely that he will successfully consolidate his position as the new savior of Peronism.

7.4 CONCLUSION

This chapter has documented the spasmodic pattern in which charismatic movements unfold. Following a crisis, a valiant leader surges to power, promising to rescue the people from their suffering. To substantiate his capacities as an all-powerful redeemer, the leader concentrates authority by cultivating deeply emotional bonds with voters, fragmenting political parties, and overriding institutional constraints. Through this process, the leader establishes a political movement rooted in his charismatic appeal.

Eventually, the founder's seemingly extraordinary, yet inherently unsustainable, performance begins to falter. Having undermined institutional safeguards in the name of concentrating power, the founder's government stands on the brink of collapse. Because the founder dies or disappears before the moment of doom arrives, he escapes blame for the ensuing disaster. Nevertheless, the inevitable eruption of a crisis – compounded by the sudden absence of the founder's charismatic authority – causes the movement to recede from politics. Crucially, this retreat from power is temporary; it does not cause the movement's permanent demise, nor does it set in motion a process of institutionalization. Instead, the citizens' profound, affective identification with the founder persists and helps perpetuate his movement in politically latent form.

During this period of crisis, the followers' worldview remains rooted in the founder's personalistic authority. The followers mourn the loss of their beloved savior and desperately wish for a symbolic reincarnation to appear and take charge of the chaotic situation. Meanwhile, thanks in large part to the founder's aggressive quest for supreme power, political parties remain deeply fragmented and political institutions remain weak. I contend that these conditions do not lend themselves to reconstructing a routinized party system. Instead, they create opportunities for new politicians to revive the movement by embodying the founder's charismatic style.

Thus, out of the ashes of the movement's first collapse, a new leader has the opportunity to rise and restore the movement to power. Like the founder, the successor accomplishes this by tapping into the followers' unmediated emotional attachments and implementing daring reforms, which she achieves by overpowering parties and weakening institutions that threaten her executive power. These personalistic tactics help the successor resuscitate the movement, yet their viability rests on short-lived policies and poor political infrastructure. Paradoxically, then, the successor's victory plants the seeds for another collapse. While this failure may discredit the leader in question, however, the movement – whose legitimacy rests primarily on the charismatic legacy of the founder – survives. The cycle therefore repeats, perpetuating the movement while generating recurrent political and economic volatility. In the following chapter, I reflect on the self-reinforcing nature of charismatic movements and draw broader conclusions about the consequences for democracy.

8

Theoretical Implications and Broader Conclusions

8.1 THEORETICAL IMPLICATIONS

8.1.1 Central Findings

This book has investigated how two paradigm-shifting political movements founded by charismatic leaders, Argentine Peronism and Venezuelan Chavismo, have lived on and dominated politics for years after the disappearance of their founders. Conventional understandings of charisma would predict that the survival of these movements would require their transformation into institutionalized parties. Yet both movements have persisted by sustaining their original, deeply personalistic nature.

Perón and Chávez established their movements by rising in the midst of serious crises, recognizing people's suffering, and delivering on the promise to provide swift and thorough relief. In Argentina, Perón granted unprecedented benefits to millions of workers and poor migrants, including stable jobs, decent wages, paid vacation, housing, and healthcare. In Venezuela, Chávez established social "missions" that delivered to poor citizens a tidal wave of aid including food, water, healthcare, housing, and education. Through these impressive actions, the two leaders fostered profound, unmediated emotional attachments with their followers. Furthermore, the leaders used these bonds with their followers to overpower actors, parties, and institutions that threatened their supremacy.

Due to the unsustainable magnitude of their ambitious benefit programs, the founders' seemingly miraculous performance predictably declined, unleashing economic and political instability that would undermine democracy and harm their own supporters. Nevertheless, the followers would remember the initial, astounding performance of the policies rather than their eventual exhaustion and collapse. Moreover, because Perón was ousted by a coup and Chávez died before the implosion of his reforms, their followers exculpated them from blame, helping solidify the leaders' charismatic legacies.

Based on the logic of routinization, the affective intensity of followers' attachments should have dissipated after the founders disappeared. In turn, the depersonalization of these bonds should have transformed the movements into more conventional, institutionalized political parties. Yet in both cases, the deep, affective quality of citizens' attachments to the founders proved strikingly resilient.

Upon the deaths of Perón and Chávez, the followers' emotional attachments grew even more intense. When Perón passed away in 1974, his followers stampeded Congress, where his body was displayed, and "succumb[ed] to emotion" at the loss of their savior (Page 1983, 494). While different factions of the movement violently opposed each other in subsequent years, they remained unified in their unwavering loyalty to Perón. Similarly, when Chávez died of cancer in early 2013, the masses thronged the streets of Caracas to mourn his death in an amazing display of public mourning. Afterward, shrines commemorating the founder appeared in private homes and public spaces across Venezuela, evidencing the ongoing sway of his charismatic influence. Even as followers grew increasingly divided depending on their support for Chávez's handpicked successor, Nicolás Maduro, they all remained devoted to the founder.

Today, at least one-third of voters in Argentina and Venezuela continue to express emotional attachments to Peronism and Chavismo. Moreover, the personalistic character of the two movements remains strong, whereas their programmatic trademarks and organizational infrastructures remain underdeveloped. These characteristics suggest that the followers' loyalty is still rooted in the movements' charismatic foundations and cast doubt on the argument that the movements have routinized.

To explain this surprising outcome, my theory of charismatic movement emergence and revival examines the nature and trajectory of followers' support for the founder and movement (the demand side of charisma), as well as the strategies and conditions used by new leaders to connect with the followers and consolidate power (the supply side of charisma). Drawing insights from political psychology on the nature and behavior of political identities, I explain why citizens' charismatic attachments persist and demonstrate how new leaders can reactivate those bonds by claiming to be heirs of the adored founder. In turn, I analyze the interplay between structure and agency to determine the conditions under which successors can revive the movement and establish their own charismatic authority. Finally, I weave together the perspectives of followers and leaders to illustrate how charismatic movements can develop self-reinforcing, spasmodic trajectories that weaken democracy. Based on this research, I show that charismatic movements can persist in personalistic form and dominate politics for years and even decades after their founders disappear, rather than disintegrating or transforming into institutionalized parties.

To begin, I contend that the foundation for a movement's emergence and survival rests on citizens' charismatic attachments. As shown in Chapter 3, the founder of the movement fulfills three conditions to establish these attachments with his supporters. He directly recognizes the people's suffering; promises and enacts bold policies that provide the people with desperately needed relief; and crafts a narrative that praises him as a savior, depicts his opponents as enemies, and stresses his quasi-religious mission to provide the people with transcendence. Although existing literature documents the importance of these conditions for the formation of charismatic bonds, it underestimates the downstream impact of these factors on the followers' political attitudes and behaviors. Conversely, my research shows that the founder's direct recognition, seemingly miraculous performance, and symbolic narrative form the basis of citizens' worldview and understanding of politics for years after the founder has disappeared.

The followers' original, charismatic attachments have a profound and lasting influence on their attitudes and behaviors because these bonds develop into a resilient political identity. As suggested by political psychologists, the *nature* of this identity is enduring; however, its *intensity* fluctuates over time. Thus, when the charismatic founder disappears and his policies collapse, the personalistic nature of citizens' attachments remains intact. Under these circumstances, the political significance of the bonds is likely to decline – at least temporarily. Indeed, struck by the absence of the founder and devastated by the ensuing crisis, the followers are likely to withdraw from politics, causing the movement to retreat from power.

Crucially, as illustrated in Chapter 4, citizens' fervent devotion to the founder and movement persists because even in the founder's absence, the followers remain intimately attached to his narrative, which glorifies his heroic leadership and keeps alive his promise of salvation from evil (opposition) forces. Over time, the followers preserve this narrative and pass it to new generations by recounting cherished memories and holding onto symbols that commemorate the founder's selflessness and extraordinary qualities. This personalistic mechanism preserves the charismatic nature of citizens' identification with the movement and sustains their hope that a new savior will eventually rise up, assume the founder's mantle, and restore the movement to power. Thus, while citizens' attachments become politically latent when the founder disappears, their bonds have the potential to be reactivated by successors who prove themselves worthy of the founder's role.

To resuscitate the political significance of the followers' deep, affective bonds and consolidate power, I argue that successors must satisfy symbolic and material conditions similar to those fulfilled by the founder. In particular, new leaders must promise and implement audacious policies that deliver tangible benefits to the followers in order to demonstrate their capacity to take the founder's place. In addition, the new leaders must weave themselves into the movement's symbolic narrative to demonstrate their intention to revive the founder's redemptive mission. As demonstrated in the survey experiments in Chapter 5, successors who achieve these strategies cause followers to express stronger emotional attachment to the movement. Moreover, the movement's supporters come to view such leaders as more charismatic and worthier of electoral support. Thus, the findings indicate that it is possible to reactivate the intensity of citizens' resilient, *charismatic* attachments.

In sum, analysis from the demand side demonstrates that followers' unmediated emotional attachments to the founder create a base for the long-term survival of charismatic movements. Yet, on the supply side, the capacity of successors to return these movements to power depends on an additional set of conditions related to both structure and agency, as outlined in Chapter 6. First, successors must seek power independently, as self-starters, and often do so years after the founder has disappeared. Unlike the weakling successors whom the founders directly anoint, self-starters have greater autonomy to reshape and update the movement's narrative without appearing to undermine the founder's legacy. Second, new leaders must seek power under conditions of crisis, when the followers' craving for a hero intensifies. Only then does the opportunity emerge for the new leaders to prove their extraordinary ability to rescue the people, thus reviving the founder's mission of salvation. Finally, because of the charismatic nature of the followers' identity, successors must conform to the founder's personalistic style. This final condition is essential for rekindling the followers' affective attachments and convincing these devotees that the successors are worthy of the founder's mantle.

By combining the perspectives of movement followers and leaders, my theory demonstrates that charismatic movements tend to develop spasmodic trajectories that are self-reinforcing. To substantiate their charismatic potential, successors implement daring reforms that lack long-term sustainability, but carry a powerful, initial impact. Achieving this impressive material performance is necessary: each successor's legitimacy as an heir of the founder depends on it. Invariably, however, the unsustainable nature of the policies causes them to break down, which eventually erodes the new leader's charismatic authority. When the successor falls from grace, the movement recedes from power and the political salience of citizens' attachments declines once again. But, this temporary slump does not change the resilient, charismatic nature of the followers' bonds with the movement. In fact, by producing a crisis, this downturn actually creates the opportunity for a new self-starter to rise up and reactivate the followers' ties to the movement. The new leader achieves this in the same fashion as her predecessor: by implementing impressive, yet shortsighted, policies and tying herself to the symbolic legacy of the founder. This process therefore repeats the abovementioned cycle. In short, the movement lives on, but it unfolds in an erratic pattern characterized by the periodic resurgence of charismatic leadership followed by temporary, leaderless recessions.

In addition to preserving personalistic leadership, the fitful life cycle of charismatic movements perpetually undermines party system development, encourages authoritarian leader tendencies, accelerates institutional decay, and generates economic instability. While charismatic leaders' policies tend to produce abbreviated periods of impressive economic growth and social well-being, eventually they collapse and unleash terrible crises. These downturns are compounded by the disproportionate concentration of power in the executive branch, the weakness of political parties, and the relative absence of institutional safeguards – characteristics that are reinforced with the rise of each successor. Thus, charismatic movements cause countries to suffer unusually high levels of political and economic volatility.

Argentina's seventy-five-year experience of Peronism, detailed in Chapter 7, underscores the negative consequences of charismatic movement revival for programmatic development, economic stability, and democracy. Indeed, while the tumultuous character of the country's history predates Perón, the frequency and intensity of nationwide crises dramatically increased starting with the charismatic founder's rise to power in 1946. Since then, the economic and political highs and lows experienced in Argentina have been extreme, even in comparison to other Latin American countries known for volatility and institutional weakness (Levitsky and Victoria Murillo 2013; Mora y Araujo 2011).

Although Chavismo has unfolded more recently than Peronism, the political chaos and economic devastation it produced in Venezuela has made the country stand out in Latin America as uniquely unstable and undemocratic. Some scholars and pundits optimistically predict that the failed leadership of Chávez's terribly unappealing handpicked successor, Nicolás Maduro, has planted the seeds for the movement's self-destruction (Denis 2015; López Maya 2014; Rondón 2017). Conversely, my theory predicts that, in light of the impressive resilience of the followers' attachments and the opposition's monumental struggles to unify and gain the trust of the poor masses, Chavismo has significant potential to endure. In fact, the movement's current chapter is not unlike that of Isabel Perón, whose failed leadership following the death of her husband precipitated Argentina's 1976–83 military dictatorship. It is possible that, similar to Peronism, Chavismo will temporarily implode under the strain of Maduro's authoritarian rule and reemerge years later under a more compelling self-starter, when conditions are more favorable.

In conclusion, my theory provides a novel explanation for the remarkable persistence of political movements founded by charismatic leaders. Rather than transforming into routinized parties, I show that the original, personalistic nature of these movements fuels their perpetuation. Thus, these movements can live on and dominate politics for long stretches of time. However, their fitful trajectories generate perpetual institutional weakness, social upheaval, and economic volatility. Unlike routinization, which encourages the gradual development of programmatic continuity and organizational infrastructure, the revival of charismatic movements infuses democracies with enduring illiberal tendencies and perpetually destabilizes party systems.

8.1.2 Theoretical Contributions

8.1.2.1 *Routinization versus Revival*

To my knowledge, this study is the first to directly challenge the routinization thesis and provide an alternative explanation for the striking resilience of charismatic movements. While some scholars have produced insightful theories about the survival of charisma, their analyses are firmly rooted in the logic of routinization. Weber's original theory of charisma and its routinization provides the foundation for these studies (1922/1978). According to Weber, charisma is inherently unstable in its pure form. Yet, he argues, charismatic movements have the potential to transform into alternative forms of authority: namely traditional authority, rational authority, or a combination of the two (ibid., 246). Based on this reasoning, Weber discusses several potential pathways of routinization. For instance, charisma might be "traditionalized" into a form of hereditary succession, in which next-of-kin inherits the original leader's legitimacy (ibid., 248). Alternatively, charisma might be "rationalized" by transferring from the leader to a series of offices, rules, and procedures used to govern society (ibid.).

Building on Weber, Shils (1965) develops a theory in which the leader's charisma disperses to a series of inanimate offices, groups, and laws. He claims that charisma survives by detaching from the individual leader and injecting meaning and value into associated "collectivities," as well as inanimate "roles and rules" (ibid., 205). Citizens' faith in and attachments to the leader therefore transfer to these institutions, strengthening and stabilizing the bureaucracy that develops in the charismatic leaders' place (ibid.).

Alternatively, Jowitt argues that charismatic movements and parties can survive if their *platform*, rather than (or in addition to) their leader, embodies a heroic and transformative mission. Under these circumstances, he states that the "[charismatic] Party is called on to sacrifice, struggle, and exercise continual vigilance to maintain its purpose" (Jowitt 1992, 11). Unlike Shils, who states that the charisma originally associated with an individual leader "disperses" to institutions, Jowitt contends that the institutions can develop a form of "impersonal" charisma from the outset (ibid.; Shils 1965, 205). To illustrate his theory, Jowitt traces the history of Leninism, which he argues was always rooted at least as much in a "charismatic" platform as in Lenin's personal appeal (Jowitt 1992, 8–12).

Despite the differences across these authors regarding the origin of charismatic authority, they all conclude that charisma can only persist in *depersonalized* form. In contrast, my theory of charismatic movement revival stresses that charisma lives on precisely by sustaining its *personalistic* core. The followers help maintain the personalistic nature of their identity with the movement when the founder disappears by recounting their individual experiences of his heroic leadership. This reinforces the citizens' direct, emotional attachments to the founder and his movement, rather than transforming their bonds into respect for bureaucratic offices and procedures that are indirectly associated with the founder, as Shils would argue. Moreover, whereas routinization theories insist that only depersonalized party organizations can perpetuate charisma, I argue that new leaders who *personally* embody the founder can revive charisma in its original form. Using this strategy, successors can become powerful charismatic leaders themselves – if only temporarily. By developing this personalistic mechanism of survival, my theory makes a novel and important contribution to the literature on charisma.

8.1.2.2 *Structure versus Agency*
In documenting and explaining the personalistic revival of charisma, this book also contributes to key debates about the roles of structure and agency in politics. Scholars debate the extent to which charisma relies on one or the other. On the one hand, some define charisma as a fixed personality trait with inscrutable origins (e.g., Antonakis et al. 2016; Hoffman and Hoffman 1968; House and Howell 1992; Keller 2006: Maranell 1970). This interpretation, which underscores the magnetic appeal of individual leaders, focuses disproportionately on agency at the expense of structure. Unsurprisingly, many social scientists have criticized this understanding of charisma as too slippery, ambiguous, and subjective to warrant rigorous analysis (e.g., Bendix 1967; Schlesinger 1960; Smith 2000; Van der Brug and Mughan 2007; Worsley 1957).

On the other hand, some authors stress that structure plays an indispensable role in the establishment of charismatic authority. For instance, Weber states that charismatic leaders must rise "in times of psychic, physical, economic, ethical, religious, [or] political distress" to prove their extraordinary capacities to their potential disciples (Weber 1968, 18). Similarly, Madsen and Snow underscore the importance of a crisis for generating feelings of low self-efficacy, which initiates the process of charismatic bonding between leaders and followers (1991, 9–14). These theories of charisma highlight important structural conditions. However, they risk becoming overly deterministic. Indeed, given the intensely personal and subjective nature of this type of authority, it would seem problematic to overlook the individual agency of charismatic leaders.

My study sheds greater light on the distinct influences of agency and structure on charisma by tracing the long-term trajectories of charismatic movements. I illustrate how structure and agency interact to facilitate new leaders' ability to reactivate citizens' charismatic attachments and inherit the founder's mantle. I show that the capacity of successors to revive the movement depends in part on their agency. Without their own personal appeal, skill, and experience, these leaders could not achieve extraordinary performance reminiscent of the founder, nor could they tap into the followers' emotional bonds.

Nevertheless, my theory stresses the centrality of structural conditions in the revival of charismatic movements. To begin, the eruption of a crisis provides the indispensable opening for successors to prove their heroic potential because it makes citizens crave a new savior in the first place. The method by which new leaders are selected and the timing of their rise also greatly influence their prospects for success. In addition, the preexisting, charismatic nature of citizens' identification with the movement structures the way these leaders govern. Specifically, these leaders must use a personalistic style and tie themselves to the founder's legacy to fulfill the followers' expectations for a savior. Thus, while charismatic successors often manage to exercise largely independent authority for a period of time, these structural conditions impose crucial constraints on their power. Paradoxically, these conditions also strengthen the movement's momentum and help extend its survival beyond the abbreviated rules of its successors.

By clarifying the roles of structure and agency in the spasmodic trajectories of charismatic movements, this study also demonstrates that the impact of charisma on politics is far less ephemeral than previously assumed (Eatwell 2006; Jowitt 1992; Kitschelt et al. 2010; Madsen and Snow 1991; Weber 1922/ 1978). I show that the resilience of citizens' affective attachments to the charismatic founder underpins the survival of these movements in their original, personalistic form. In turn, the emergence of structural conditions conducive to the rise of a new savior – namely, the eruption of a crisis – encourage new, ambitious, and talented leaders to reactivate citizens' attachments, return the movement to power, and consolidate a new wave of personalistic authority. As illustrated in Argentina and Venezuela, charisma can therefore exert a profound, destabilizing influence on politics for years or even decades.

8.1.2.3 *Political Identity, Cleavages, and Partisanship*
In contrast to previous studies that emphasize the short-lived nature of charismatic attachments, my theory indicates that these attachments can develop into a resilient political identity. Although the content of this identity remains rooted in the heroic legacy of individual leaders and therefore differs from more traditional political identities based on programmatic content and/or robust social networks, it has a similar capacity to endure, cross over to new generations, and profoundly shape citizens' worldviews, attitudes, and behaviors. Whereas programmatic and organizational identities "help bind voters to parties" and therefore facilitate party system institutionalization (Roberts 2014, 20), the charismatic identity tethers citizens to a weakly institutionalized movement that thrives off of, and reinforces, volatile cycles of personalistic leadership. Thus, my theory stresses that the charismatic identity can result in unique consequences for the political system.

Like other forms of partisanship, the charismatic identity establishes a cleavage that organizes society into two groups: the "in-group" constitutes true believers while the "out-group" incorporates individuals who do not belong to the movement (Tajfel 1974). In programmatic settings, these in- and out-groups tend to be rooted in left–right ideology and substantive policies as much as affect; thus, while the people in an out-group possess a negative identification with one party, they often also possess a *positive* identity with another party. For example, in the United States, many conservative individuals negatively identify with Democrats, but also positively identify as Republicans, and vice versa.

In contrast, the charismatic identity links up with a *personalistic* cleavage, which organizes in- and out-groups based on profound (positive or negative) emotions toward individual leaders and has little to do with programmatic content. Because the out-group coalesces based exclusively on a strong rejection of the charismatic leader and movement, the group struggles to develop a positive identification with its own group or party. Thus, these individuals' anti-identification with the movement, defined by negative emotions rather than substantive policies, predominates. Even more than in programmatic party systems, affective (rather than programmatic or ideological) polarization between followers and opponents becomes a defining quality of the political system (Abramowitz and McCoy 2019, Iyengar et al. 2019). As some studies have noted (Ostiguy 2009; Ostiguy and Roberts 2016), the personalistic cleavage generated by a charismatic identity can undermine the relevance of more traditional ideological or social divisions thought to facilitate party system institutionalization (Lipset and Rokkan 1967). By demonstrating how charismatic attachments emerge and develop into a resilient identity, my theory sheds light on the mechanisms through which such a personalistic cleavage can structure the political system in ways that intensify affective polarization and harm programmatic development.

8.1.2.4 A Novel Explanation for Enduring Institutional Weakness

Finally, my theory of charismatic movement revival contributes to the literature on institutional weakness and its consequences for democracy. My analysis reinforces the findings of several important studies that highlight the detrimental impact of personalism, elites' top-down control of parties, stark programmatic reversals, and severe crises on party system institutionalization (Gervasoni 2018; Kostadinova and Levitt 2014; Lupu 2013, 2014; Mainwaring 2018; Mainwaring and Scully 1995; Roberts 2007, 2014). For example, my finding that charismatic movements can remain dormant for years before suddenly becoming revived by new leaders complements Mainwaring's observation that, in Latin America, countries with seemingly stable party systems can experience surprisingly rapid institutional and ideological change, at times "unravel[ing] quickly and dramatically" (2018, 35, 62). Furthermore, the fits and starts of charismatic movements emphasized by my study align with Roberts' analysis of the "ebb and flow of populist waves" in several Latin American countries, including Argentina and Venezuela (2007, 4, 12).

My theory of charismatic movement revival contributes an alternative explanation for recurrent institutional weakness that rests on the self-reinforcing, spasmodic trajectories of charismatic movements. Specifically, as detailed in Chapter 7, I argue that the emergence of these movements sets into motion an endogenous cycle of personalistic leadership that establishes – and subsequently perpetuates – problems of institutional weakness highlighted by the previously mentioned authors. Moreover, because the charismatic core of such movements persists over time rather than succumbing to routinization, my theory suggests that it can undermine democratic development for decades. Indeed, as shown in Chapter 7, the periodic revival of charismatic movements encourages executive aggrandizement, promotes shortsighted policies whose inevitable collapse harms citizens' well-being, exacerbates affective polarization, hinders programmatic party structuration, and makes it difficult for both citizens and institutions to hold leaders accountable.

Importantly, my explanation of persistent institutional weakness extends only to countries where charismatic movements have taken root.[1] Nonetheless, I argue that its contribution to the broader literature is valid and useful for two reasons. First, while they have hitherto not been very common, my research shows that charismatic movements have a powerful and enduring impact on political systems. Second, the growing trend toward the "personalization" of politics, combined with the recent rise of charismatic leaders in countries around the world, suggest that my theory may become increasingly relevant in diverse contexts (Dalton and Wattenberg 2000; Garzia 2011; Gervasoni 2018; Kyle and Mounk 2018; McAllister 2007; Roberts 2014). It is particularly notable that the recent surge in charismatic leaders and movements has coincided with the alarming global retreat of democracy (Freedom House 2020). My theory suggests not only that these trends are related, but also that the threats to democracy posed by these charismatic movements could be more enduring than previously thought. The next section demonstrates how the central components of my theory generalize to four additional cases within and beyond Latin America.

8.2 CHARISMATIC MOVEMENT REVIVAL IN COMPARATIVE PERSPECTIVE

Does the theory presented in this book – that charismatic movements survive by sustaining their personalistic nature – provide valid and useful insights for cases beyond Argentina and Venezuela? A brief examination of movements in Peru,

---

[1] An important exception to this rule exists where charismatic movement founders have irrevocably tarnished their legacy by overshadowing their magnetic appeal with excessive brutality. In such cases, the abhorrent nature of the founder's legacy is more likely to stigmatize it in collective memory, greatly undermining its impact on the political system (see Art 2006; Manucci 2020). For example, the memory of Hitler's unspeakable genocide against the Jewish people far outweighs that of his charismatic bonds with his Nazi followers or his vision for transforming Germany (and the world). Because his abhorrent legacy has been condemned by Germany and the international community alike, his charisma has had little, if any, impact on German political institutions.

Italy, Thailand, and China – a set of cases that approximates a "most different systems" design – suggests that it does (Przeworski and Teune 1970, 34). While an in-depth, multimethod investigation of these cases lies beyond the scope of this study, I rely on secondary literature to assess the relevance of different aspects of my theory across the four cases. First, I consider to what extent leaders in these countries fostered charismatic bonds with their followers. Next, I examine whether these leaders used their authority to establish charismatic movements that overpowered existing parties and institutions. Subsequently, I analyze the trajectories of these movements after their founders' departure from the political scene, paying special attention to the status of citizens' attachments and the movements' impact on the party system.

This short analysis illustrates that, despite emerging in diverse contexts, key characteristics of the four movements under examination appear strikingly similar to those of Peronism and Chavismo. Like their Argentine and Venezuelan counterparts, the founders of all four movements established unmediated, emotional attachments with a large group of citizens and used charismatic authority to dominate politics, weakening (or attempting to weaken) important parties and political institutions along the way. The four founders also remained remarkably popular after stepping down from power. Furthermore, immediate successors – whether anointed by the founder or supported by opposition forces – struggled to establish independent legitimacy and govern effectively. Finally, in some cases, the widespread and persistent public adoration of the followers suggests the potential for revival of the movement when the right conditions emerge. In other cases, movement revival seems unlikely. Nevertheless, I demonstrate that, even in these cases, the charismatic legacies of the movement founder continue to influence politics in important ways that undermine programmatic and institutional development.

8.2.1 Peru

As described in Chapter 6, Alberto Fujimori rose to power in 1990 as a political outsider amidst a severe crisis of hyperinflation and "brutal insurrectionary violence" (Weyland 2006, 14). The urban lower classes and rural poor, who suffered disproportionately from the crisis, saw in Fujimori the potential for miraculous relief. Indeed, unlike Mario Vargas Llosa – Fujimori's elite competitor who allied with existing parties and proposed a detailed platform for economic recovery – Fujimori rose independently and campaigned on a simple promise that resonated with the suffering masses: "honesty, technology, and work" (Weyland 2002, 102–3). In office, Fujimori followed through on his promise by enacting a series of daring reforms to combat hyperinflation; next, he launched a campaign to defeat Peru's most violent insurrectionary group, the Shining Path, and soon captured its top leaders (ibid., 150–58). To the poor, Fujimori's straightforward promises and audacious performance seemed extraordinary – especially compared to the incompetence of past administrations.

Thus, although the founder's emotional appeal was less pronounced than that of Perón or Chávez, he cultivated a powerful narrative that celebrated his reputation for "getting things done," denounced his adversaries (including Congress and the Supreme Court) as obstructionist, and solidified deep, unmediated attachments with Peru's underprivileged masses.

By fulfilling the three conditions necessary for establishing charismatic attachments, Fujimori enjoyed tremendous popular support. By 1992, just two years into his presidency, he achieved an approval rating as high as 82 percent (Weyland 2002, 171–72). Even eight years later, when the impressive performance of his policies began to wane and allegations of corruption and wrongdoing surfaced, his approval remained well above 50 percent (Arce and Carrión 2010, 37–38; Wise 2006, 220).[2] Notably, poor voters offered particularly strong and enduring devotion to the leader. In fact, by 2000, his approval among the very poor was seventeen points higher than among the upper class (Carrión 2006, 130).

Having established his personalistic authority, Fujimori trampled on the already-fragmented party system and dismantled democratic institutions over the course of his ten-year rule. When he rose to power in 1990, Peruvians had already lost faith in established parties. In this context, Fujimori seemed especially appealing due to his lack of affiliation and the fact that "he hadn't done anything yet" (Weyland 2002, 102). As president, the leader capitalized on public sentiments to concentrate power and further undermine the party system. For example, rather than building a new party, he created four transient coalitions to support each of his election campaigns: "Change 90" in 1990, "New Majority" in 1995, "Let's Go Neighbors" in 1998, and "Peru 2000" in 1999/2000. He subjugated each of these coalitions to his personal will and let them fade away when he no longer needed their services, extinguishing opportunities to develop them into nascent parties (Carrión 2006, 7; Levitsky 1999, 82).

In addition to accelerating the disintegration of the party system, Fujimori challenged democratic institutions that constrained his power. In April 1992, he orchestrated a military-backed self-coup in which he "closed the Congress, suspended the constitution, and purged the judiciary" (Levitsky 1999, 78). Shortly thereafter, he enacted a new constitution that permitted his overwhelmingly popular reelection in 1995 (ibid.). Like other charismatic leaders, Fujimori reinstated elections to demonstrate his tremendous popular support, the most essential source of his legitimacy. Yet he also maintained a tight grip

---

[2] In particular, Wise states that Fujimori's initially impressive reforms were rather superficial in the long run: they failed to "tackle glaring reform gaps in such areas as income distribution, the restructuring and modernization of small and medium-sized firms, and export promotion" (2010, 220). Thus, "although the Fujimori coalition was patently successful in launching the first phase of market reforms in Peru, this same coalition emerged as the main bottleneck in the pursuit of second-phase market reforms" (ibid., 224).

on other democratic institutions, enabling him to exercise unquestioned authority for eight more years (Carrión 2006, 6). In doing so, he single-handedly carried out policies to sustain his supreme power without fear of reprisal.

In 2000, under pressure from Congress, in the wake of a major corruption scandal, Fujimori reluctantly resigned and fled to Japan after being elected for a third, unconstitutional term (Levitsky and Zavaleta 2016, 433). Crucially, many of his poor followers remained loyal to him even after he was forced from power. In fact, his abrupt departure, which was initiated by politicians in Congress, strengthened the antiestablishment appeal of Fujimorismo for these voters (Meléndez 2019). Conversely, anti-Fujimorista voters did not develop strong political attachments to other parties or leaders in the aftermath of the charismatic leader's demise. Peru's subsequent presidents therefore rose to power as "free agents," garnering support through their *negative* association with Fujimorismo rather than through building their own parties with *positive*, coherent identities (Levitsky and Zavaleta 2016, 412; Meléndez 2019). Many anti-Fujimorista voters supported these leaders simply because they represented "the least-worst option" (Meléndez 2019). Because of their incapacity to construct lasting attachments with voters, these presidents struggled to achieve legitimacy and suffered low approval ratings, even though most of them oversaw substantial economic growth during their terms (Dargent and Muñoz 2016, 147; Tanaka 2011, 77). For these reasons, while its charismatic founder has been absent from politics for nearly two decades, Fujimorismo has survived as the country's *only* cohesive political identity (Levitsky and Zavaleta 2016, 432; Meléndez 2019; Tanaka 2011, 80).

As discussed in Chapter 6, Fujimori's daughter, Keiko, made an impressive attempt to restore Fujimorismo to power by running for president in 2011 and again in 2016. Although she invested greater resources in constructing an organized party than her father did, she also revived his personalistic connections to his mass following, relied heavily on her symbolic association with him, and personally embodied his reputation for miraculously resolving the people's most pressing problems (Dargent and Muñoz 2016, 152; Meléndez 2019). Keiko failed to win the presidency in either year due primarily to the absence of a severe crisis, which tempered voters' desire for a charismatic savior to relieve their suffering. Even so, her personalistic image and association with her father reactivated the support of many of his followers (Dargent and Muñoz 2016, 155; Meléndez 2019; Tanaka 2011, 81). Thus, in the 2016 election, she won the first round of the elections by more than 18 percentage points and lost in the second round by a razor-thin margin of 0.24 percentage points (Dargent and Muñoz 2016, 145). Moreover, Keiko's opponent, Pedro Pablo Kuczynski, won the election due to his anti-Fujimorista status rather than his own platform or identity. In fact, as an illustration of his weak mandate, the new president resigned less than two years into his tenure, under threat of impeachment, based on accusations of corruption (Vergara 2018, 65).

In sum, Alberto Fujimori's movement has continued to shape Peruvian politics since the charismatic leader's departure nearly two decades ago. Millions of followers have continued to express profound attachments to his legacy. Meanwhile, parties have remained extremely fragmented, while non-Fujimorista leaders have struggled to establish independent authority. To be sure, the absence of an economic crisis, as well as multiple corruption scandals and recent rifts between Keiko Fujimori and her brother, Kenji, have threatened the movement's future prospects. In particular, since Keiko's loss in 2016, each sibling has hurled accusations of malfeasance at the other – Keiko for accepting campaign money from the corrupt Brazilian construction company, Odebrecht, and Kenji for making backdoor deals with former president Kuczynski to pardon the siblings' father, Alberto – decreasing the likelihood that Fujimorismo will return to power in the near future (Collyns 2018).

Nevertheless, the resilience of the followers' loyalty to Fujimorismo and the movement's ongoing personalistic influence on the political system are impressive – especially in light of the political drama surrounding the Fujimori family. While a future victory for Keiko (or Kenji) seems improbable at the time of writing, the historical trajectory of Fujimorismo since their father's fall from power in 2000 reflects marked similarities with other charismatic movements – namely in its resilient charismatic nature, its capacity to maintain the emotional devotion of its followers, and its profound and often destabilizing influence on Peru's fragmented party system.

8.2.2 Italy

Similar to Chávez in Venezuela, Silvio Berlusconi rose to power from the ashes of Italy's collapsed party system in 1994. From 1948 until Berlusconi's precipitous political debut, Italy had been governed by a rigid "partyocracy" dominated by Christian Democracy (DC), a party characterized by intense factionalism and deeply entrenched patronage (Koff and Koff 2000, 32–33). Although Italy had a multiparty system during this period, the DC controlled every cabinet and all but two premierships, while the second-largest party, the Italian Communist Party (PCI), perpetually stood in second place yet remained excluded from government power (Koff and Koff 2000, 32–33). In the early 1990s, however, the explosion of a massive corruption scandal called *Tangentopoli* (kickback city) – which implicated the vast majority of parties and leaders from across the political system – caused Italian voters to abandon the DC along with the entire political establishment. The scandal implicated an estimated 5,000 politicians; over half of parliament was indicted and 400 city and town councils were forced to close down (ibid., 1–3). This scandal, combined with the 1989 fall of the Berlin Wall and the decline in Communist identification, caused voters to thoroughly reject the political establishment and seek out an inspirational figure to rectify the situation (ibid.).

In answer to voters' cries for help, Berlusconi "burst upon the political scene" with his brand-new personalistic movement, *Forza Italia* (FI), in January 1994, promising far-reaching change (ibid., 31). By March of that year, he transformed from a political novice into the country's most popular politician, winning elections and, in May, becoming Prime Minister. Unlike existing politicians, whom voters perceived as complicit in a system of rules that had long benefited the political class at the expense of the people, Berlusconi connected on an emotional level with the masses and "gave voice" to their widespread frustration (Donovan 2015, 12, 19). Drawing on his outsider profile and his status as a wealthy media tycoon, he vowed to "transfer" his fabulous success to ordinary Italians. As he confidently implored, "Trust me, because I can make Italy as rich as I did myself" (Fabbrini 2013, 159). He also appealed to the increasingly middle-class electorate through promises to dramatically cut taxes, slash the unemployment rate, enact massive public works projects, and increase pensions for retirees. Lastly, the charismatic leader created a symbolic narrative that resonated deeply with his followers. This narrative praised Berlusconi for his "mission and sacrifice" to rescue Italy from the grips of selfish politicians and deliver both material success and happiness to the people (McDonnell 2016, 723).

By recognizing the anger and suffering of citizens who felt excluded by the political establishment, promising wealth and other tangible benefits, and crafting a narrative that depicted him as the savior who would rescue the people from the morally bankrupt political system, Berlusconi founded a powerful charismatic movement and consolidated deep, affective bonds with a large base of followers. Riding this wave of support, he served as Prime Minister three times – in 1994, 2001–6, and 2008–11 – during which he achieved high approval ratings that peaked at 63 percent and established "full personal control" over politics (Fabbrini 2013, 154–55; Sexton 2009).[3]

During his premierships, Berlusconi took advantage of his virtual monopoly over national media to project his personal appeal and showcase seemingly extraordinary (though superficial) reforms (Fabbrini 2013, 159–60). He also constructed a loyal coalition in Congress by weaving together "a complex set of personal deals dressed up in populist appeals to xenophobic nationalism and crude consumerism" (Bellamy 2006, 351). In doing so, the charismatic leader further destabilized Italy's practically collapsed party system and reaffirmed his supremacy. He also undermined democratic institutions that threatened his power. For instance, he "used his control on national television to de-legitimize

---

[3] Due to Italy's parliamentary system, Berlusconi's executive power differed from that of other charismatic leaders under examination. In particular, he served as Prime Minister rather than as President, and did so during intermittent periods (1994, 2001–6, and 2008–11). Nevertheless, similar to his charismatic counterparts in other countries, he consolidated a massive, loyal following and concentrated tremendous, personalistic authority over the political system during his premierships (Donovan 2015; Fabbrini 2013; McDonnell 2016).

independent bodies such as magistrates or newspapers and other critics" (Fabbrini 2013, 160). He also brazenly engaged in scandalous behavior ranging from tax fraud to sexual exploits, trusting that his charismatic appeal and reverent group of followers would nevertheless protect his image as a national hero (Donadio 2018). Finally, like Chávez, Perón, and Fujimori, Berlusconi resisted attempts to institutionalize the FI or share power with a "second leader" or "potential successor" (Koff and Koff 2000, 44).

Over the course of his rule, Berlusconi's dramatic promises of economic reform failed to fully materialize. As the "Euro crisis" loomed and "ungovernable Italian public debt" threatened the stability of other European states, he faced mounting pressure and ultimately resigned in November 2011 (Fabbrini 2013, 167). Crucially, for his charismatic legacy, the leader's retreat from power resulted more from *external* pressure, coming from other European leaders, than from discontent among Italian voters. Moreover, Berlusconi's departure left a power vacuum that was filled by an uninspiring technocrat, Mario Monti, and "a cabinet composed of university professors, bankers, and high-level public officials" (ibid., 168). Building on his image as a victim bullied by elite European powers (especially Germany) and on the poor performance of the government that succeeded him, Berlusconi was therefore able to make an impressive comeback in 2013 (Reinbold 2013). Indeed, just two years after resigning, he courageously revived his FI movement and campaigned to become Prime Minister for a fourth time.

Ultimately, Berlusconi was barred from running due to allegations of tax fraud and did not return to power. Nevertheless, his movement won about 30 percent of the votes and one-third of the seats in both houses of Congress (Alsop 2013). Moreover, Berlusconi's supporters continued to express profound faith in him. One follower passionately stated, "Now Silvio is back and I believe again" (Reinbold 2013). Another proclaimed, "I have always loved Silvio; he stands for everything that is good in the world" (ibid.). Based on this outpouring of support, a journalist incredulously stated at the time, "adoration of Berlusconi remains widespread. In the parallel universe occupied by followers, there is no room for doubt about Berlusconi and lines are clearly drawn. Silvio is good and the others are bad" (ibid.).

Throughout the 2010s, Italy continued to struggle with political fragmentation and economic decline (Donadio 2018). Thus, support for parties – especially the bumbling center–left coalition led by Matteo Renzi and, subsequently, Paolo Gentiloni – remained low. Meanwhile, Berlusconi's followers continued to express deep attachments to their beloved leader, causing him to run for the premiership yet again in 2018. Technically, the charismatic leader's criminal record barred him from political office; he also failed to win sufficient votes. Nevertheless, Berlusconi did not disappear from politics. In fact, in 2019, with his ban from office lifted, he ran for and won a seat in the European Parliament ("Silvio Berlusconi: Italy's Perpetual Powerbroker," 2019).

In sum, Berlusconi founded a charismatic movement that dominated politics in Italy for almost two decades. Rather than fading away or routinizing when the leader resigned in 2011, his legacy and movement, backed by the ongoing devotion of millions of followers, continued to shape Italian politics. Consequently, the political system remains deeply fragmented, personalistic, and volatile (Donovan 2015, 15). In light of the leader's electoral defeat in 2018, some have declared, "the Berlusconi era is over" (Giuffrida 2018). However, given the leader's regular reappearances as well as the resilience of his followers' emotional support, it seems unlikely that his charismatic mark on politics will easily fade. In fact, as the economic crisis deepens and Italian leaders fail to address it, it is possible that voters' wistful memories of "recent times under Berlusconi when they felt richer" could facilitate the movement's return to power under Berlusconi or, eventually, another alluring self-starter (Natanson 2018).

8.2.3 Thailand

Similar to the other countries under analysis, in Thailand the 1997 Asian Financial Crisis created favorable conditions for a charismatic leader to rise up and transform politics. The political and economic collapse produced by the crisis discredited the incumbent Democrat Party (DP) and facilitated the meteoric rise of Thaksin Shinawatra, a successful businessman who portrayed himself to his fellow Thais as a "breath of fresh air" (Phongpaichit and Baker 2004, 62). Although Thaksin had previously entered politics, briefly serving as Foreign Minister from October 1994 to January 1995, he abandoned his post after just five months. Then, on the heels of the crisis in July 1998, he founded his own political movement, Thai Rak Thai (TRT – Thais Helping Thais) (ibid., 64). Unlike existing political parties, Thaksin stifled the organizational development of the TRT and instead used it as a personalistic vehicle to launch himself into executive power (McCargo and Pathmanand 2005, 110). In 2001, Thaksin became the most popular Prime Minister in Thai history (Phongpaichit and Baker 2004, 62).

On the campaign trail and during his first years in office, Thaksin cultivated intensely emotional bonds with the poor masses, especially in the long-neglected countryside. First, he directly recognized the two groups who had suffered the most during the 1997 crisis: small business owners and the rural poor. He appealed to the former group, which consisted largely of low- and middle-income individuals operating family owned businesses, by acknowledging their feelings of abandonment by the outgoing government, which had embraced the painful stabilization policies recommended by the International Monetary Fund. For instance, in a public speech in 2000, Thaksin stated, "a lot of my brothers and sisters are still enduring great suffering and my business friends still cannot find money from banks … don't worry for me but for the country" (in Phongpaichit and Baker 2004, 74). Even more important than these constituents, Thaksin vowed to rescue poor citizens, who resided in the rural north and northeastern regions of the country and constituted 69 percent of the national population, from their miserable living conditions. On the campaign trail, he declared, "Nothing will stand in my way. I am determined to devote myself to politics in order to lead the Thai people out of poverty – I think the people want Thai Rak Thai to take the government's reins and solve the country's problems" (in Phongpaichit and Baker 2004, 80).

As Prime Minister, Thaksin followed through on his promise by enacting three audacious policies that delivered immediate relief to his struggling constituents: a three-year debt moratorium for farmers, a development fund of one million baht (approximately US$32,000) for every Thai village, and a health-care program that provided direct access to services to all Thais for 30 baht (less than US$1) (McCargo and Pathmanand 2005, 89). Many analysts viewed Thaksin's policies as ideologically vacuous and logistically unworkable (ibid., 90). However, for poor Thais, the swift and impressive impact of the policies – referred to colloquially as "Thaksinomics" – made the leader appear extraordinary (Phongpaichit and Baker 2004, 99).

In addition to his bold programs, Thailand's new savior wove his appeals and policies into a symbolic narrative that resonated deeply with his followers. Similar to Berlusconi in Italy, he confirmed his heroic status by playing up his extraordinary success as a self-made billionaire – an image that appealed to traditional Thai values and contrasted with the corrupt reputation of established politicians (ibid., 77). Additionally, Thaksin promoted a dichotomous view of the world with good, hardworking people on one side and selfish, backward enemies on the other. He warmly embraced his devotees as members of the former group while lambasting the political establishment, the IMF, and other "outside forces" as members of the latter group (ibid., 76). Finally, he stressed his dedication to a deeper mission to transform Thailand into a peaceful paradise for its humble, deserving citizens (ibid., 64). Unlike his cold and distant predecessors, Thaksin communicated this narrative to his followers in an open and intimate fashion through direct contact, off-the-cuff speeches, and a weekly radio show that was broadcast to virtually every station in the country (McCargo and Pathmanand 2005, 168; Phongpaichit and Baker 2004, 96).

As Prime Minister, Thaksin further consolidated his charismatic authority by weakening institutions that threatened his power. Like his counterparts in other countries, he filled his cabinet with sycophants upon becoming Prime Minister (Phongpaichit and Baker 2004, 92). He also reformed the constitution to make it costly for cabinet members and congressmen to challenge his authority, resulting in a weak and deferential parliament. Meanwhile, he pushed his aggressive policy agenda through by using "cabinet decisions and executive decrees" (ibid., 96–97). He also stifled dissent by launching "blistering attacks" on his critics and maintaining a tight grip on media outlets (McCargo and Pathmanand 2005, 199).

Although Thaksin's illiberal actions weakened Thailand's young democracy, his followers' adoration of him intensified over the course of his premiership. He therefore swept the February 2005 elections, winning 375 of 500 seats in parliament – a full 127 seats more than he had captured in 2001 – and "came to feel virtually invincible" (Pongsudhirak 2012, 47–48). However, the combination of Thaksin's concentrated power, his overwhelming popularity, and the potentially disastrous consequences of his bold policies led opposing forces – comprised of the military, the crown, and old-guard politicians – to overthrow him a year later, in September 2006 (ibid., 49).

Similar to the junta that ousted Perón in 1955, the Thai military established a caretaker government after forcing Thaksin into exile, outlawed his party, and attempted to eradicate his influence. Yet, as in Argentina, this strategy proved ineffective, and Thaksin continued to exercise his charismatic authority from afar. Despite his physical absence, his movement – represented by a new proxy, the People's Power Party (PPP) – won elections in 2006 and 2007, both of which the military annulled; when it won again in 2008, the military begrudgingly allowed Thaksin's hand-chosen replacement, Samak Sundaravej, to serve a brief nine months as Prime Minister (Phongpaichit and Baker 2013, 610; Pongsudhirak 2012, 55).

A typical anointed successor, Samak lacked the appeal and capacity to stabilize the political situation, which was increasingly characterized by chaos and anti-government protests ("Thai Parliament in emergency session," 2008). This led the military and Constitutional Tribunal to intervene again in September 2008, removing Samak on a legal technicality (Pongsudhirak 2012, 55). In the following month, another of Thaksin's protégés – his brother-in-law, Somchai Wongsawat – stepped in as Prime Minister, only to be quickly overwhelmed by opposition protests (ibid.). By December, the military and Constitutional Tribunal once again banned the leaders of three pro-Thaksin parties from politics until 2012 and helped usher the unelected DP leader, Abhisit Vejjajiva, into the premiership (ibid., 49).

Abhisit's tenure as the military-backed Prime Minister lasted for less than two years. Lacking sufficient political legitimacy, the new leader ratcheted up repression, outlawed dissent, and cracked down on (pro-Thaksin) protests to a much greater degree than Thaksin himself had done during his rule (Hewison 2012, 28). In response to Abhisit's poor leadership, Thaksin's faithful rank-and-file held massive "red shirt" protests demanding the restoration of democracy in 2010 (Thabchumpon and McCargo 2011, 993). In response, the military called for elections in July 2011 and permitted the participation of the pro-Thaksin party – now called the Pheu Thai Party (PTP) – though not of Thaksin himself. As with each prior election since Thaksin's initial rise to power in 2001, the PTP won the elections in a landslide due to the massive support of Thaksin's followers (Hewison 2012, 28).

Unable to personally return to power as Prime Minister, Thaksin once again demonstrated his charismatic style by handpicking a replacement who would not overshadow his authority: his younger sister, Yingluck Shinawatra. Yingluck, who "had no background in politics" and "had previously worked in the family real-estate business," posed little threat to Thaksin's power (Pongsudhirak 2012, 50). To enhance her image and ensure her electoral success, Thaksin referred to Yingluck as "his clone," while his followers demonstrated support by wearing masks with Thaksin's face during the election campaign (Hewison 2012, 30; Phongpaichit and Baker 2013, 617). The strategy worked: the PTP nominated Yingluck as their candidate in May 2011, and she became Thailand's first female Prime Minister with the party's massive victory in the July elections.

As a handpicked successor, however, Yingluck encountered several challenges during her premiership that ultimately led to her ouster in 2014. While she enjoyed the support of the majority of the Thai population upon rising to power, she struggled to control the eruption of opposition ("yellow shirt") protests, which spread across Bangkok in December 2013 and January 2014 and enjoyed the implicit support of the military, the crown, and several businesses (McCargo 2015, 338). Furthermore, she lacked the political skills and independent authority to navigate the fragile truce between her government and the powerful military–crown alliance. Meanwhile, she failed to meet the grand expectations of her brother's followers, who hoped that her government would carry out her brother's transformative mission and, after years of suffering under the military-backed DP rule, deliver peace and prosperity.

In the ultimate demonstration of her weak leadership, Yingluck allowed a dysfunctional and fraudulent snap election to proceed in the spring of 2014, even though the contest was widely perceived to be rigged against her (Mahtani 2014). In contrast to previous elections, which Thaksin's followers took as an opportunity to demonstrate their fervent support, turnout in the 2014 election was less than 50 percent. Pro-Thaksin candidates up and down the ballot campaigned in a "half-hearted" manner, illustrating their reservations about Yingluck's leadership (McCargo 2015, 341–42). Thus, in the midst of rising political unrest, the military ousted Yingluck and staged a coup in May 2014. Subsequently, the Army Commander General, Prayut Chan-o-cha, declared himself Prime Minister (ibid., 343–44).

Amazingly, despite Yingluck's political failure and Prayut's undemocratic rule, which has persisted from 2014 to the time of writing in 2020, Thaksin's disciples have continued to profess faith that their beloved leader will return to Thailand and rescue them from their misery. For example, in the lead-up to sham elections held by the military-backed party in March 2019, Thaksin's followers in the northeast thronged the streets to demonstrate their fervent hope for his return. His symbolic narrative, which claims to "believe in the majority of farmers, in the little people," speaks to these individuals, who recall that "Thaksin was the first to pay attention to this region" almost two decades earlier (Schmidt and Thanthong-Knight 2019). Furthermore, while the military government dubiously declared victory after the 2019 election, Thaksin's PTP won more votes than any other opposition party, arousing suspicions that the military artificially inflated its own vote tally (Tanakasempipat and Thepgumpanat 2019). Although Prayut remains Prime Minister today, Thaksin maintains his position as Thailand's most popular leader – a remarkable feat, given that he has not physically returned to the country since fleeing in 2006. In fact, his charismatic movement appears to be waiting for the right conditions to return to power, perhaps under the authority of its original founder.

In short, Thaksin's TRT provides yet another example of the remarkable resilience of charismatic movements. Thaksin rose in the wake of a severe crisis and consolidated profound, emotional attachments with millions of poor Thais. When the military and opposition forces ousted him in 2006, his charismatic appeal grew more – not less – intense among his followers. Moreover, his followers' loyalty has persisted despite the failures of his anointed successors, indicating the intensely personalistic nature of the followers' attachments. Given their ongoing, fervent support for the charismatic founder, it is possible that Thaksin could return to power in the future, not unlike Juan Perón in 1973.

8.2.4 China

In China, Mao Zedong founded a far more violent, totalitarian, and ideologically coherent party than the other charismatic leaders analyzed in this book. However, from his establishment of the Chinese Communist Party (CCP) in 1949 until his death in 1976, he also struggled against forces of routinization from within his party and on several occasions subordinated the organization to his personal authority. From the outset, Mao used "extraordinary charismatic powers" to establish deep attachments with millions of Chinese citizens (Pye 1976, 250). Similar to other charismatic founders, he achieved this by recognizing the suffering of rural peasants, launching a transformative program of modernization, and constructing a "romantic vision" of the common man with which the people personally identified (ibid.). To do so, he drew on his peasant background to sympathize with his followers while simultaneously glorifying himself as "the greatest figure in Chinese history" (Schram 1967, 386). He also portrayed his revolution as an all-out war against traditional Chinese society and, more than advancing Marxist–Leninist doctrine per se, promised his followers that he would emancipate them from the evils of old society (ibid., 384). In short, it is Mao's profoundly personalistic appeal – rather than his position atop the totalitarian CCP – that caused his followers to pledge their fervent devotion to his movement.

Over the course of his rule, Mao battled against the routinization of his movement and insisted on "plac[ing] the leader above the Party as the sole source of authority and the sole source of truth" (ibid., 386). For example, in 1958, Mao attacked the CCP bureaucracy, which had been growing in size and competence, with the Great Leap Forward – an impractical, haphazard, and ambitious program that clearly aimed to subjugate the party to his personal authority. In contrast to the CCP's prior policies, which had been bureaucratic and modest in scope, the Great Leap Forward "was utopian in substance and chaotic in implementation," reinforcing Mao's charismatic leadership style (Teiwes and Sun 1999, 5). The extraordinarily ambitious and poorly organized nature of the program unleashed a catastrophic famine that caused the death of an estimated 15 to 46 million people (ibid.), causing Mao to back down in 1962 (ibid., 183–84). This disaster led Mao to temporarily cede power to other CCP officials, who sought to deemphasize his charismatic leadership and routinize the party.

Despite the massive failure of the Great Leap Forward, however, Mao staged an impressive comeback four years later in 1966 by launching the Cultural Revolution. Similar to his prior effort, he advanced the Cultural Revolution to attack the CCP organization, which had once again given way to the forces of routinization (Andreas 2007, 439). In particular, Mao used his direct, affective connections with students, workers, and peasants across the country to rebel against entrenched party officials in the name of his larger mission of physical and spiritual transcendence. In contrast to the increasingly rigid and institutionalized CCP, the Cultural Revolution had a "fluid and volatile" structure that hinged exclusively on Mao's charismatic authority (ibid., 441, 451). Unlike the Great Leap Forward, this second violent upheaval was successful: Mao confirmed his position as China's supreme savior and greatly weakened the party beneath him, effectively reversing the impressive efforts of lower-ranking officials to routinize his movement.

When faced with death in 1976, Mao further asserted his charismatic authority by choosing Hua Guofeng, a sycophant, to replace him. Like other anointed successors, Hua was "a relatively unknown figure with a fairly ordinary political legacy [who] lacked the charismatic authority enjoyed by his predecessor" (Weatherly 2010, 141). Hua attempted to shore up legitimacy by arresting more compelling leaders in the CCP, whom he viewed as threats, and – similar to Maduro in Venezuela – used propaganda to stress his personal connection to Mao (ibid.). To avoid betraying the heroic legacy of his predecessor, Hua also pledged to continue outdated, Soviet-era economic policies rather than embrace the market economy (Vogel 2011, 188). Consequently, Hua ultimately failed to establish independent authority. Instead, his "power stemmed entirely from his selection by Mao and from the official positions he held in the party and governmental bureaucracies" (ibid., 185). Just two years into his rule, in December 1978, the ambitious Deng Xiaoping sidelined Hua (ibid., 200).

Unlike Hua, Deng was a far more experienced and talented leader. He also distinguished himself from Mao: unlike the charismatic founder, Deng strengthened the CCP bureaucracy, deemphasized Mao's romantic and utopian visions, and embraced a pragmatic political style that integrated socialism with free market policies (Wong and Lam 2017, 37–38). Interestingly, Deng never sought the chief executive office himself, but rather appointed others to serve in the symbolic role as Chairman or Secretary General while wielding de facto authority from behind the scenes (Zhiyue 2017, 124). Ironically, however, while claiming to prioritize party over personal authority, Deng held a tight grip on Chinese politics up until his death in 1997, creating another succession crisis similar to the one following Mao's death three decades earlier. Indeed, in the aftermath of Deng's demise, China's leadership consisted of "a mostly faceless group of longtime party engineers who have scaled the ranks not by fighting in wars or developing political and economic ideologies but rather by cultivating higher-ranking bureaucrats and divulging as little as possible about their ideas and plans" (Kurlantzick 2011).

In contrast to the bland party officials who succeeded Deng, China's current leader, Xi Jinping, has sought to carve out a new chapter of CCP history based on his own charismatic cult of personality since rising to power in 2012. To do so, he has invoked strategies remarkably similar to the other ambitious self-starters analyzed in this book. For example, Xi has deemphasized the significance of Deng's legacy and has instead played up his symbolic connections to Mao (Myers 2018), "reinstitut[ing] many of Mao's norms and ambitions with gusto" (Wong and Lam 2017, 31). Xi has also enacted bold reforms – such as the "Belt and Road Initiative," an ambitious and expensive project to link China to European countries by building infrastructure along the historic Silk Road. Not only has this initiative bathed the leader in a heroic glow, but also has "been compared to chairman Mao's bold plans in the 1950s to become the proud leader of the Third World" (ibid., 42).

Additionally, Xi has toured the country to communicate directly with ordinary people and "put himself on a pedestal with Mao Zedong, to rekindle a populist image" (Hernández 2018). He has also used his massive propaganda machine to launch programs of social control, such as "Xi Jinping thought" and "Xi Study Strong Nation," all of which incorporate symbols of Mao such as the "Little Red Book" (Bandurski 2019; Myers 2018). To be sure, China's coercive, post totalitarian setting makes it difficult to parse out popular from coerced support. Moreover, Xi's personalistic rise has not coincided with a serious crisis – a necessary condition for consolidating charismatic authority. Nevertheless, his efforts to associate himself with Mao's heroic legacy mimic the strategies of other self-starters in charismatic movements and indicate the broad relevance of these leadership strategies – which appear to be important even in strongly authoritarian settings.

In sum, charismatic movements from across the world have persisted for long stretches of time without undergoing routinization. Although the leaders of these movements have fallen from power or died, their followers have continued to express profound attachments to the leaders' heroic legacies. Moreover, in most cases, new leaders have attempted to tap into the founders' legacies and rekindle citizens' attachments to consolidate independent authority, albeit with varying degrees of success. Although these movements have developed in diverse settings, where variations in regime type (democratic vs. authoritarian), institutional system (presidential vs. parliamentary), and political orientation (from left to right) are marked, the strategies and behaviors of charismatic founders and their successors across these movements seem remarkably similar. Determining the extent to which citizens' attachments to these leaders and movements persist and become reactivated through a personalistic mechanism requires further analysis. Nevertheless, the preliminary evidence suggests that my theory of charismatic revival has broader validity in a geographically and historically diverse set of political movements.

8.3 CONCLUSION

This book has illustrated that, rather than fading away or routinizing, charismatic movements can persist in personalistic form for years after the disappearance of their founders. Consequently, these movements can infuse democracies with illiberal qualities. Specifically, followers' enduring, emotional attachments to the founder and his mission of salvation generate perverse incentives for subsequent politicians to act in similarly heroic ways. To do so, new leaders seek power in times of crisis, when citizens are most vulnerable. Next, to prove they are worthy of the followers' devotion, the new leaders forgo programmatic objectives to implement more dramatic and impressive, yet irresponsible, policies. The leaders enact such policies by draining resources and overriding constraints imposed by political parties and democratic institutions, including the legislative and judiciary branches. In these ways, successors reinforce authoritarian leader behaviors, undermine the development of parties, and perpetuate problems of institutional weakness.

In addition to undermining responsible leadership and party system development, the bold yet fragile nature of successors' policies impedes the quality of democratic representation. At the outset, such programs deliver substantial benefits to many citizens. Yet the extreme and programmatically untethered nature of the policies, combined with their inevitable exhaustion, ends up harming those same individuals. Most insidiously, these audacious policies unleash severe crises that are difficult to overcome, especially in contexts of institutional weakness. Yet rather than delegitimizing the charismatic movement, these crises generate conditions for the movement's regeneration under the leadership of new, yet similarly personalistic, self-starters.

In short, charismatic movements develop fitful but resilient trajectories that perpetually undermine institutional development and democratic representation. The self-reinforcing nature of these movements makes them difficult to overcome. Indeed, my theory suggests that transforming charismatic movements into routinized parties would require a powerful, exogenous force to break the self-perpetuating cycle of personalistic leadership. Future studies should explore the conditions that make such a path of routinization possible.

This book focuses on Peronism and Chavismo. Yet charismatic movements have dominated political systems across the world, including Fujimorismo in Peru, Berlusconi's FI in Italy, Thaksin's PTP in Thailand, and Maoism in China. More recently, charismatic leaders including Viktor Orbán (Hungary), the Kaczyński brothers (Poland), Recep Tayyip Erdoğan (Turkey), and Donald Trump (United States) have risen to power and established transformative movements. These movements have posed alarming threats to democracy and have shown few signs of routinizing. My study reveals an alternative pathway such movements can take after the disappearance of their founders: revival in personalistic form. Furthermore, my theory provides a generalizable framework with which to evaluate the behaviors and relative success of new leaders who attempt to replace their charismatic predecessors. Above all, my findings indicate that charismatic movements have the potential to survive, generate instability, and undermine democracy for years to come.

Bibliography

Abdelal, Rawi, Yoshiko M. Herrera, Alastair Iain Johnston, and Rose McDermott. 2009. "Identity as a Variable." In *Measuring Identity: A Guide for Social Scientists*, eds. Rawi Abdelal, Yoshiko M. Herrera, Alastair Iain Johnston, and Rose McDermott. Cambridge: Cambridge University Press, 17–32.

Abramowitz, Alan, and Jennifer McCoy. 2019. "United States: Racial Resentment, Negative Partisanship, and Polarization in Trump's America." *The Annals of the American Academy* 681: 137–56.

Achen, Christopher H. 1992. "Social Psychology, Demographic Variables, and Linear Regression: Breaking the Iron Triangle in Voting Research." *Political Behavior* 14(3): 195–211.

2002. "Parental Socialization and Rational Party Identification." *Political Behavior* 24(2): 151–70.

Aldrich, John Herbert. 1995. *Why Parties? The Origin and Transformation of Political Parties in America*. Chicago: The University of Chicago Press.

Allison, Paul. 2012. "When Can You Safely Ignore Multicollinearity?" http://statistical horizons.com/multicollinearity (accessed February 1, 2016).

Allison, Scott T., Dafna Eylon, James K. Beggan, and Jennifer Bachelder. 2009. "The Demise of Leadership: Positivity and Negativity Biases in Evaluations of Dead Leaders." *The Leadership Quarterly* 20(2): 115–29.

Alsop, Harry. February 26, 2013. "Italy Elections: Results Breakdown of Lower and Upper Chambers." *Telegraph*. www.telegraph.co.uk/news/worldnews/europe/ italy/9894625/Italy-elections-results-breakdown-of-lower-and-upper-chambers .html (accessed May 1, 2019).

February 13, 2019. "Italy Elections: Results Breakdown of Lower and Upper Chambers." *Telegraph*. www.telegraph.co.uk/news/worldnews/europe/italy/ 9894625/Italy-elections-results-breakdown-of-lower-and-upper-chambers.html (accessed May 1, 2019).

Andreas, Joel. 2007. "The Structure of Charismatic Mobilization: A Case Study of Rebellion During the Chinese Cultural Revolution." *American Sociological Review* 72: 434–58.

Andrews-Lee, Caitlin. 2019a. "The Power of Charisma: Investigating the Neglected Citizen-Politician Linkage in Hugo Chávez's Venezuela." *Journal of Politics in Latin America* 11(3): 298–322.

2019b. "The Revival of Charisma: Experimental Evidence from Argentina and Venezuela." *Comparative Political Studies* 52(5): 687–719.

2020. "The Politics of Succession in Charismatic Movements: Routinization versus Revival in Argentina, Venezuela, and Peru." *Comparative Politics* 52(2): 289–316.

Antonakis, John, Nicolas Bastardoz, Philippe Jacquart, and Boas Shamir. 2016. "Charisma: An Ill-Defined and Ill-Measured Gift." *Annual Review of Organizational Psychology and Organizational Behavior* 3(1): 293–319.

Aponte, Carlos. 2014. "La política social durante las gestiones presidenciales de Hugo Chávez (1999–2012)." Doctoral book, Center for Development Studies, the Central University of Venezuela, Caracas.

Arce, Moisés E., and Julio F. Carrión. 2010. *"Presidential Support in a Context of Crisis and Recovery in Peru, 1985–2008." Journal of Politics in Latin America* 2(1): 31–51.

"Argentina cancela su deuda de 9.810 millones de dólares con el Fondo Monetario Internacional." *El País*, January 3, 2006. https://elpais.com/economia/2006/01/03/actualidad/1136277177_850215.html (accessed May 1, 2019).

"Argentina: Results from the 1995 Presidential Elections." June 31, 1999. Political Database of the Americas; Georgetown University and the Organization of the American States. https://pdba.georgetown.edu/Elecdata/Arg/arg95.html (accessed May 5, 2017).

"Argentine Peso Collapses as Macri's Re-election Chances Drop." *The New York Times*, August 12, 2019. www.nytimes.com/2019/08/12/business/argentine-peso.html (accessed September 25, 2019).

Arias, María Fernanda. 1995. "Charismatic Leadership and the Transition to Democracy: The Rise of Carlos Saúl Menem in Argentine Politics." LANIC Etext Collection, Teresa Lozano Long Institute of Latin American Studies. https://lanic.utexas.edu/project/etext/llilas/tpla/9502.html (accessed April 4, 2019).

Art, David. 2006. *The Politics of the Nazi Past in Germany and Austria*. New York: Cambridge University Press.

Arza, Camila. 2012. "The Politics of Counter-Reform in the Argentine Pension System: Actors, Political Discourse, and Policy Performance: The Politics of Counter-Reform." *International Journal of Social Welfare* 21: 46–60.

Ascher, William. 1984. *Scheming for the Poor: The Politics of Redistribution in Latin America*. Cambridge, MA: Harvard University Press.

Auyero, Javier. 2001. *Poor People's Politics: Peronist Survival Networks and the Legacy of Evita*. Durham, NC: Duke University Press.

Baker, Andy, and Kenneth F. Greene. 2011. "The Latin American Left's Mandate: Free-Market Policies and Issue Voting in New Democracies." *World Politics* 63(1): 43–77.

Bandura, Albert. 1982. "Self-Efficacy Mechanism in Human Agency." *American Psychologist* 37(2): 122–47.

Bandurski, David. December 18, 2018. "Xi Jinping's Story of Reform." *China Media Project*. https://chinamediaproject.org/2018/12/18/putting-numbers-on-chinas-reform-legacy/ (accessed May 1, 2019).

February 13, 2019. "The Dawn of the Little Red Phone." *China Media Project.*
https://chinamediaproject.org/2019/02/13/the-dawn-of-the-little-red-phone/ (accessed
May 1, 2019).

Bass, Bernard M., and Bruce J. Avolio. 1995. "Multifactor Leadership Questionnaire
(MLQ)." http://doi.apa.org/getdoi.cfm?doi=10.1037/t03624–000 (accessed July
22, 2020).

Becerra, Martín. 2015. "Transgresión, Propaganda, Convergencia y Concentración. El
Sistema de Medios en el Kirchnerismo." In *Década ganada? Evaluando el legado
del Kirchnerismo*, eds. Carlos Gervasoni and Enrique Peruzzotti. Buenos Aires:
Debate.

Bellamy, Richard. 2006. "An Italian Story? Berlusconi and Contemporary Democratic
Politics." *Modern Italy* 11(3): 347–51.

Bendix, Reinhard. 1967. "Reflections on Charismatic Leadership." *Asian Survey* 7(6):
341–52.

Bennett, Andrew. 2009. "Process Tracing: A Bayesian Perspective." In *The Oxford
Handbook of Political Methodology*, Edited by Janet M. Box-Steffensmeier,
Henry E. Brady, and David Collier. Oxford University Press, 702–21.

Berg, Bruce L. 2001. *Qualitative Research Methods for the Social Sciences*, 4th ed.
Boston: Allyn & Bacon.

Bernhard, Michael et al. 2020. "Weasel Words and the Analysis of 'Postcommunist'
Politics: A Symposium." *East European Politics and Societies: and Cultures* 34(2):
283–325.

Bersch, Katherine. 2016. "The Merits of Problem-Solving Over Powering: Governance
Reforms in Brazil and Argentina." *Comparative Politics* 48(2): 205–25.

Birnbaum, Sarah. December 25, 2017. "Family Ties and a Presidential Pardon." Public
Radio International. www.pri.org/stories/2017-12-25/family-ties-and-presidential-
pardon-its-greek-tragedy-playing-out-peru (accessed June 1, 2018).

Bohm, Jonathan, and Laurence Alison. 2001. "An Exploratory Study in Methods of
Distinguishing Destructive Cults." *Psychology, Crime & Law* 7(2): 133–65.

Brader, Ted, and Joshua A. Tucker. 2008. "Pathways to Partisanship: Evidence from
Russia." *Post-Soviet Affairs* 24(3): 263–300.

Brambor, Thomas, William Roberts Clark, and Matt Golder. 2006. "Understanding
Interaction Models: Improving Empirical Analyses." *Political Analysis* 14(1):
63–82.

Briceño, Héctor. 2015a. *"Chavistas no Maduristas. Los nuevos actores políticos.
Parte 1." Política UCAB* (67): 1–3.

2015b. "La ùltima elección. Venezuela en la encrucijada eectoral." *Em Debate* 7(4):
16–33.

Brownlee, Jason. 2007. "Hereditary Succession in Modern Autocracies." *World Politics*
59(4): 595–628.

Brubaker, Rogers, Mara Loveman, and Peter Stamatov. 2004. "Ethnicity as Cognition."
Theory and Society 33: 31–64.

Burns, James MacGregor. 1978. *Leadership.* 1st ed. New York: Harper & Row.

Cafiero, Antonio. 2011. *Militancia sin tiempo: Mi vida en el Peronismo.* Buenos Aires:
Planeta.

"Cafiero v. Menem: Un partido con enigmas." July 1, 1988. *La Nación*: 5 (April 10,
2019).

Calvo, Ernesto, and M. Victoria Murillo. 2012. "Argentina: The Persistence of Peronism." *Journal of Democracy* 23(2): 148–61.
Campbell, Angus, Philip E. Converse, Warren E. Miller, and Donald E. Stokes. 1960. *The American Voter.* Unabridged ed. Chicago: University of Chicago Press.
Capriata, Laura. April 13, 2008. "Kirchner Firmó Cada Seis Días Un Decreto de Necesidad y Urgencia." *La Nación.* www.lanacion.com.ar/politica/kirchner-firmo-cada-seis-dias-un-decreto-de-necesidad-y-urgencia-nid1003971 (accessed April 25, 2019).
Capriles, Colette. 2012. "La política por otros medios: Espectáculo y Cesarismo del siglo XXI." *Cuadernos Unimetanos* 30: 54–61.
Carlin, Ryan E., Jonathan Hartlyn, Timothy Hellwig, Gregory Love, Cecilia Martínez-Gallardo, and Matthew Singer. 2016. "Executive Approval Database 1.0." *Executive Approval Project.* www.executiveapproval.org (accessed August 1, 2019).
Carrión, Julio F. 2006. "Public Opinion, Market Reforms, and Democracy in Fujimori's Peru." In *The Fujimori Legacy*, ed. Julio F. Carrión. University Park: Pennsylvania State University Press, 126–49.
Carroll, Rory. 2013. *Comandante: Myth and Reality in Hugo Chávez's Venezuela.* Penguin Press: New York.
Cassese, Nicolás. October 19, 1999. "Cavallo se ilusiona con fagocitar al PJ." *La Nación* 10. www.lanacion.com.ar/politica/cavallo-se-ilusiona-con-fagocitar-al-pj-nid157871/ (accessed April 10, 2019).
cfkargentina.com. "Cristina y Néstor, en fotos." *Sitio Oficial de Cristina Fernández de Kirchner.* www.cfkargentina.com/fotos/ (accessed May 1, 2019).
Chávez, Hugo. February 2, 1999. "Toma de Posesion del Comandante Presidente Hugo Rafael Chávez Frías." *todo Chávez en la web.* www.todochavez.gob.ve/todocha vez/3013-toma-de-posesion-del-comandante-presidente-hugo-rafael-chavez-frias (accessed December 14, 2015).
September 29, 2003a. "Aló Presidente No. 165." *Sistema Bolivariana de Comunicación e Información.* www.alopresidente.gob.ve (accessed December 14, 2015).
October 1, 2003b. "Discurso en el acto de homenaje a los trabajadores de PdVSA y Marinos Mercantes." In *Hugo Chávez Frías: Discursos e intervenciones, Diciembre de 2002 - Enero de 2003*, ed. Fidel Ernesto Vásquez. La Habana: Ediciones Plaza, 11–18.
2003c. "Intervención del Comandante Presidente Hugo Chávez en el estado Cojedes." *todo Chávez en la web.* www.todochavez.gob.ve/todochavez/1463-intervencion-del-comandante-presidente-hugo-chavez-en-el-estado-cojedes (accessed December 14, 2015).
2012. "Golpe de Timón: autocritica para rectificar." In *Golpe de Timón: I consejo de ministros del nuevo ciclo de La Revolución Bolivariana*, eds. Michel Bonnefoy and Francisco Avila. Caracas: Imprenta Nacional y Gaceta Oficial, 17–21.
Cherny, Nicolás. 2014. "La Relación Presidente-Partido de Gobierno en el Kirchnerismo." In *Peronismo y Democracia: Historia y Perspectivas*, Ensayo, eds. Marcos Novaro and Samuel Amaral. Buenos Aires: Edhasa, 143–60.
Ciria, Alberto. 1974. "Peronism Yesterday and Today." *Latin American Perspectives* 1(3): 21–41.

Collier, David. 2011. "Understanding Process Tracing." *PS: Political Science & Politics* 44(4): 823–30.

Collyns, Dan. October 10, 2018. "Peru Opposition Leader Keiko Fujimori Detained over 'Money Laundering.'" *The Guardian.* https://www.theguardian.com/world/2018/oct/10/peru-opposition-leader-keiko-fujimori-detained-in-financial-investigation (accessed August 15, 2019).

Colonna, Lucas. April 25, 2003. "Rodríguez Saá: 'Tienen miedo de que el pueblo pueda votar.'" *La Nación.* www.lanacion.com.ar/politica/rodriguez-saa-tienen-miedo-de-que-el-pueblo-pueda-votar-nid491462/ (accessed April 10, 2019).

Comas, José. *March 28, 1993.* "*Entrevista: 'Estoy haciendo lo que hubiera hecho Perón en esta época.'*" *El País.* https://elpais.com/diario/1993/03/28/internacional/733273209_850215.html (accessed May 24, 2017).

Conover, Pamela Johnston. 1984. "The Influence of Group Identifications on Political Perception and Evaluation." *The Journal of Politics* 46(3): 760–85.

"Consejo Nacional Electoral." www.cne.gob.ve (accessed January 22, 2016).

Consultores 21. 2014. *Public Opinion Data on Government Support, 1999–2008.* Caracas: Consultores 21. Unpublished raw data.

2019. *Perfil 21: Servicio de análisis de entorno.* Caracas. Public Opinion Data.

Converse, Philip E. 1969. "Of Time and Partisan Stability." *Comparative Political Studies* 2(2): 139–71.

Coppedge, Michael. 1997. *Strong Parties and Lame Ducks: Presidential Partyarchy and Factionalism in Venezuela.* Stanford, CA: Stanford University Press.

Corach, Carlos. 2011. *18,885 Días de política: Visiones irreverentes de un país complicado.* Buenos Aires: Sudamericana.

Córdova, Abby. 2009. "Methodological Note: Measuring Relative Wealth Using Household Asset Indicators." *AmericasBarometer Insights* (6): 1–9.

Corrales, Javier, and Michael Penfold. 2015. *Dragon in the Tropics: The Legacy of Hugo Chávez.* 2nd ed. Washington, DC: The Brookings Institution.

Cramer, Katherine J. 2016. *The Politics of Resentment: Rural Consciousness in Wisconsin and the Rise of Scott Walker.* Chicago/London: University of Chicago Press.

Citrin, Jack, and David O. Sears. 2009. "Balancing National and Ethnic Identities: The Psychology of E Pluribus Unum." In *Measuring Identity: A Guide for Social Scientists,* Cambridge/New York: Cambridge University Press.

Cyr, Jennifer. 2013. "Que veinte años no es nada: Hugo Chávez, las elecciones de 2012 y el Continuismo Político Venezolano." *Revista de Ciencia Política* 33(1): 375–91.

2016. "The Pitfalls and Promise of Focus Groups as a Data Collection Method." *Sociological Methods & Research* 45(2): 231–59.

Cyr, Jennifer, and Carlos Meléndez. 2015. "*Understanding (Anti-) Chavismo and (Anti-) Fujimorismo: A Demand-Side Perspective.*" Paper Presented at the Latin American Studies Association Congress. San Juan, Puerto Rico.

Dagatti, Mariano. 2013. "El Quinto Peronismo: Acerca de los Discursos Públicos de *Néstor Kirchner como Presidente del Partido Justicialista.*" Paper presented at the First International Congress of Rhetoric and Interdiscipline (I Congreso Internacional de Retórica e Interdisciplina). Mendoza, Argentina.

Dalton, Russell J., and Martin P. Wattenberg. 2000. "Unthinkable Democracy." In *Parties without Partisans*, eds. Russell J. Dalton and Martin P. Wattenberg. Oxford/New York: Oxford University Press, 3–16.

Damill, Mario, and Roberto Frenkel. 2015. "La economía bajo los Kirchner." In *Década Ganada? Evaluando el legado del Kirchnerismo*, eds. Carlos Gervasoni and Enrique Peruzzotti. Buenos Aires: Debate.

Dargent, Eduardo, and Paula Muñoz. 2016. "Peru: A Close Win for Continuity." *Journal of Democracy* 27(4): 145–58.

Datanálisis: Encuesta Nacional Ómnibus. July 2020. *Indicadores Opinión Pública*. Caracas: National Public Opinion Survey.

"Datanálisis: Oposición aventaja 35 puntos en las elecciones Parlamentarias." November 17, 2015. *informe21.com*. https://informe21.com/politica/datanalisis-opo sicion-aventaja-35-puntos-en-las-elecciones-parlamentarias (accessed December 14, 2015).

Datz, Giselle. 2012. "The Inextricable Link between Sovereign Debt and Pensions in Argentina, 1993–2010." *Latin American Politics and Society* 54(1): 101–26.

Davies, Wyre. November 24, 2015. "Argentina's Macri Faces No Shortage of Challenges." *BBC News*. www.bbc.com/news/world-latin-america-34909489 (accessed April 25, 2019).

D'Elia, Yolanda, and Thais Maingon. 2009. *La Política Social en el Modelo Estado/ Gobierno Venezolano*. Caracas: Instituto Latinoamericano de Investigaciones Sociales.

Democracy in Retreat. 2019. Freedom House. https://freedomhouse.org/report/free dom-world/2019/democracy-retreat (accessed August 20, 2020).

Denis, Roland. September 28, 2015. "Adiós al Chavismo." www.aporrea.org/ideologia/ a214599.html (accessed October 24, 2015).

Di Giorgio, Sebastián. August 8, 2020. "El Albertómetro: qué *dicen las encuestas sobre la cuarentena, la deuda, la justiciar y la inseguridad.*" *Diagonales*. https://diagonales .com/contenido/el-albertmetro-qu-dicen-las-encuestas-sobre-la-cuarentena-la-deuda- la-justicia-y-la-inseguridad/22038?fbclid=IwAR3bEf9PZ2xss6ut2fdlLkm2SpSPK_ l1vkFR3ebSYoA1kVHY4kGwQUO62IA (accessed August 31, 2020).

de Souza, Amaury. 2011. "The Politics of Personality in Brazil." *Journal of Democracy* 22(2): 75–88.

Di Tella, Guido. 1983. *Argentina Under Perón, 1973–76*. St. Antony's/Macmillan Series. London: Palgrave.

Díaz, Joaquín Mugica. January 16, 2018. "Nuevo tiempo en el Peronismo: Quién es quién en la negociación por la unidad." *Infobae*. www.infobae.com/politica/2018/ 01/16/nuevo-tiempo-en-el-peronismo-quien-es-quien-en-la-negociacion-por-la-uni dad/ (accessed May 5, 2019).

Donadio, Rachel. February 28, 2018. "Why Is Silvio Berlusconi Back (Again)?" *The Atlantic*. www.theatlantic.com/international/archive/2018/02/silvio-berlusconi-ital ian-elections/554447/ (accessed April 29, 2019).

Donovan, Mark. 2015. "Berlusconi's Impact and Legacy: Political Parties and the Party System." *Modern Italy* 20(1): 11–24.

Downs, Anthony. 1957. *An Economic Theory of Democracy*. Boston: Addison Wesley.

Druckman, James N., Donald P. Green, James H. Kuklinski, and Arthur Lupia. 2011. "Experimentation in Political Science." In *Cambridge Handbook of Experimental*

Political Science, eds. James N. Druckman, Donald P. Green, James H. Kuklinski, and Arthur Lupia. Cambridge: Cambridge University Press, 3–11.

Eatwell, Roger. 2006. "The Concept and Theory of Charismatic Leadership." *Totalitarian Movements and Political Religions* 7(2): 141–56.

Eberhardt, Lindsay, and Jennifer L. Merolla. 2017. "Shaping Perceptions of Sarah Palin's Charisma: Presentations of Palin in the 2008 Presidential Election." *Journal of Women, Politics & Policy* 38(2): 103–27.

Eisenstadt, S.N. 1968. "Introduction." In *Max Weber: On Charisma and Institution Building*, ed. S.N. Eisenstadt. Chicago: University of Chicago Press, ix–lvi.

Ellner, Steve. 2003. "Introduction: The Search for Explanations." In *Venezuelan Politics in the Chávez Era*, eds. Steve Ellner and Daniel Hellinger. Boulder, CO: Lynne Rienner.

2010. *Rethinking Venezuelan Politics: Class, Conflict, and the Chávez Phenomenon.* Boulder, CO: Lynne Rienner.

2011. "Venezuela's Social-Based Democratic Model: Innovations and Limitations." *Journal of Latin American Studies* 43(3): 421–49.

Ellsworth, Brian. February 2, 2018. "Abstention Looms over Venezuela Opposition in Upcoming Election." *Reuters*. www.reuters.com/article/us-venezuela-politics-absten tion/abstention-looms-over-venezuela-opposition-in-upcoming-election-idUSKBN1F M0IB (accessed March 26, 2018).

España, Luis Pedro. 2014. *Encuesta sobre condiciones de vida (ENCOVI): Venezuela 2014.* Caracas: Universidad Católica Andrés Bello. *Poverty survey.*

"Evita votaría a Cristina, Perón votaría a Taiana, y los dos Juntos a Unidad Ciudadana." October 16, 2017. *Infobae*. www.infobae.com/politica/2017/10/16/ cristina-kirchner-cierra-su-campana-en-racing/ (accessed May 1, 2019).

Fabbrini, Sergio. 2013. "The Rise and Fall of Silvio Berlusconi: Personalization of Politics and Its Limits." *Comparative European Politics* 11(2): 153–71.

Flores-Macias, Gustavo. 2012. *After Neoliberalism? The Left and Economic Reforms in Latin America.* Oxford/New York: Oxford University Press.

Fierman, Julia. 2020. "'I Embrace You with the Affection and Loyalty of Always': Personalism and Exchange in Argentine Populism." *The Journal of Latin American and Caribbean Anthropology* 25(1): 104–22.

Fiorina, Morris P. 1981. *Retrospective Voting in American National Elections.* New Haven, CT: Yale University Press.

Fox, John. 2008. "Detecting Collinearity." In *Applied Regression Analysis and Generalized Linear Models*, Thousand Oaks: Sage Publications, 308–9.

Freedom in the World 2019: Democracy in Retreat. 2020. Freedom House. https:// freedomhouse.org/report/freedom-world/2019/democracy-retreat (accessed August 20, 2020).

Fusco, Pinélides. September 2, 2017. *"Fusco, el fotógrafo del mito de Perón y Evita."* *El País*. https://elpais.com/elpais/2017/08/30/album/1504108014_834194.html#foto_ gal_1 (accessed May 1, 2019).

Gantman, Ernesto R. 2012. "Un modelo fallido de desarrollo: la experiencia Argentina (1989–2001)." *Cuadernos de Relaciones Laborales* 30(2): 327–54.

García-Guadilla, María Pilar. 2012. "Democracia, inclusión y metodologías participa-tivas: La experiencia de los consejos comunales En Venezuela." In *Construyendo democracias y metodologías participativas desde El Sur*, eds. Tomás R Villasante et al. Santiago: Lom Ediciones, 217–42.

Garzia, Diego. 2011. "The Personalization of Politics in Western Democracies: Causes and Consequences on Leader–Follower Relationships." *The Leadership Quarterly* 22(4): 697–709.

Gauna, Aníbal F. 2018. "Populism, Heroism, and Revolution. Chávez's Cultural Performances in Venezuela, 1999–2012." *American Journal of Cultural Sociology* 6(1): 37–59.

GBAO Strategies. 2019. *Venezuela: National Public Opinion Survey*. Caracas. National Public Opinion Survey.

Gélineau, François. 2007. "*Presidents, Political Context, and Economic Accountability: Evidence from Latin America.*" *Political Research Quarterly* 60(3): 415–28.

Gervasoni, Carlos. 2015. "Libertades y derechos políticos, 2003–2014: El Kirchnerismo evaluado desde siete modelos de democracia." In *¿Década Ganada? Evaluando el legado del kirchnerismo*, eds. Carlos Gervasoni and Enrique Peruzzotti. Buenos Aires: Debate.

2018. "Argentina's Declining Party System." In *Party Systems in Latin America*, ed. Scott Mainwaring. New York: Cambridge University Press, 255–90.

Gervasoni, Carlos, and Enrique Peruzzotti. 2015. "Introducción: La larga década krchnerista, ganada, perdida o desperdiciada?" In *Década Ganada? Evaluando el legado del Kirchnerismo*, eds. Carlos Gervasoni and Enrique Peruzzotti. Buenos Aires: Debate.

Gilbert, Jonathan. December 6, 2015. "Her Time Is Up, but Argentina's President Is Not Going Quietly." *New York Times*. www.nytimes.com/2015/12/07/world/americas/her-time-is-up-but-argentinas-president-is-not-going-quietly.html (accessed April 2, 2019).

Gill, Timothy M. December 4, 2017. "No, a Coup Isn't Likely in Venezuela." *The Monkey Cage*. www.washingtonpost.com/news/monkey-cage/wp/2017/12/04/no-a-coup-isnt-likely-in-venezuela-and-if-one-happens-its-unlikely-to-bring-democracy/ (accessed February 2, 2018).

Gillespie, Patrick, and Jorgelina Do Rosario. July 8, 2019. "Macri's Odds of Winning Argentina Race Are Rising, Pollster Says." *Bloomberg*. www.bloomberg.com/news/articles/2019-07-08/macri-s-odds-of-winning-argentina-race-are-rising-pollster-says (accessed June 18, 2020).

Gillespie, Richard. 1982. *Soldiers of Perón: Argentina's Montoneros*. Oxford [Oxfordshire]/New York: Clarendon Press/Oxford University Press.

Giuffrida, Angela. May 9, 2018. "Berlusconi Vows Not to Veto Pact between Italy's Populist Parties." *The Guardian*. www.theguardian.com/world/2018/may/09/berlusconi-vows-not-to-veto-pact-between-italys-populist-parties (accessed April 30, 2019).

Goodwyn, Lawrence. 1978. *The Populist Moment: A Short History of the Agrarian Revolt in America*. New York: Oxford University Press.

Granovetter, Mark S. 1973. "The Strength of Weak Ties." *American Journal of Sociology* 78(6): 1360–80.

Gravil, Roger. 1984. "Guido Di Tella: Argentina under Peron 1973–1976: The Nation's Experience with a Labour-Based Government." *Journal of Latin American Studies* 16(1): 203.

Green, Donald P., Bradley Palmquist, and Eric Schickler. 2002. *Partisan Hearts and Minds: Political Parties and the Social Identities of Voters*. New Haven, CT/London: Yale University Press.

Guadalupe, Alan Soria. October 31, 2020. "A 150 días de la cuarentena, la aprobación de Fernández Detuvo su caída pero crece la preocupación por la economía." *La Nación*. www.lanacion.com.ar/politica/a-150-dias-cuarentena-aprobacion-fernandez-detuvo-nid2420351 (accessed August 31, 2020).

Haberman, Clyde. October 11, 2015. "Children of Argentina's 'Disappeared' Reclaim Past, with Help." *New York Times*. www.nytimes.com/2015/10/12/us/children-of-argentinas-disappeared-reclaim-past-with-help.html (accessed June 1, 2019).

Haslam, S. Alexander, Stephen Reicher, and Michael Platow. 2011. *The New Psychology of Leadership: Identity, Influence, and Power*. New York: Psychology Press.

Hassan, Steven. 1990. *Combatting Cult Mind Control*. Rochester, VT: Park Street Press.

Hawkins, Kirk Andrew. 2010. *Venezuela's Chavismo and Populism in Comparative Perspective*. New York: Cambridge University Press.

Hawkins, Kirk A., and David R. Hansen. 2006. "Dependent Civil Society: The Círculos Bolivarianos in Venezuela." *Latin American Research Review* 41(1): 102–32.

Hawkins, Kirk A., Guillermo Rosas, and Michael E. Johnson. 2011. "The Misiones of the Chávez Government." In *Venezuela's Bolivarian Democracy: Participation, Politics, and Culture under Chávez*, eds. David Smilde and Daniel Hellinger. Durham: Duke University Press, 186–218.

Hawkins, Kirk Andrew, Ryan E. Carlin, Levente Littvay, and Cristóbal Rovira Kaltwasser, eds. 2019. *The Ideational Approach to Populism: Concept, Theory, and Analysis*. London/New York: Routledge.

"Hay que enfrentar la crisis y pulverizarla, dijo Menem." May 7, 1989. *La Nación* 14.

Hernández, Javier C. September 28, 2018. "For Xi Jinping, Being a Man of the People Means Looking the Part." *The New York Times*. www.nytimes.com/2018/09/28/world/asia/xi-jinping-china-propaganda.html (accessed May 1, 2019).

Hewison, Kevin. 2012. "Avoiding Conflict: Thailand after the Red Shirt Uprising." *Political Insight* 3(3): 28–31.

Hicks, Raymond, and Dustin Tingley. 2011. "Causal Mediation Analysis." *The Stata Journal* 11(4): 605–19.

"Histórico: El país saldará en un solo pago la deuda con el FMI." December 16, 2005. *La Nación*. www.lanacion.com.ar/politica/historico-el-pais-saldara-en-un-solo-pago-la-deuda-con-el-fmi-nid765314 (accessed July 5, 2019).

Hoffman, Stanley, and Inge Hoffman. 1968. "The Will to Grandeur: De Gaulle as Political Artist." *Daedalus* 97(3): 829–87.

Hogg, Michael A. 2001. "A Social Identity Theory of Leadership." *Personality and Social Psychology Review* 5(3): 184–200.

Hogg, Michael A., and Scott A. Reid. 2006. "Social Identity, Self-Categorization, and the Communication of Group Norms." *Communication Theory* 16(1): 7–30.

Horwitz, Luisa. June 4, 2020. "Approval Rating Update: Argentina's Alberto Fernández." *Americas Society/Council of the Americas*. www.as-coa.org/articles/approval-rating-update-argentinas-alberto-fernández (accessed August 18, 2020).

House, Robert J., and Jane M. Howell. 1992. "Personality and Charismatic Leadership." *Leadership Quarterly* 3(2): 81–108.

"How Will the Belt and Road Initiative Advance China's Interests?" China Power." May 8, 2017. *China Power Team*. https://chinapower.csis.org/china-belt-and-road-initiative/ (accessed May 1, 2019).

Huckfeldt, Robert. 2001. "The Social Communication of Political Expertise." *American Journal of Political Science* 45(2): 425.

Huckfeldt, Robert, and John Sprague. 1992. "Political Parties and Electoral Mobilization: Political Structure, Social Structure, and the Party Canvass." *American Political Science Review* 86(01): 70–86.

Huddy, Leonie. 2001. "From Social to Political Identity: A Critical Examination of Social Identity Theory." *Political Psychology* 22(1): 127–56.

2013. "From Group Identity to Political Cohesion and Commitment." In *Oxford Handbook of Political Psychology*, eds. Leonie Huddy, David O. Sears, and Jack Levy. New York: Oxford University Press, 737–73.

Hunter, Wendy. 2010. *The Transformation of the Workers' Party in Brazil, 1989–2009*. New York: Cambridge University Press.

Hunter, Wendy, and Timothy J. Power. 2019. "Bolsonaro and Brazil's Illiberal Backlash." *Journal of Democracy* 30(1): 68–82.

Ibrahim, Zuraidah, and John Power. January 5, 2019. "Middle Class and Frustrated in Asia? Populist Politicians Are Seeking You Out in 2019." *South China Morning Post*. www.scmp.com/week-asia/politics/article/2180786/poll-dance-how-asias-politicians-are-mobilising-voting-masses (accessed February 6, 2019).

Imai, Kosuke, Luke Keele, and Dustin Tingley. 2010. "A General Approach to Causal Mediation Analysis." *Psychological Methods* 15(4): 309–34.

"Intervención del Comandante Presidente Hugo Chávez en concentración ¡Triunfo del pueblo!" October 7, 2012. *Todo Chávez en la Web*. www.todochavez.gob.ve/todochavez/26-intervencion-del-comandante-presidente-hugo-chavez-en-concentracion-triunfo-del-pueblo (accessed December 14, 2015).

Iyengar, Shanto. 1994. *Is Anyone Responsible? How Television Frames Political Issues*. Chicago: University of Chicago Press.

Iyengar, Shanto, Yphtach Lelkes, Matthew Levendusky, Neil Malhotra, and Sean J. Westwood. 2019. "The Origins and Consequences of Affective Polarization in the United States." *Annual Review of Political Science* 22(1): 129–46.

James, Daniel. 1988. *Resistance and Integration: Peronism and the Argentine Working Class, 1946–1973*. Cambridge: Cambridge University Press.

Jourdan, Adam, and Eliana Raszewski. May 18, 2019. *Reuters*. https://af.reuters.com/article/worldNews/idAFKCN1SO0C4 (accessed August 15, 2019).

Jowitt, Kenneth. 1992. *New World Disorder: The Leninist Extinction*. Berkeley: University of California Press.

Kampwirth, Karen. 2010. "Introduction." In *Gender and Populism in Latin America*. University Park: Pennsylvania State University Press, 1–24.

Keller, Robert T. 2006. "Transformational Leadership, Initiating Structure, and Substitutes for Leadership: A Longitudinal Study of Research and Development Project Team Performance." *Journal of Applied Psychology* 91(1): 202–10.

Kelly, Janet, and Pedro A. Palma. 2004. "The Syndrome of Economic Decline and the Quest for Change." In *The Unraveling of Representative Democracy in Venezuela*, eds. Jennifer L. McCoy and David J. Myers. Baltimore: Johns Hopkins University Press, 202–30.

Kenny, Paul D. 2017. *Populism and Patronage: Why Populists Win Elections in India, Asia, and Beyond*. 1st ed. Oxford/New York, NY: Oxford University Press.

Key, V.O. 1966. *The Responsible Electorate*. Cambridge: Harvard University Press.

"Kirchner acusó a Menem de dar un 'golpe a la democracia.'" May 14, 2003. *La Nación*. www.lanacion.com.ar/politica/kirchner-acuso-a-menem-de-dar-un-golpe-a-la-democracia-nid496131 (accessed May 1, 2019).

"Kirchner anunció un plan de empleo para los desocupados." October 24, 2003. *La Nación*. www.lanacion.com.ar/politica/kirchner-anuncio-un-plan-de-empleo-para-los-desocupados-nid538547 (accessed April 10, 2019).

Kirkpatrick, Jeane J. 1971. *Leader and Vanguard in Mass Society: A Study of Peronist Argentina*. Cambridge, MA: MIT Press.

Kitschelt, Herbert. 2000. "Linkages between Citizens and Politicians in Democratic Polities." *Comparative Political Studies* 33(6–7): 845–79.

Kitschelt, Herbert, Kirk A. Hawkins, Juan Pablo Luna, Guillermo Rosas, and Elizabeth J. Zechmeister. 2010. "Introduction." In *Latin American Party Systems*, eds. Herbert Kitschelt et al. Cambridge: Cambridge University Press, 1–57.

Klar, Samara. 2013. "The Influence of Competing Identity Primes on Political Preferences." *The Journal of Politics* 75(4): 1108–24.

Koff, Sondra Z., and Stephen P. Koff. 2000. *Italy, from the First to the Second Republic*. London/New York: Routledge.

Koivumaeki, Riitta-Ilona. 2015. "Evading the Constraints of Globalization: Oil and Gas Nationalization in Venezuela and Bolivia." *Comparative Politics* 48(1): 107–25.

Kornblith, Miriam. 2013. "Chavismo after Chávez?" *Journal of Democracy* 24(3): 47–61.

Kostadinova, Tatiana, and Barry Levitt. 2014. "Toward a Theory of Personalist Parties: Concept Formation and Theory Building: Concept Formation and Theory Building." *Politics & Policy* 42(4): 490–512.

Kovalski, Manuel Alcalá. September 5, 2019. "Lessons Learned from the Argentine Economy under Macri." *Brookings*. www.brookings.edu/blog/up-front/2019/09/05/lessons-learned-from-the-argentine-economy-under-macri/ (accessed August 18, 2020).

Krauss, Clifford. December 20, 2001. "Reeling from Riots, Argentina Declares a State of Siege." *The New York Times*. www.nytimes.com/2001/12/20/world/reeling-from-riots-argentina-declares-a-state-of-siege.html (accessed July 5, 2019).

Kronick, Dorothy. November 27, 2015. "Chavismo You'll Have to Bargain With." *Caracas Chronicles*. www.caracaschronicles.com/2015/11/27/you-wont-pick-power-up-off-the-street-youll-have-to-bargain-for-it/ (accessed February 2, 2018).

Kurlantzick, Joshua. September 27, 2011. "After Deng: On China's Transformation." *The Nation*. www.thenation.com/article/after-deng-chinas-transformation/ (accessed August 23, 2019).

Kyle, Jordan, and Yascha Mounk. March 9, 2018. "Why It's so Difficult to Kill a Populist Movement." *The Washington Post*. www.washingtonpost.com/outlook/why-its-so-difficult-to-kill-a-populist-movement/2018/03/09/28e2a7d2-22e6-11e8-badd-7c9f29a55815_story.html?utm_term=.088abc7b932d (accessed March 15, 2018).

Laclau, Ernesto. 2005. *On Populist Reason*. London: Verso.

Lasswell, Harold Dwight. 1948. *Power and Personality*. New York: Norton.

"Latinobarómetro Survey 1996-2015." 2017. *Latinobarómetro*. www.latinobarometro.org/latContents.jsp.

Levitsky, Steven. 1999. "Fujimori and Post-Party Politics in Peru." *Journal of Democracy* 10(3): 78–92.

2003. *Transforming Labor-Based Parties in Latin America: Argentine Peronism in Comparative Perspective.* Cambridge/New York: Cambridge University Press.

2011. "A Surprising Left Turn." *Journal of Democracy* 22(4): 84–94.

Levitsky, Steven, and María Victoria Murillo. 2005. "Building Castles in the Sand? The Politics of Institutional Weakness in Argentina." In *Argentine Democracy: The Politics of Institutional Weakness*, eds. Steven Levitsky and María Victoria Murillo. University Park: Pennsylvania State University Press, 21–44.

Levitsky, Steven, and María Victoria Murillo. 2013. "Building Institutions on Weak Foundations." *Journal of Democracy* 24(2): 93–107.

Levitsky, Steven, and Mauricio Zavaleta. 2016. "Why No Party-Building in Peru?" In *Challenges of Party-Building in Latin America*, eds. Steven Levitsky, James H. Loxton, Brandon Van Dyck, and Jorge Domínguez. New York: Cambridge University Press, 412–39.

Lewis-Beck, Michael S., ed. 2008. *The American Voter Revisited.* Ann Arbor: University of Michigan Press.

Lipset, Seymour Martin, and Stein Rokkan. 1967. "Cleavage Structures, Party Systems, and Voter Alignments: An Introduction." In *Party Systems and Voter Alignments: Cross-National Perspectives*, eds. Seymour Martin Lipset and Stein Rokkan. New York: The Free Press, 1–64.

López Maya, Margarita. 2003. "Hugo Chávez Frías: His Movement and His Presidency." In *Venezuelan Politics in the Chávez Era*, eds. Steve Ellner and Daniel Hellinger. Boulder, CO: Lynne Rienner, 73–92.

2014. "Venezuela: The Political Crisis of Post-Chavismo." *Social Justice* 40(4): 68–87.

2016. *El ocaso del Chavismo.* Caracas: Editorial Alfa.

López Maya, Margarita, and Luis E. Lander. 2000. "La popularidad de Chávez: Base para un proyecto popular?" *Cuestiones Políticas* (24): 8–21.

2011. "Participatory Democracy in Venezuela." In *Venezuela's Bolivarian Democracy: Participation, Politics, and Culture under Chávez*, eds. David Smilde and Daniel Hellinger. Durham: Duke University Press, 58–79.

Love, Gregory J., and Leah C. Windsor. 2018. "Populism and Popular Support: Vertical Accountability, Exogenous Events, and Leader Discourse in Venezuela." *Political Research Quarterly* 71(3): 532–45.

Lowenthal, Abraham F., and David Smilde. June 11, 2019. "Negotiating Venezuela's Transition." *The New York Times.* www.nytimes.com/2019/06/11/opinion/guaido-venezuela-norway.html (accessed July 5, 2019).

Loxton, James, and Steven Levitsky. 2018. "Personalistic Authoritarian Successor Parties in Latin America." In *Life after Dictatorship*, eds. James Loxton and Scott Mainwaring. Cambridge: Cambridge University Press, 113–42.

Loxton, James, and Scott Mainwaring, eds. 2018. *Life after Dictatorship: Authoritarian Successor Parties Worldwide.* Cambridge: Cambridge University Press.

Luna, Juan Pablo. 2014. *Segmented Representation: Political Party Strategies in Unequal Democracies.* Oxford University Press.

Luna, Juan Pablo, and David Altman. 2011. "Uprooted but Stable: Chilean Parties and the Concept of Party System Institutionalization." *Latin American Politics and Society* 53(2): 1–28.

Lupu, Noam. 2013. "Party Brands and Partisanship: Theory with Evidence from a Survey Experiment in Argentina: Party Brands and Partisanship." *American Journal of Political Science* 57(1): 49–64.

2014. "Brand Dilution and the Breakdown of Political Parties in Latin America." *World Politics* 66(4): 561–602.

2015. "Partisanship in Latin America." In *The Latin American Voter*, eds. Ryan E. Carlin, Matthew M. Singer, and Elizabeth J. Zechmeister. Ann Arbor: University of Michigan Press, 226–45.

2016. "The End of the Kirchner Era." *Journal of Democracy* 27(2): 35–49.

Lupu, Noam, and Rachel Beatty Riedl. 2013. "Political Parties and Uncertainty in Developing Democracies," eds. Noam Lupu and Rachel Beatty Riedl. *Comparative Political Studies* 46(11): 1339–65.

Lupu, Noam, and Susan Stokes. 2010. "Democracy, Interrupted: Regime Change and Partisanship in Twentieth-Century Argentina." *Electoral Studies* 29(1): 91–104.

Machado, Jesús. 2008. *Estudio sobre cooperativas en cuatro estados de Venezuela.* Caracas: Fundación Centro Gumilla. Survey Report.

2009. *Estudio cuantitativo de opinión sobre los consejos comunales.* Caracas: Fundación Centro Gumilla. Survey Report.

Madsen, Douglas, and Peter G. Snow. 1991. *The Charismatic Bond: Political Behavior in Time of Crisis.* Cambridge: Harvard University Press.

Mahtani, Shibani. March 25, 2014. "'Rigged' and 'Robbed': Thaksin Shinawatra Says Thai Elections Weren't Free or Fair." *The Washington Post.* www.washingtonpost .com/world/asia_pacific/rigged-androbbed-thaksin-shinawatra-says-thai-elections-werent-free-or-fair/2019/03/25/88345d0e-4cbe-11e9-8cfc-2c5d0999c21e_story.html (accessed August 15, 2019).

Maingon, Thais. 2004. "Política social en Venezuela: 1999–2003." *Cuadernos del CENDES* 21(55): 47–73.

2016. "La política social y el *régimen de bienestar.*" *Estudios Latinoamericanos, Nueva Época (38):* 115–43.

Mainwaring, Scott. 2012. "From Representative Democracy to Participatory Competitive Authoritarianism: Hugo Chávez and Venezuelan Politics." *Perspectives on Politics* 10(4): 955–67.

2014. "Party System Institutionalization: Reflections Based on the Asian Cases." In *Party System Institutionalization in Asia: Democracies, Autocracies, and Shadows of the Past*, eds. Allen Hicken and Erik Martinez Kuhonta. New York: Cambridge University Press, 328–48.

2016. "Party System Institutionalization, Party Collapse and Party Building." *Government and Opposition* 51(4): 691–716.

2018. "Introduction." In *Party Systems in Latin America*, ed. Scott Mainwaring. Cambridge: Cambridge University Press, 1–14.

Mainwaring, Scott, and Timothy Scully, eds. 1995. *Building Democratic Institutions: Party Systems in Latin America.* Stanford: Stanford University Press.

Mainwaring, Scott, and Edurne Zoco. 2007. "Political Sequences and the Stabilization of Interparty Competition: Electoral Volatility in Old and New Democracies." *Party Politics* 13(2): 155–78.

Mander, Benedict. April 27, 2020. "Covid-19 Has Silver Linings for Argentina's President." *Financial Times.* www.ft.com/content/0c43684d-3aae-4b0d-a368-1bcfb401b85c (accessed August 17, 2020).

Manucci, Luca. 2020. *Populism and Collective Memory: Comparing Fascist Legacies in Western Europe*. Abingdon, Oxon: Routledge.

Maranell, Gary M. 1970. "The Evaluation of Presidents: An Extension of the Schlesinger Polls." *The Journal of American History* 57(1): 104–13.

"Martha Chávez aplaude ataque a monumento 'Ojo que Llora.'" September 25, 2007. *Perú 21*. http://archivo.peru21.pe/noticia/64913/martha-chavez-aplaude-ataque-monumentoojo-que-llora (accessed July 30, 2020).

Martínez Meucci, Miguel Angel, and Rebecca V. de Lustgarten. 2014. "La Narrativa revolucionaria del Chavismo." Paper presented at the Latin American Studies Association Congress, Chicago.

McAllister, Ian. 2007. "The Personalization of Politics." In *The Oxford Handbook of Political Behavior*, eds. Russell J. Dalton and Hans-Dieter Klingemann. New York: Oxford University Press, 571–88.

McCargo, Duncan. 2015. "Thailand in 2014: The Trouble with Magic Swords." *Southeast Asian Affairs* 337–58.

McCargo, Duncan, and Ukrist Pathmanand. 2005. *The Thaksinization of Thailand*. Copenhagen S, Denmark: NIAS Press.

McClintock, Cynthia. 2006. "A 'Left Turn' in Latin America? An Unlikely Comeback in Peru." *Journal of Democracy* 17(4): 95–109.

McDonnell, Duncan. 2016. "Populist Leaders and Coterie Charisma." *Political Studies* 64(3): 719–33.

McGuire, James. 1995. "Political Parties and Democracy in Argentina." In *Building Democratic Institutions*, eds. Scott Mainwaring and Timothy R. Scully. Stanford: Stanford University Press, 200–46.

1997. *Peronism without Perón: Unions, Parties, and Democracy in Argentina*. Stanford: Stanford University Press.

2014. "Sources of Populist Resilience: Peronismo, Getulismo, and Chavismo." Unpublished Manuscript.

Medina, Medófilo. 2003. "La ley habilitante o el detonante 'A' de la crisis política." In *Venezuela: Confrontación social y polarización política*, eds. Medófilo Medina and Margarita López Maya. Bogotá: Ediciones Aurora, 20–35.

Meléndez, Carlos. 2019. *El mal menor: Vínculos políticos en el Perú posterior al colapso del sistema de partidos*. Lima: Instituto de Estudios Peruanos.

Meléndez, Carlos, and Cristóbal Rovira Kaltwasser. 2019. "Political Identities: The Missing Link in the Study of Populism." *Party Politics* 25(4): 520–33.

"Menem, candidato presidencial del PJ." July 10, 1988. *La Nación*: 1 (April 10, 2019).

"Menem: 'No ofrezco falsas promesas, sino trabajo y más trabajo.'" May 6, 1989. *La Nación*: (April 10, 2019)

Merolla, Jennifer L., and Elizabeth J. Zechmeister. 2009a. "Las percepciones de liderazgo en el contexto de las elecciones mexicanas de 2006." *Política y Gobierno* Special Volume: 41–81.

2009b. *Democracy at Risk: How Terrorist Threats Affect the Public*. Chicago: The University of Chicago Press.

2011. "The Nature, Determinants, and Consequences of Chávez's Charisma: Evidence from a Study of Venezuelan Public Opinion." *Comparative Political Studies* 44(1): 28–54.

Merolla, Jennifer L., Jennifer M. Ramos, and Elizabeth J. Zechmeister. 2007. "Crisis, Charisma, and Consequences: Evidence from the 2004 U.S. Presidential Election." *The Journal of Politics* 69(1): 30–42.

Michelutti, Lucia. 2017. "'We Are All Chávez': Charisma as an Embodied Experience." *Latin American Perspectives* 44(1): 232–50.

Moffitt, Benjamin. 2015. "How to Perform Crisis: A Model for Understanding the Key Role of Crisis in Contemporary Populism." *Government and Opposition* 50(2): 189–217.

Moffitt, Benjamin and Simon Tormey. 2014. "Rethinking Populism: Politics, Mediatisation and Political Style." *Political Studies* 62: 381–97.

Mora y Araujo, Manuel. 2011. *La Argentina bipolar: Los vaivenes de la opinión pública: 1983–2011*. Buenos Aires: Sudamericana.

Morales, Maru P. July 3, 2016. "Ni los Chavistas quieren que Maduro siga gobernando Venezuela." *La Patilla*. www.lapatilla.com/2016/07/03/ni-los-chavistas-quieren-que-maduro-siga-gobernando-venezuela/ (accessed October 2, 2017).

Morgan, Jana. 2007. "Partisanship during the Collapse of Venezuela's Party System." *Latin American Research Review* 42(1): 78–98.

2011. *Bankrupt Representation and Party System Collapse*. University Park: Pennsylvania State University Press.

Mudde, Cas. 2007. *Populist Radical Right Parties in Europe*. Cambridge: Cambridge University Press.

Mudde, Cas, and Cristóbal Rovira Kaltwasser. 2017. *Populism: A Very Short Introduction*. New York, NY: Oxford University Press.

Murillo, María Victoria, and S.J. Rodrigo Zarazaga. 2020. "Argentina: Peronism Returns." *Journal of Democracy* 31(2): 125–36.

Myers, Steven Lee. November 5, 2018. "China's Leader, Hogging Spotlight, Elbows Communist Titan Aside." *The New York Times*. www.nytimes.com/2018/11/05/world/asia/china-xi-jinping-deng-xiaoping.html (accessed May 1, 2019).

Natanson, Phoebe. February 25, 2018. "Despite Ban from Public Office, Berlusconi Seeks Political Comeback at 81." *ABC News*. https://abcnews.go.com/International/ban-public-office-berlusconi-seeks-political-comeback-81/story?id=53249770 (accessed May 1, 2019).

Niemi, Richard G., and M. Kent Jennings. 1991. "Issues and Inheritance in the Formation of Party Identification." *American Journal of Political Science* 35(4): 970.

Nogueira, Roberto Martínez. 2015. "La Gestión Pública Durante El Kirchnerismo." In *Década ganada? Evaluando el legado del Kirchnerismo*, eds. Carlos Gervasoni and Enrique Peruzzotti. Buenos Aires: Debate.

O'Donnell, Guillermo A. 1996. "Illusions about Consolidation." *Journal of Democracy* 7(2): 34–51.

Ollier, María Matilde. 2010. "El liderazgo político en democracias de baja institucionalización (El caso del Peronismo en la Argentina)." *Revista de sociología* (24): 127–50.

2015. "El ciclo de las presidencias dominantes: *Néstor y Cristina Kirchner (2003–2013)*." In *Década ganada? Evaluando el legado del Kirchnerismo*, eds. Carlos Gervasoni and Enrique Peruzzotti. Buenos Aires: Debate.

"ONPE ya tiene resultados al 100% de actas procesadas." April 21, 2016. *El Comercio*. https://elcomercio.pe/politica/elecciones/onpe-resultados-100-actas-procesadas-395110 (accessed May 1, 2019).

Ostiguy, Pierre. 2009. "Argentina's Double Political Spectrum: Party System, Political Identities, and Strategies, 1944–2007." Kellogg Institute. Working Paper #361.

Ostiguy, Pierre. 2017. "Populism: A Socio-Cultural Approach." In *The Oxford Handbook of Populism*, eds. Cristóbal Rovira Kaltwasser, Paull Taggart, Paulina Ochoa Espejo, and Pierre Ostiguy. New York: Oxford University Press, 73–97.

Ostiguy, Pierre, and Kenneth M. Roberts. 2016. "Putting Trump in Comparative Perspective: Populism and the Politicization of the Sociocultural Low." *Brown Journal of World Affairs* 23(1): 25–50.

Page, Joseph A. September 20, 1981. "Evita: The True Life and Strange Cult of the Long-Running Legend." *The Washington Post*. www.washingtonpost.com/archive/lifestyle/style/1981/09/20/evita-the-true-life-and-strange-cult-of-the-long-running-legend/0b98a070-dd65-44e1-846e-35f8c20c918b/ (accessed July 27, 2020).

Page, Joseph A. 1983. *Perón, a Biography*. 1st ed. New York: Random House.

Paladini, Eduardo. April 14, 2019. "Tres nuevas encuestas: La pelea Macri – Cristina y efecto Lavagna en el Balotaje." *Clarín*. www.clarin.com/politica/nuevas-encuestas-pelea-macri-cristina-efecto-lavagna-balotaje_0_rxJ58kRIl.html (accessed July 10, 2019).

Panebianco, Angelo. 1988. *Political Parties: Organization and Power*. Cambridge/New York: Cambridge University Press.

Pappas, Takis S. 2012. "Political Charisma Revisited, and Reclaimed for Political Science." Committee on Concepts and Methods, Working Paper Series.

  2016. "Are Populist Leaders 'Charismatic'? The Evidence from Europe." *Constellations* 23(3): 378–90.

  2019. *Populism and Liberal Democracy: A Comparative and Theoretical Analysis*. 1st ed. Oxford: Oxford University Press.

Parker, Dick. 2005. "Chávez and the Search for an Alternative to Neoliberalism." *Latin American Perspectives* 32(2): 39–50.

"Pedro Pablo Kuczynski y *César Acuña en segundo lugar tras Keiko Fujimori, según Ipsos.*" January 17, 2016. Diario Correo. https://diariocorreo.pe/politica/pedro-pablo-kuczynski-y-cesar-acuna-en-segundo-lugar-tras-keiko-fujimori-segun-ipsos-647235/ (accessed May 1, 2019).

Perón, Juan Domingo. 1974. *La comunidad organizada*. Buenos Aires: Fundación Evita.

"Peru's Fujimori, Pardon Annulled, Forced Back to Prison." January 23, 2019. *Reuters*. www.reuters.com/article/idUSKCN1PI0BL (accessed May 1, 2019).

Phongpaichit, Pasuk, and Christopher J. Baker. 2004. *Thaksin: The Business of Politics in Thailand*. Chiang Mai, Thailand: Silkworm Books.

  2013. "Reviving Democracy at Thailand's 2011 Election." *Asian Survey* 53(4): 607–28.

Pion-Berlin, David. 1983. "Political Repression and Economic Doctrines: The Case of Argentina." *Comparative Political Studies* 16(1): 37–66.

Plotkin, Mariano Ben. 2002. *Mañana es san Perón: A Cultural History of Peron's Argentina*. Wilmington: Scholarly Resources.

Pongsudhirak, Thitinan. 2012. "Southeast Asia: Thailand's Uneasy Passage." *Journal of Democracy* 23(2): 47–61.

Primera, Maye. July 1, 2011. "Chávez anuncia que tiene cáncer." *El País*. https://elpais.com/internacional/2011/07/01/actualidad/1309471203_850215.html (accessed July 16, 2019).

"Progresar Ya No Es Una Política Focalizada Sino Que Pasamos a Universalizar El Derecho a Estudiar." March 12, 2015. *Sitio Oficial de Cristina Fernández de Kirchner*. www.cfkargentina.com/cristina-kirchner-discurso-progresar-estudiantes/ (accessed April 26, 2019).

Przeworski, Adam, and Henry Teune. 1970. *The Logic of Comparative Social Inquiry*. New York: Wiley-Interscience.

Pye, Lucian W. 1976. *Mao Tse-Tung: The Man in the Leader*. New York: Basic Books.

Quiroga, Hugo. 2005. *La Argentina en Emergencia Permanente*. Buenos Aires: Edhasa.

Ramirez, Leo. March 5, 2014. "5 Myths about the Venezuela Crisis." www.pri.org/stories/2014-03-05/5-myths-about-venezuela-crisis (accessed May 1, 2019).

Rapoza, Kenneth. April 17, 2019. "It's Looking Terrible Right Now for President Macri in Argentina." *Forbes*. www.forbes.com/sites/kenrapoza/2019/04/17/its-looking-terrible-right-now-for-president-macri-in-argentina/#1e6174b4356f (accessed May 1, 2019).

Raszewski, Eliana. June 18, 2015. "Scioli Será Único Candidato Oficialista En Primarias de Argentina Tras Dimisión de Rival." *Reuters*. https://lta.reuters.com/articulo/latinoamerica-politica-argentina-eleccio-idLTAKBN0OY1BZ20150618 (accessed April 20, 2019).

Rebossio, Alejandro. September 1, 2012. "Argentina Comienza a Debatir una Segunda Reeleción de Fernández." *El País*. https://elpais.com/internacional/2012/09/01/actualidad/1346521869_615086.html (accessed August 13, 2020).

Reinbold, Fabian. February 20, 2013. "'Only Silvio Can Save Italy.'" *Spiegel International*. www.spiegel.de/international/europe/silvio-berlusconi-followers-loyal-as-ever-ahead-of-italian-elections-a-884532.html (accessed April 30, 2019).

"Replanteo En El Justicialismo Tras El Triunfo de Carlos Menem." July 11, 1988. *La Nación*: 6 (April 10, 2019).

Rhodes-Purdy, Matthew. 2015. "Participatory Populism: Theory and Evidence from Bolivarian Venezuela." *Political Research Quarterly* 68(3): 415–27.

Riedl, Rachel Beatty. 2014. *Authoritarian Origins of Democratic Party Systems in Africa*. Cambridge/New York: Cambridge University Press.

Roberts, Kenneth M. 2007. "Latin America's Populist Revival." *SAIS Review* 27(1): 3–15.

2008. "The Mobilization of Opposition to Economic Liberalization." *Annual Review of Political Science* 11(1): 327–49.

2013. "Market Reform, Programmatic (De)Alignment, and Party System Stability in Latin America" *Comparative Political Studies* 46(11): 1422–52.

2014. *Changing Course in Latin America: Party Systems in the Neoliberal Era*. New York: Cambridge University Press.

Rodríguez, Martín. April 26, 2019. "Órden Queremos Todos." *La Política Online*. www.lapoliticaonline.com/nota/martin-rodriguez-orden-queremos-todos/?fbclid=IwAR1dOFrdlchOhR1QHUM06XGgkhIw3F4sftoIldTqbTMDBxRJq9fqlIPi4ls (accessed April 26, 2019).

Rodríguez, Martín, and Pablo Touzon. 2020. *La Grieta Desnuda: El Macrismo y su Época*. 2nd ed. Autonomous City of Buenos Aires: Capital Intelectual.

Romer & Associates: Survey 11, May–June 1992 [dataset]. Estudio Graciela C. Romer Y Asociados [producer]. Ithaca, NY: Roper Center for Public Opinion Research, *RoperExpress* [distributor] (February 25, 2019).

Romero, Simon. May 27, 2011. "A Second Fujimori Contends for Peru's Presidency." *The New York Times*. https://www.nytimes.com/2011/05/28/world/americas/ 28peru.html (accessed July 30, 2020).

Rondón, Andrés Miguel. *June 29, 2017*. "The Long, Slow Death of Chavismo." *The Atlantic*. www.theatlantic.com/international/archive/2017/06/maduro-venezuela-protest-chavez/532149/ (accessed February 8, 2018).

Rossi, Federico M. 2013. "Peronism." In *The Wiley-Blackwell Encyclopedia of Social and Political Movements*, eds. David A. Snow, Donatella della Porta, Bert Klandermans, and Doug McAdam, 1–3. https://doi.org/10.1002/9780470674871 .wbespm366

Rovira Kaltwasser, Cristóbal, Paul Taggart, Paulina Ochoa Espejo, and Pierre Ostiguy. 2017. "Populism: An Overview of the Concept and the State of the Art." In *The Oxford Handbook of Populism*, eds. Cristóbal Rovira Kaltwasser, Paul Taggart, Paulina Ochoa Espejo, and Pierre Ostiguy. Oxford: Oxford University Press, 1–23.

Sachs, Jeffrey D. 1989. "Social Conflict and Populist Policies in Latin America." *NBER Working Paper*, 2897.

Salvia, Agustín. 2015. "Heterogeneidades estructurales y desigualdades sociales persistentes." In *Década ganada? Evaluando el legado del Kirchnerismo*, eds. Carlos Gervasoni and Enrique Peruzzotti. Buenos Aires: Debate.

Samuels, David, and Cesar Zucco. 2014. "The Power of Partisanship in Brazil: Evidence from Survey Experiments." *American Journal of Political Science* 58(1): 212–25.

2015. Crafting Mass Partisanship at the Grass Roots. *British Journal of Political Science* 45(4): 755–75.

Scharfenberg, Ewald. April 2, 2013. "Maduro dice que un 'pajarito' con el espíritu de Chávez lo bendijo." *El País*. https://elpais.com/internacional/2013/04/02/actuali dad/1364930548_441291.html (accessed May 1, 2018).

Schattschneider, E.E. 1942. *Party Government*. Westport, CT: Greenwood Press.

Schlesinger, Arthur M. 1960. *The Age of Roosevelt. 3: The Politics of Upheaval*. Boston: Houghton Mifflin Comp.

Schlozman, Daniel. 2015. *When Movements Anchor Parties: Electoral Alignments in American History*. Princeton: Princeton University Press.

Schmidt, Blake, and Randy Thanthong-Knight. March 19, 2019. "An Exiled Billionaire Haunts Thailand." *Bloomberg Businessweek*. www.bloomberg.com/news/articles/ 2019-03-19/exiled-billionaire-thaksin-shinawatra-haunts-thailand-s-elections (accessed September 11, 2019).

Schram, Stuart R. 1967. "Mao Tse-Tung as a Charismatic Leader." *Asian Survey* 7(6): 383–88.

Sears, David O. 2001. "The Role of Affect in Symbolic Politics." In *Citizens and Politics*, ed. James H. Kuklinski. Cambridge: Cambridge University Press, 14–40.

Seawright, Jason. 2012. *Party-System Collapse: The Roots of Crisis in Peru and Venezuela*. Stanford, CA: Stanford University Press.

Seawright, Jason, and John Gerring. 2008. "Case Selection Techniques in Case Study Research: A Menu of Qualitative and Quantitative Options." *Political Research Quarterly* 61(2): 294–308.

Sexton, Renard. December 15, 2009. "Berlusconi the Survivor." *FiveThirtyEight*. https://fivethirtyeight.com/features/berlusconi-survivor/ (accessed April 30, 2019).

Shils, Edward. 1965. "Charisma, Order, and Status." *American Sociological Review* 30(2): 199.

"Silvio Berlusconi: Italy's Perpetual Powerbroker." May 29, 2019. *BBC News*. www .bbc.com/news/world-europe-11981754 (accessed August 10, 2019).

Singer, Margaret. 2003. *Cults in Our Midst: The Continuing Fight Against Their Hidden Menace*. Revised Edition. San Francisco: Jossey-Bass.

Smilde, David. 2011. "Introduction: Participation, Politics, and Culture." In *Venezuela's Bolivarian Democracy: Participation, Politics, and Culture under Chávez*, eds. David Smilde and Daniel Hellinger. Durham: Duke University Press, 1–27.

Smith, Philip. 2000. "Culture and Charisma: Outline of a Theory." *Acta Sociologica* 43(2): 101–11.

Spruyt, Bram, Gil Keppens, and Filip Van Droogenbroeck. 2016. "Who Supports Populism and What Attracts People to It?" *Political Research Quarterly* 69(2): 335–46.

Steffens, Niklas K., Kim Peters, S. Alexander Haslam, and Rolf van Dick. 2017. "Dying for Charisma: Leaders' Inspirational Appeal Increases Post-Mortem." *The Leadership Quarterly* 28(4): 530–42.

Stoyan, Alissandra T. 2020. "Ambitious Reform via Constituent Assemblies: Determinants of Success in Contemporary Latin America." *Studies in Comparative International Development* 55: 99–121.

Streb, Jorge M. 2015. "Evaluaciones econtradas sobre el desempeño económico Argentino 2003–2013." In *Década Ganada? Evaluando el legado del Kirchnerismo*, eds. Carlos Gervasoni and Enrique Peruzzotti. Buenos Aires: Debate.

Sturzenegger, Federico. September 4, 2019. "Macri's Macro: The Meandering Road to Stability and Growth." *Brookings*. www.brookings.edu/bpea-articles/macris-macro-the-meandering-road-to-stability-and-growth/ (accessed August 18, 2020).

Sued, Gabriel. April 25, 2003. "Soy el mejor discípulo de Perón." *La Nación*. www .lanacion.com.ar/politica/menem-soy-el-mejor-discipulo-de-peron-nid491459 (accessed April 15, 2019).

Sugiyama, Natasha Borges, and Wendy Hunter. 2013. "Whither Clientelism? Good Governance and Brazil's Bolsa Família Program." *Comparative Politics* 46(1): 43–62.

Tajfel, H. 1974. "Social Identity and Intergroup Behaviour." *Social Science Information* 13(2): 65–93.

Tanaka, Martín. 2011. "A Vote for Moderate Change." *Journal of Democracy* 22(4): 75–83.

Tanakasempipat, Patpicha, and Panarat Thepgumpanat. April 7, 2019. "Manipulation Suspicions Mount in Thailand's Post-Coup Election." *Reuters*. www.reuters.com/ article/us-thailand-election-establishment-analy/manipulation-suspicions-mount-in-thailands-post-coup-election-idUSKCN1RJ07E (accessed May 1, 2019).

Taub, Amanda, and Max Fisher. May 6, 2017. "In Venezuela's Chaos, Elites Play a High-Stakes Game for Survival." *The New York Times*. www.nytimes.com/2017/ 05/06/world/americas/venezuela-unrest-protests.html?mcubz=0&_r=0 (accessed May 1, 2019).

Taylor, Verta. 1989. "Social Movement Continuity: The Women's Movement in Abeyance." *American Sociological Review* 54(5): 761.

"Thai Parliament in Emergency Session." August 31, 2008. *The New York Times*. https://www.nytimes.com/2008/08/31/world/asia/31iht-thai.1.15765157.html? searchResultPosition=1 (accessed September 12, 2019).

Tegel, Simeon. December 27, 2017. "Pardon of Peruvian Autocrat Fujimori Brings His Powerful Family Back into the Spotlight." *The Washington Post*. www .washingtonpost.com/world/the_americas/pardon-of-peruvian-autocrat-amid-political-maelstrom-brings-fujimoris-back-to-spotlight/2017/12/27/2a88b736-ea90-11e7-956e-baea358f9725_story.html (accessed June 1, 2018).

Teiwes, Frederick C., and Warren Sun. 1999. *China's Road to Disaster: Mao, Central Politicians, and Provincial Leaders in the Unfolding of the Great Leap Forward, 1955–1959*. Armonk, NY: M.E. Sharpe.

Thabchumpon, Naruemon, and Duncan McCargo. 2011. "Urbanized Villagers in the 2010 Thai Redshirt Protests." *Asian Survey* 51(6): 993–1018.

The AmericasBarometer: Venezuela, 2007. The Latin American Public Opinion Project (LAPOP). Public Opinion Data. www.LapopSurveys.org.

The World Bank Open Data: Argentina 2018. 2018. The World Bank. Public Opinion Data. www.data.worldbank.org (accessed February 15, 2018).

The World Bank in Peru: Overview. April 2019. The World Bank. www.worldbank .org/en/country/peru/overview (accessed September 10, 2019).

"Triumph for Perón." 1973. *The New York Times*: 42 (August 1, 2019).

Tucker, Robert C. 1968. "The Theory of Charismatic Leadership." *Daedalus* 97(3): 731–56.

United States Information Agency [USIA]. USIA Poll # 1985-I85110: Youth Attitudes Survey [dataset]. 1985-I85110. Consultoria Interdisciplinaria en Desarrollo S.A. (CID) [producer]. Ithaca, NY: Roper Center for Public Opinion Research, Roper*Express* [distributor] (February 25, 2019).

Urbinati, Nadia. 2019. *Me the People: How Populism Transforms Democracy*. Cambridge: Harvard University Press.

Usborne, David. March 6, 2013. "Death of Venezuelan President Hugo Chavez Leaves Tears – and a Nation Divided." *Independent*. www.independent.co.uk/news/world/americas/death-of-venezuelan-president-hugo-chavez-leaves-tears-and-a-nation-divided-8521706.html (accessed May 1, 2018).

USIA Poll #1985-I85110: Youth Attitudes Survey, October–November 1985 [dataset]. Consultoria Interdisciplinaria en Desarrollo S.A. (CID) [producer]. Ithaca, NY: Roper Center for Public Opinion Research, Roper*Express* [distributor] (April 2, 2019).

Van der Brug, Wouter, and Anthony Mughan. 2007. "Charisma, Leader Effects and Support for Right-Wing Populist Parties." *Party Politics* 13(1): 29–51.

Van Vugt, Mark, and Claire M. Hart. 2004. "Social Identity as Social Glue: The Origins of Group Loyalty." *Journal of Personality and Social Psychology* 86(4): 585–98.

Vavreck, Lynn. 2009. *The Message Matters: The Economy and Presidential Campaigns*. Princeton, NJ: Princeton University Press.

Venezuela Profile. 2018. Freedom House. https://freedomhouse.org/report/freedom-world/2018/venezuela (accessed February 18, 2018).

Ventura, Adrián. April 14, 1999. "Menem conducirá el PJ hasta el 2003." *La Nación* 6.

Vergara, Alberto. 2018. "Latin America's Shifting Politics: Virtue, Fortune, and Failure in Peru." *Journal of Democracy* 29(4): 65–76.

Villasmil Bond, Ricardo. 2005. *Lecciones aprendidas de política económica en Venezuela: 1936–2004*. 1st ed. Caracas: Ildis.

Vogel, Ezra F. 2011. *Deng Xiaoping and the Transformation of China*. Cambridge: The Belknap Press of Harvard University Press.

@VTVcanal8. December 8, 2016. "Un Chávez luminoso caminó por las calles de Caracas este día de la Lealtad [Twitter Post]." https://twitter.com/vtvcanal8/status/807018444340109312 (accessed December 2, 2017).

Waisman, Carlos H. 1987. *Reversal of Development in Argentina: Postwar Counterrevolutionary Policies and Their Structural Consequences*. Princeton, NJ: Princeton University Press.

Ware, Alan. 1996. *Political Parties and Party Systems*. Oxford/New York: Oxford University Press.

Weatherly, Robert. 2010. *Mao's Forgotten Successor: The Political Career of Hua Guofeng*. New York/Cambridge, UK: Palgrave Macmillan.

Weber, Max. 1968. "The Sociology of Charismatic Authority." In *Max Weber: On Charisma and Institution Building*. ed. S.N. Eisenstadt. Chicago: University of Chicago Press, 18–27.

1922/1978. *Economy and Society: An Outline of Interpretive Sociology*. Eds. Guenther Roth and Claus Wittich. Berkeley: University of California Press.

Weyland, Kurt. 2001. "Clarifying a Contested Concept: Populism in the Study of Latin American Politics." *Comparative Politics* 34(1): 1.

2002. *The Politics of Market Reform in Fragile Democracies: Argentina, Brazil, Peru, and Venezuela*. Princeton/Oxford: Princeton University Press.

2003. "Economic Voting Reconsidered: Crisis and Charisma in the Election of Hugo Chávez." *Comparative Political Studies* 36(7): 822–48.

2006. "The Rise and Decline of Fujimori's Neopopulist Leadership." In *The Fujimori Legacy: The Rise of Electoral Authoritarianism in Peru*, ed. Julio F. Carrión. State College: Penn State University Press, 13–38.

2013. "The Threat from the Populist Left." *Journal of Democracy* 24(3): 18–32.

2017. "Populism: A Political-Strategic Approach." In *The Oxford Handbook of Populism*, eds. Cristóbal Rovira Kaltwasser, Paul Taggart, Paulina Ochoa Espejo, and Pierre Ostiguy. Oxford: Oxford University Press, 48–72.

Wiarda, Howard. 1973. "Toward a Framework for the Study of Political Change in the Iberic-Latin Tradition: The Corporative Model." *World Politics* 25(2): 206–35.

2009. "The Political Sociology of a Concept: Corporatism and the 'Distinct Tradition.'" *The Americas* 66(1): 81–106.

Willner, Ann Ruth, and Dorothy Willner. 1965. "The Rise and Role of Charismatic Leaders." *The ANNALS of the American Academy of Political and Social Science* 358(1): 77–88.

Wilpert, Gregory. 2007. *Changing Venezuela by Taking Power: The History and Policies of the Chavez Government*. New York: Verso.

Wise, Carol. 2006. "Against the Odds: The Paradoxes of Peru's Economic Recovery in the 1990s." In *The Fujimori Legacy: The Rise of Electoral Authoritarianism in Peru*, ed. Julio F Carrión. University Park: Pennsylvania State University Press, 201–26.

Wong, Yiu-Chung, and Willy Wo-Lap Lam. 2017. "The Legacy of Mao Zedong." In *Routledge Handbook of the Chinese Communist Party*, ed. Willy Wo-Lap Lam. London: Routledge, 31–46.

World Development Indicators: Urbanization. 2015. The World Bank. World Bank Data. www.worldbank.org (accessed February 17, 2016).

World Values Survey: Round Four – Country-Pooled Datafile 2000-2004. 2018. Madrid: JD Systems Institute. Public Opinion Data. www.worldvaluessurvey.org/WVSDocumentationWV4.jsp.

Worsley, Peter. 1957. *The Trumpet Shall Sound: A Study of "Cargo" Cults in Melanesia*. London: MacGibbon & Kee.

Wortman, Ana. 2015. "La construcción simbólica del poder Kirchnerista." In *Década ganada? Evaluando el legado del Kirchnerismo*, eds. Carlos Gervasoni and Enrique Peruzzotti. Buenos Aires: Debate.

Wynia, Gary W. 1978. *Argentina in the Postwar Era: Politics and Economic Policy Making in a Divided Society*. 1st ed. Albuquerque: University of New Mexico Press.

Ybarra, Gustavo. April 25, 2003. "Masivo Cierre de Campaña de Kirchner." *La Nación*. www.lanacion.com.ar/politica/masivo-cierre-de-campana-de-kirchner-nid491449/ (accessed December 1, 2016).

Zelaznik, Javier. 2013. "Unión cívica radical: Entre el tercer movimiento histórico y la lucha por la subsistencia." *Revista SAAP* 7(2): 423–31.

Zhiyue, Bo. 2017. "Factional Politics in the Party-State Apparatus." In *Routledge Handbook of the Chinese Communist Party*, ed. Willy Wo-Lap Lam. London: Routledge, 122–34.

Zimbardo, Philip. 1997. "What Messages Are Behind Today's Cults?" *American Psychological Association Monitor* 14. https://www.icsahome.com/articles/what-messages-behind-cults-zimbardo (accessed July 10, 2020).

"Zotero | Your Personal Research Assistant." www.zotero.org/ (accessed May 6, 2019).

Zúquete, José Pedro. 2008. *"The Missionary Politics of Hugo Chávez." Latin American Politics and Society* 50(1): 91–121.

    2013. "Missionary Politics – A Contribution to the Study of Populism: Missionary Politics." *Religion Compass* 7(7): 263–71.

Index

Milton Keynes UK
Ingram Content Group UK Ltd.
UKHW010610250424
441733UK00008B/41